Data Warehousing and Business Intelligence for e-Commerce

Alan R. Simon & Steven L. Shaffer

Data Warehousing and Business Intelligence for e-Commerce

MORGAN KAUFMANN PUBLISHERS

AN IMPRINT OF ACADEMIC PRESS

A Harcourt Science and Technology Company

SAN FRANCISCO   SAN DIEGO   NEW YORK   BOSTON
LONDON   SYDNEY   TOKYO

Executive Editor	Diane D. Cerra
Publishing Services Manager	Scott Norton
Senior Production Editor	Cheri Palmer
Assistant Editor	Belinda Breyer
Production Assistant	Mei Levenson
Editorial Assistant	Mona Buehler
Cover Design	Yvo Riezebos Design
Cover Image	© Bill Bachmann/Stock, Boston/PictureQuest
Text Design	Stuart L. Silberman Graphic Design
Composition/Illustration	Technologies 'N Typography
Copyeditor	Ken DellaPenta
Proofreader	Jennifer McClain
Indexer	Ty Koontz
Printer	Courier Corporation

Morgan Kaufmann Publishers
340 Pine Street, Sixth Floor, San Francisco, CA 94104–3205, USA
http://www.mkp.com

ACADEMIC PRESS
A Harcourt Science and Technology Company
525 B Street, Suite 1900, San Diego, CA 92101–4495, USA
http://www.academicpress.com

Academic Press
Harcourt Place, 32 Jamestown Road, London, NW1 7BY, United Kingdom
http://www.academicpress.com

Library of Congress Cataloging-in-Publication Data
Simon, Alan R.
  Data warehousing and business intelligence for e-commerce / Alan R. Simon, Steven L. Shaffer.
    p.   cm
  Includes index.
  ISBN 1–55860–713–7
    1. Electronic commerce.   2. Business intelligence.   3. Data warehousing.
  4. Industrial marketing.   I. Shaffer, Steven L.   II. Title.
  HF5548.32.S56   2001
  658.8'4—dc21   2001018796

This book is printed on acid-free paper.

For Ann.

—Alan Simon

I would like to thank my wonderful wife, Joan, and our children, Jordan and Dylan, for their support and encouragement. I love you!

—Steve Shaffer

Foreword

by Dr. Ramon C. Barquin
President, Barquin and Associates

Just a few months ago, Amazon.com announced that it was building a data warehouse that was expected to reach 3 petabytes. This planned size would surpass the Wal-Mart data warehouse by a substantial margin—and any other data warehouse in the commercial space for that matter. The battle between real and virtual business, between traditional commerce and e-commerce, seemed to be moving into a new arena. In many ways bricks and clicks appeared to be converging in their reliance on data warehousing as their primary source for business intelligence.

Data warehousing, as any truly dynamic discipline, has evolved significantly since its inception. In the decade that's elapsed since Bill Inmon coined the term and articulated the base definition, we have seen data warehousing move in several directions, following the demands of the marketplace.

From the earliest days of data warehousing it has been clear that the discipline was focused on analysis. In effect, it was rare to see data warehousing addressed without some reference to the OLAP (On-Line Analytical Processing) theme. Today, however, we're much more likely to see data warehousing being positioned broadly in the context of business intelligence or business intelligence solutions. Analysis is implicit in the mix, but the fact that we're looking for solutions to specific business problems has moved data warehousing from the notion of the static store of data that purists insisted had no applications, to the dynamic repository of integrated content aimed at solving some aspect of an enterprise's business problems.

Together with this movement has come the appearance of a number of distinct types of data warehousing entities as well as the emergence of more specific application spaces for data warehousing. With respect to the different data warehousing entities—note that we do not necessarily call them "data warehouses"—we've seen the development and interaction of data marts, operational data stores, OLAP servers, data mining servers, MOLAP/ROLAP/DOLAP hypercubes, as well as virtual data warehouses. It has also become clear that any large and complex enterprise will need some combination of data warehousing entities architected into a purposeful data warehousing environment that serves as a business intelligence laboratory.

The second aspect of our observation is that we've moved beyond data warehousing and into specific application areas. The most important of these areas is so-called customer relationship management (CRM). Given the importance that the customer has in any enterprise, it's only logical to assume that obtaining business intelligence about the customer is a high-priority activity.

In traditional commercial enterprises, business intelligence about the customers tends to be reduced to understanding customer behavior. We start by analyzing customer performance: what has each customer bought, over time, total volumes, trends, and so on. Most of these pursuits necessitated capturing transactions and eventually building some data warehousing entity with the historical information available to query over the time dimension. It was very seldom the case 10 years ago that understanding the customer entailed bringing in data at every customer touch point. Yet that concept started to emerge as a necessary and important activity in order to target products and manage promotions and marketing campaigns. The work pioneered by the database marketing community was one of the foundations of the data mining discipline, and this in turn started to point the way to CRM, specially e-CRM.

Enter e-commerce. Now we need to know not only past performance on the purchasing front, but also how the customer—or prospect—behaves as he or she enters our virtual store, the Web site or portal. To the already demanding requirement to capture transaction data for further analysis, we must now also capture the clicks of the mouse that define where the visitor has been on our Web site. What pages has he or she visited? What colors attract more positive attention? What shapes? What icons? What fonts? In the search for the holy grail of "stickiness," we know that a prime factor is personalization. And for this we need to warehouse the clicks and, at the speed of thought, identify the visitor, if possible, and personalize the page.

We can start to see the importance and magnitude of the task that Alan Simon and Steven Shaffer have tackled. *Data Warehousing and Business Intelligence for e-Commerce* is an essential contribution to the body of knowledge linking data warehousing and e-commerce. As e-commerce emerges as the foundation of the new economy, there will be an increasing need to build the data warehousing environments and infrastructures that support it. A reference source is needed on how to address the data warehousing aspects of electronic commerce.

e-Commerce encompasses the universe of electronic transactions between consumers (C), businesses (B), government (G), and employees (E). Each facet presents different challenges and demands certain attention to specific details. Business-to-business data warehousing is not necessarily the same as business-to-consumer data warehousing. The alphabet soup characterizing the different types of e-commerce transactions—B2C, B2B, C2C, C2B, G2C, B2G, B2E—will each require special treatment. Simon and Shaffer do exactly that, dedicating a chapter to each one of these areas.

Furthermore, they address a number of additional aspects of the data warehousing and e-commerce equation by providing ample attention to the core technologies, protocols, tools, and techniques, as well as to the often ignored but critical factors of security and data quality.

We are quickly moving into an economic world characterized by three major information-related spaces: content, distribution, and processing. In the future the vast majority of content will sit in data warehouses somewhere in cyberspace, with all access to that content and its delivery taking place through the application of processing tools via the Web. This is where we are going—the extraction of knowledge from data warehouses through the Web. Simon and Shaffer are giving us a good template to start building in that direction.

Contents

Preface

The evolution of data warehousing technology, products, and architecture that occurred during the 1990s is now going through a period of "creative chaos" in which old assumptions are being discarded and a new generation of capabilities is taking hold, all driven by the needs of e-commerce environments.

The focus of this book is to provide readers with a solid end-to-end grounding in how data warehousing—one of the most successful "technology movements" of the 1990s—can best be adapted to meet the challenges brought about by the Internet revolution and e-commerce. Given that the rules of e-commerce are still being established by the marketplace as a whole, we devote a significant portion of our discussion throughout the book to e-commerce strategy and technology.

It's likely that some data-warehousing-oriented readers might simply dismiss that material as "belonging to the transactional side and having little to do with data warehousing." However, it's our strong belief that in the e-commerce era, the traditional *old-fashioned* demarcation between a business's transactional side (i.e., the source applications that provide content to the data warehouse, whether Internet-based or not) and the informational and analytical side (i.e., the data warehousing and business intelligence environment) *must* cease to exist.

Data warehousing evolved through the 1990s to environments that typically featured batch-oriented "stocking" and "restocking" of the data warehouse, primarily for purposes of after-the-fact reporting and analysis. However, as we'll discuss throughout this book, all forms of e-commerce—business-to-consumer (B2C), business-to-business (B2B), and other variations we'll visit—require not only the after-the-fact business intelligence to achieve their full potential but also demand the close integration of "classical" data warehousing technology and content with e-commerce transactional content (for example, the contents of an online consumer's shopping cart). Further, on-the-fly decisions using this integrated data content must be made by a company's e-commerce environment and, perhaps, presented to online shoppers in a B2C environment, or to the purchasing agent from some other company in a B2B setting, to influence buy-or-not decisions.

We don't mean to imply that classical data warehousing is totally passé in the e-commerce era, but rather that it has only *part* of the overall solutions architecture and must be augmented with new methods and approaches to use data as an integral part of business operations. There are many texts that discuss the many aspects of classical data warehousing,[1] such as methodologies, data modeling and designing dimensional databases, ETL (extraction, transformation, and loading) procedures and rules, and user-facing, front-end tools. The reader is directed to one or more of the many excellent sources for information about the classical side of data warehousing (including background material about the subject itself) since, as noted, that discipline is still very much a part of the e-commerce picture.

We focus our discussion in this book on extending the classical side of data warehousing into new models of business intelligence—intelligent business, if you prefer that term—for various types of e-commerce environments. The "rules" governing this space have yet to be defined to the level of widespread acceptance that has hallmarked 1990s-era data warehousing. The material we present comes very much from the "real world" as organizations struggle to take the lessons learned from initial forays into e-commerce and move past the late 1990s model of simply building a Web site—perhaps augmented with some rudimentary, consumer-specific "personalized touches"—and then waiting for the crowds to begin ordering online.

Consequently, applying business intelligence and underlying data warehousing capabilities is now, in many organizations, a "green field" process: those companies are throwing away conventional wisdom, developing e-commerce strategies to take them well into the 2000–2010 decade, and then moving from their current first-generation e-commerce efforts into far more comprehensive online environments.

In the aftermath of so many dot-com "Internet pure-play" companies in financial trouble or having gone out of business, many "old economy" companies that had frantically slapped together strategies for getting on the Internet (and had been sneered at by the "new economy" crowd as having come to the party late, perhaps too late) were *putting their own e-commerce efforts on hold.* They were doing so not because they were backing away from their respective e-commerce initiatives, but rather with the dot-com "pure-play" threat seeming to have subsided, many larger corporations were now taking a step back and devoting their energies to developing long-range, viable e-commerce strategies. Collectively, the new conventional wisdom seemed to be that rather than continuing to proceed down a "quick strike" path, trying to develop an Internet presence as quickly as possible just to get their companies online, it was time to focus on strategy and architecture.

We strongly believe that a key part of this "OK, let's slow down and do it right" approach to e-commerce *must* involve a thorough look at how data warehousing and business intelligence fit into these firms' overall Internet strategies. And again, as we noted above, this entire discipline will be fertile ground during the first half of the 2000–2010 decade as the old rules of data warehousing and e-commerce evolve to much more closely related, technology-enabled architecture and implementation.

Acknowledgments

We would like to thank Craig Kaley for his outstanding technical contribution to this project. We'd also like to thank the editors at Morgan Kaufmann Publishers with whom we worked on this book—Diane Cerra, Belinda Breyer, and Cheri Palmer for their assistance and support throughout the project.

---

1. Including Alan Simon's *Data Warehousing for Dummies* (IDG Books, 1997) and *90 Days to the Data Mart* (John Wiley & Sons, 1998).

Part I

Foundations: Concepts and Business Models

Part I provides the reader with the foundations upon which subsequent discussion about core technology, products, and integrated e-commerce systems architecture will be based. The focus of Part I is at the conceptual level: that is, we focus on the "what" and "why" aspects of e-commerce business intelligence and data warehousing rather than the in-depth "how" orientation of later chapters in this book.

Sufficient discussion about e-commerce basics and business models is provided for readers with only peripheral exposure to doing business on the Internet, but we avoid going into too much depth. Rather, this discussion will serve as the backdrop for the conceptual material in Part I about data warehousing in different facets of e-commerce:

- *Business-to-consumer (B2C)*

- *Two variants of B2C in the form of consumer-to-consumer (C2C) and consumer-to-business (C2B)*

- *Business-to-business (B2B)*

- *Two types of e-government models: government-to-citizen (G2C) and business-to-government (B2G)*

- *Business-to-employee (B2E)*

1

Background, Terminology, Opportunity, and Challenges

As indicated by its title, this first chapter will provide the foundations upon which the approaches, technical discussion, solutions, and other material found throughout this book will be built. Readers who have some amount of experience and accomplishments in one or more of the book's major subject areas—data warehousing, customer relationship management (CRM), or e-commerce—may wish to skim this chapter, while those readers new to all of these various disciplines will likely want to spend a bit more time with the material contained in this introductory chapter.

We *strongly* recommend, however, that all readers spend at least a little time with this chapter before moving on to the more in-depth, solutions-focused content found in subsequent chapters, for several reasons:

- We are in the early stages of a "great convergence" of the most significant technology disciplines of the 1990s, and, as we'll discuss shortly, there are a number of lessons to be learned from what we did right in the 1990s *as well as what we did wrong* that are important to understand with regard to the foundation for e-commerce-based data warehousing and data management.

- Terminology in all of the underlying disciplines we'll discuss—particularly data warehousing, but also in e-commerce and CRM—has evolved to a hodgepodge of multiple, often conflicting meanings for commonly used terms and phrases. For the sake of consistency and common understanding, we will be very specific in this chapter about the terms we will use throughout this book and the context in which we will use them.

- As we'll discuss near the end of this chapter, there are some significant challenges with regard to organizations' efforts to apply data warehousing principles and technology to their respective e-commerce initiatives. Understanding these challenges—and how to overcome them—is every bit as important as understanding the concepts, architecture, and technology that we'll discuss in this chapter and throughout this book.

Background: A Look Back at the 1990s

The period from 1990 through 1999 was a remarkable decade in which many core computing and communications technologies and developments from the prior decade all came together and transformed the way in which business in the United States and throughout much of the world was done. Information systems broke out of the back office, where, for the most part, earlier generations of computer applications had been used primarily for permitting repetitive business processes to be accomplished faster and to encompass significantly larger volumes of data than if manual processes had still been used. The major product and architectural advances of the 1980s—desktop computers (PCs, as well as larger, more powerful workstations), networking technology (particularly local area networks, or LANs), and relational database management systems (RDBMSs)—converged to permit whole new classes of information systems and applications to be created and successfully deployed. At the same time, core telephony and other communications technology saw similar dramatic advances, and likewise converged with computer technology to provide a much deeper set of tools from which advanced information systems could be constructed.

But what was most notable about information systems throughout the 1990s was not just the continuing advancement in and synergies among different types of computer and communications technologies, but rather how that technology led to the birth and widespread acceptance of certain classes of applications. Specifically, we saw the following occur:

1. Enterprise Resource Planning (ERP) applications take hold.

2. CRM catches on.

3. Organizations pursue data warehousing to provide business intelligence.

4. The Internet evolves to a phenomenally successful e-commerce engine.

Let's discuss each of these points in turn.

ERP Applications Take Hold

From the earliest days of corporate computing systems until the end of the 1980s, nearly all large and mid-sized organizations pursued a mix-and-match, highly heterogeneous (read: disjointed) approach to their core back-office systems (finance, human resources, purchasing, inventory management, etc.), consisting of often poorly integrated custom and multivendor commercial applications. The 1990s saw, for the first time, many companies embrace product offerings from companies such as SAP AG, Peoplesoft, and Oracle that provided (or at least intended to provide) a single integrated package framework upon which most or all of a company's core business processes could be implemented, deployed, and used throughout the enterprise. By the mid-1990s, when belated awareness of the impending Y2K problem finally caught the attention of corporate information technology strategists and planners, the ERP "movement" got a boost from companies who chose to pursue a strategy of replacing non-Y2K compliant legacy systems rather than fixing them. For many organizations, ERP implementation and deployment *was* their Y2K fix.

Although many organizations had less-than-satisfactory experiences with their ERP package efforts—there were more than a few high-profile, high-cost failed ERP efforts—one significant fringe benefit did come out of a decade's experience with complex ERP integrated packages. In the late 1980s and into the first few years of the 1990s, if an organization attempted to develop and deploy a complex, enterprise-scale client/server system, failure was just about guaranteed. Many studies in the 1992–1993 time frame proclaimed the failure rate for client/server projects to be anywhere from 70 to 85%, and for a brief period of time there was such a backlash directed at client/server computing that the entire distributed systems approach to computing was branded by many as a failure, and reversion to centralized, highly inflexible computer architectures built around nonintegrated legacy applications was seen by those same doomsayers as inevitable.

Fortunately, despite the high-profile ERP failures, enough successes were widely documented that organizations began expanding the breadth and reach of their core applications beyond internal business processes (e.g., finance, human resources, etc.) toward new classes of applications that crossed enterprise boundaries and involved multiple corporations. For example, supply chain automation applications began appearing, and as we'll discuss later in this book, business-to-business (B2B) e-commerce applications such as electronic procurement (e-procurement) and buyer-to-seller electronic marketplaces are directly descended from these first-generation cross-enterprise supply chain applications, which in turn owe a large portion of their growth to the tenacity of ERP proponents who persevered throughout the decade and made *successful* large-scale, complex distributed computing systems a reality.

CRM Catches On

As we noted at the beginning of this section, the 1990s saw computing technology break out of its home in corporations' back offices and become "customer-facing." Two business areas in which customer-facing applications became common, almost ubiquitous, were

- Sales force automation (SFA) applications - A company's sales force functions of contact management, lead generation and tracking, and related business processes were linked together and managed by a single integrated environment. Whereas in the pre-SFA world computer technology was typically applied to after-the-fact rudimentary business processes such as managing accounts payable following a sale, SFA applications supported customer interaction and relationships *during* the sales cycle.

- Call center applications - Requests from a company's customers and prospects for product information, postsales product support, general customer service—or pretty much anything that might be requested over the phone—were managed in an increasingly sophisticated manner. Features were supported such as automatically routing an incoming call to a particular call center agent by identifying the incoming telephone number based upon looking up a customer's "value" (e.g., identifying high-net-worth customers of a bank as compared with "the average guy"). As was noted earlier, the convergence of communications technology played an important role in development and deployment of call center packages and systems. (A commonly heard term with regard to call center projects is CTI, or "computer-telephony integration.")

These two classes of applications—SFA and call center—we will call CRM *core systems*, terminology we'll discuss further in the "Terminology" section of this chapter. What is important to realize, though, is that as with ERP applications, CRM core systems evolved during the 1990s from a basic concept at the start of that decade to, by decade's end, a nearly indispensable part of most corporations' application portfolios. Not only were SFA systems and call centers here to stay, but they were also positioned for their next step along their evolutionary path, as we'll discuss later in this chapter: convergence with Internet technologies and e-commerce business models.

Organizations Pursue Data Warehousing to Provide Business Intelligence

In the 1990s, the database management systems (DBMS) world was facing a crisis. DBMS vendors such as IBM, Digital Equipment, Oracle, Ingres, and others had spent much of the latter part of the 1980s trying to develop distributed versions of their respective core database products. With the explosion of personal computers and minicomputers during the 1980s, corporate data assets were increasingly dispersed among hundreds or even thousands of different platforms throughout the enterprise. The idea behind a distributed DBMS (DDBMS) product was that a single enterprise-wide data management layer would provide various types of transparency services (e.g., location transparency, platform transparency, and data format transparency) and treat these physically dispersed stores of data as if they were really a single, logically centralized, and homogeneous database. For example, a single query could be executed against the DDBMS layer that would, using its own directory and metadata (a database term for "data about data") information, determine that three different databases would need to be accessed at execution time to merge and organize the requested information and present the combined results back to the user or requesting application.

Without going into a lot of detail, DDBMS technology failed, and organizations entered the 1990s facing an ever-worsening "islands of data problem."[1] Data management strategists began looking at alternatives to the failed DDBMS approach to dealing with this situation, and the idea of "data warehousing" was born.[2] Basically, data warehousing took a "something old, something new" approach to the islands of data problem: if it was too difficult to reach out at execution time to many different distributed, heterogeneous stores of data throughout the enterprise, why not preload (e.g., copy) selected groups of data from different databases and file systems into a single new database, where that content would be consolidated, "cleansed," and staged, ready for use? The "something old" portion of this approach is that most organizations were doing something like this already in the form of extract files, in which they would extract data from their legacy systems and move that data into a flat file for simple querying or generation of standard reports.

Data warehousing took off, though, for a couple of reasons:

- Whereas DDBMS technology had been thought of as a solution for both transactional and informational/analytical applications, organizations who built and deployed data warehouses typically focused their usage on the informational/analytical side to generate reports, analyze trends, and so on. Eventually, the term "business intelligence" came to represent the spectrum of different analytically focused usage and interaction models for an underlying data warehouse.

- Instead of flat files, data warehouses were typically built on top of either a relational database (taking advantage of the maturation and increasing acceptance of RDBMSs as successors to earlier pointer-based, relatively inflexible database models) or a new generation of proprietary "dimensional" database products (e.g., IRI's Express or Arbor's Essbase) that were specially architected for data analysis instead of transaction processing. While many data warehousing professionals became caught up in the relational versus proprietary database wars of the mid-1990s, the reality was that both were vast improvements over flat extract files, helping to facilitate the growth and acceptance of data warehousing.

We'll discuss more about the growth of data warehousing later, particularly as the discipline began converging with and expanding the capabilities of ERP and CRM systems. But it's important to note that by the end of the 1990s, data warehousing—like ERP and CRM—was here to stay.

The Internet Evolves to a Phenomenally Successful e-Commerce Engine

As momentous as ERP, CRM, and data warehousing are, all three of those areas can arguably be categorized as belonging to the realm of "professional computing." That is, someone from the general populace is likely to be unaware of (or maybe only peripherally aware of) sales force automation, data warehousing and business intelligence, supply chain management, or the other aspects of one or the other of these various disciplines.[3]

Most people, though, are at least familiar with the Internet and have at least a rudimentary understanding of how certain aspects of the Internet are changing aspects of their lives. Many analysts and observers have documented the dramatic evolutionary path of the Internet from a text-dominated research network at the beginning of the 1990s to a home for "billboardware" (e.g., simple advertising-oriented graphical Web sites) in the middle of the decade and then, by the end of 1999, a full-fledged force for revolutionary economic change and opportunity.

It's this most recent and current role of the Internet—economic enabler—that is most important to us with regard to the subject matter of this book. Pick any term or phrase you prefer: e-commerce, e-business, new economy, digital economy (in the next section we'll talk about terminology and sometimes conflicting meanings, as well as those definitions that are hype-laden). The indisputable fact is that an entire new and very powerful toolbox is now available to every current and potential business in the world. And, later in this chapter, we'll discuss how organizations are just beginning to use that toolbox's contents to extend the dramatic accomplishments of the 1990s that we discussed in this section—ERP, CRM, data warehousing and business intelligence, and the Internet—with dramatic "1 + 1 + 1 + 1 = 1,000" synergy.

Terminology and Discussion

Before we discuss the dramatic "1 + 1 + 1 + 1 = 1,000" synergy, though, we need to briefly cover the topic of terminology. As we noted several times in the preceding section, terminology in three of the areas in particular—data warehousing, customer-facing applications, and the Internet—is decidedly nonstandard, resulting in not uncommon misunderstandings and misconceptions about how these various disciplines can and will interact with one another.

Where we believe it's important to do so, we'll provide brief explanations behind the reason for multiple overlapping terminology. But rather than getting bogged down in this subject, for the most part we'll introduce (or reintroduce) key terms and phrases and indicate *precisely* what we mean when we use that terminology throughout this book.

Data Warehousing Terminology

Data warehouse: A logically consolidated store of data drawn from one or more sources within the enterprise and/or outside the enterprise.

Discussion: Note that the commonly used, classical (circa early 1990s) definition[4] of a data warehouse—"subject-oriented, nonvolatile, time-variant" (basically, a read-only database that contains historical information and is organized for easy access)—presupposes a particular architecture and set of capabilities (e.g., "nonvolatile" presupposes periodic batch updates and one-directional flows of content into the data warehouse). As data warehousing grew and matured throughout the 1990s, organizations began implementing data warehouses that supported real-time flows of data into the data warehouse; "feedback loops" of content from the data warehouse back to source transactional systems; and other complex cross-system interactions. In the discipline of electronic commerce, this next-generation approach to data warehousing is critical, particularly in managing data content across both the Internet and other more traditional, non-Internet channels.

Note also that a data warehouse is a *logically* consolidated store of data. While most data warehouses are currently implemented in a single database instance, it will become increasingly common to find larger, more complex stores of data implemented across multiple databases that are logically related to one another as part of a data warehousing *environment*.

Data mart: A subset of content drawn from a data warehouse—and possibly enhanced with additional content drawn from non–data warehouse sources—that is typically used to support a specific set of required business functionality.

Discussion: As with the term "data warehouse," there is no official definition for a data mart. Complicating the matter is that data marts are usually defined in the context of a data warehouse (e.g., "smaller than a data warehouse"). A further complication is that many people use the terms "data warehouse" and "data mart" interchangeably; for example, a data mart may acquire all of its content directly from source applications rather than from an already existing data warehouse.

For the most part, we will avoid using the expression "data mart" in this book unless we're discussing either (1) the architecture of a particular software vendor that includes a data store labeled as a "data mart," or (2) a secondary, physically separate subset of content extracted from an existing data warehouse. To help avoid confusion, we won't use the two terms interchangeably; rather, we will use "data warehouse."[5]

Business intelligence: A portfolio of informationally focused or analytical applications established on top of a data warehouse.

Discussion: Many people with cursory familiarity with data warehousing think of a data warehouse as being *both* (1) a store of data and (2) a set of simple reporting and analysis capabilities provided as part of the data warehouse. While this approach may well have described early- and mid-1990s data warehousing, during the last half of the 1990s an entire spectrum of different types of uses for a data warehouse evolved. Therefore, it's useful to make a distinction between the data warehouse (the store of data itself) and how that warehouse's content is used (e.g., for one or more business intelligence purposes).

We find the following classification of business intelligence applications to be useful:

- Simple reporting and querying - "Tell me what happened" functionality that provides point-in-time results, comparisons between current results with those of past periods, or other rudimentary, relatively static reports or ad hoc queries.

- Online analytical processing (OLAP) - "Tell me what happened, *and why*." Processing that enables users to further analyze results of reports and queries by drilling into the underlying details, looking at results in different ways, or otherwise performing manipulation of report and query results.

- Executive information systems (EISs) - Systems that "tell me lots of things, but don't make me work too hard to get that information." Whereas OLAP functionality can provide a wealth of information at summarized levels as well as the underlying details, tools in that category have traditionally been complex to use. EISs typically take the form of electronic online briefing books, "executive dashboards," online scorecards, or some other form in which a limited set of key business indicators (KBIs) are made available to executive users in an extremely easy-to-use fashion.

- Data mining - Predictive "tell me what might happen" capabilities that sometimes also take the form of "tell me something interesting, even though I don't know which specific questions to ask." Data mining is often thought of as the modern successor to artificial intelligence technology—neural network technology is a commonly used data mining technique—but more often than not, data mining is instituted through the use of "heavy statistics." Statistical methods such as regression analysis, association, classification, and other techniques are used to build models through which either (depending on the methodology of the techniques) large volumes of data or data samples are applied, looking for patterns, hidden relationships, and so on.

In the context of this book's subject—data warehousing applied to e-commerce—it's important to note that *all* of the above types of business intelligence are applicable. However, one particular business-to-consumer (B2C) situation might require only data mining techniques for purposes of customer segmentation (as discussed in Chapter 2); another B2C situation might be better served by implementing and deploying the entire spectrum of business intelligence applications for a number of purposes throughout the organization. Where applicable, we'll refer to particular forms of business intelligence in our discussion and examples throughout the book, and we'll be consistent and specific with our recommendations.

Extraction, transformation, and loading (ETL) and data warehousing middleware: Classical data warehousing is, as we've mentioned, batch processing based. During the 1990s an entire class of tools evolved that handle part or all of the technical processes required to

- extract data from a source application's database or file system

- perform necessary data transformations such as correcting rudimentary data errors, summarizing data, converting and unifying data codes (e.g., source application #1 uses "M" for male and "F" for female, while source application #2 uses an integer of 1 for male and 2 for female; these would typically be converted to some common code in the data warehouse as data is consolidated)

- load the transformed and "cleansed" data content into the data warehouse's database

Hence, the phrase "extraction, transformation, and loading"—or ETL for short—became widely used to describe those processes. However, data warehousing ETL can also be viewed as a subset of cross-system *middleware*, or integration-focused services used to link applications, facilitate data sharing, and so on. With regard to data warehousing for e-commerce, a mix of traditional, batch-focused ETL services together with more highly functional middleware capabilities are needed. And, with regard to middleware, there will be a mix of general-purpose middleware along with other middleware products that are exclusively focused on Internet-based integration and interaction. Therefore, we will be very specific throughout this book in explaining exactly what types of middleware we are referring to in various scenarios: traditional ETL tools, general-purpose middleware, or Internet-specific middleware.

Customer Relationship Management Terminology

Customer Relationship Management (CRM): A class of applications that includes *three different subclasses*, each of which will be discussed below:

- Traditional CRM core systems

- CRM analytics

- e-CRM systems

Discussion: As was noted earlier in this chapter, the term "CRM" has been widely used to refer to those applications that are primarily "customer-facing." However, many people think of what we'll term "CRM core systems" when they hear the term "CRM." It is important to make a distinction among the three subclasses listed above and described below, so we will avoid using the all-encompassing term "CRM" in this book; rather, we will specifically mention the class of CRM to which we're referring.

Traditional CRM core systems: "Offline" (i.e., non-Internet based) applications for either SFA or call centers.

Discussion: The primary purpose of SFA and call centers is to effectively and efficiently manage *customer contacts*. SFA systems have traditionally been used in a business-to-business setting (e.g., managing interactions between an electronics company's sales force and other companies that represent their customer base and prospects). Conversely, call centers have been used primarily in business-to-customer settings: product support, telemarketing, and so on. (Note, however, that SFA can be applied as necessary to business-to-consumer situations just as call centers can be used for business-to-business support.)

Some companies have integrated their SFA and/or call center systems with other internal applications; for example, an order recorded in an SFA application is linked in a real-time (or near-real-time) manner with back-office applications such as accounts payable and inventory management. More often, though, SFA and call center environments have been loosely coupled with other applications, relying on periodic batch transfers or even manual-based work processes to exchange information.

The common thread between traditional SFA and call centers is that in both settings, customers are *not* connected with the systems themselves. That is, if you were to create an end-to-end process flow diagram covering both offline and online processes for an SFA or call center environment, those processes in which the internal company environment interfaces with the customers are typically manual: a customer placing an order with a salesperson; that same customer requesting a copy of orders from that salesperson he or she placed over the past six months; or an individual placing a phone call to the call center to discuss a billing problem.

The entire CRM discipline has evolved with the Internet, but we find it's important to make a distinction between traditional CRM core systems and, as we'll discuss shortly, Internet-driven CRM, or e-CRM.

CRM analytics: Supporting applications that draw data from CRM core systems for the purpose of "better understanding customer behavior" by producing reports, segmenting and classifying customers based on purchase patterns, and similar analytically focused functionality.

Discussion: Recall our discussion about business intelligence as a portfolio of applications sitting on top of a data warehouse, which in turn draws its contents from source applications. CRM analytics are, in effect, special-purpose data warehouses and business intelligence applications that, instead of supporting inventory analysis or financial reporting, are designed to draw content from the CRM core systems (the data sources), reorganize and restructure that content as necessary, and support special-purpose reporting, analysis, and data mining.

As will be discussed later in this chapter, CRM analytics range from simple one-to-one "data marts" (e.g., data is extracted from a single SFA application into a separate database, where segmentation, profiling, and other analysis occurs) to more complex environments in which multiple SFA applications and multiple call centers need to be considered as data sources to the database(s) upon which the CRM analytics will be applied. The latter setting is commonly found in larger corporations, especially those in which acquisitions of other companies, each with their own CRM core systems, has occurred. And, as we'll discuss, the technical processes necessary to support CRM analytics become much more complex when Internet-based CRM (e.g., e-CRM, discussed next) is included in the mix.

Finally, it's important to note that some commercial software packages that support CRM analytics support more than just analysis and reporting. For example, a package might perform customer segmentation and then, based on targeted marketing directives and company strategy, provide capabilities to support *campaign management* functions such as (1) mailing, faxing, or e-mailing offers (e.g., special promotions) to targeted customers or prospects, or (2) initiating and managing a program to reacquire former customers. Therefore, unlike traditional data warehousing and business intelligence in which the reporting and analytic activities tend to be ending points with regard to online activity, CRM analytics increasingly feed the results of those analytical processes into other transactional business processes.

e-CRM: Internet-based systems that manage customer contacts online.

Discussion: Unlike traditional CRM core systems that, as discussed above, facilitate "offline" interaction with customers, e-CRM moves *both* families of CRM core systems—sales contact management and customer support—online and, using Internet technologies, directly links the customers and prospective customers into the systems themselves.

"Pure-play" Internet companies (e.g., a B2C or B2B dot-com company that has no preexisting non-Internet business operations) would likely implement newer-generation e-CRM systems that include not only support for the core, transactionally focused functions (again, sales contact management and customer support) but also tightly integrated analytical and informational functions such as customer segmentation and profiling—a relatively straightforward proposition that often can be based on a single application package (or set of modules from a single vendor). However, companies with *both* Internet-based and non-Internet operations will inevitably find themselves needing all three classes of CRM systems discussed above, as we'll discuss throughout this book. Therefore, while next-generation e-CRM packages provide higher levels of integration between transactional and analytic business processes, "click-and-mortar" companies (a commonly used term to describe a company with a mix of non-Internet and Internet-based business)[6] will find themselves facing significantly more complexity than with earlier, mid-1990s-class CRM environments. And, as we'll discuss in the "Challenges" section, understanding this complexity (or, more precisely, *not* appreciating and understanding that complexity) can be a major impediment to successfully building data warehousing environments to support e-commerce.

Internet Terminology

Electronic commerce (e-commerce): Using the Internet as the foundation for many different types of business processes related to commerce: purchasing, online payment, order fulfillment, supply chain management, and customer support, among others.

Electronic business (e-business): Synonymous with e-commerce.

Discussion: A common point of confusion for many is the distinction—or lack thereof—between the terms "e-commerce" and "e-business." The former term was the first to appear during the dramatic growth of the Internet during the 1990s, but by the latter part of that decade the term "e-business" had come into vogue. Some consultancies and product companies define e-business as the overall framework and infrastructure of Internet-based business, while in their view e-commerce refers only to the actual online transactions (e.g., placing an online order and using your credit card for automatic payment).

We believe that the term "e-transaction" should be used for online transactions, and for all intents and purposes "e-commerce" and "e-business" can be used interchangeably. As with data warehousing and CRM, there are no official definitions provided by a standards body that explicitly and authoritatively define the meanings of these two terms. For consistency, we will use "e-commerce" throughout this book, unless we are referring to product or service offerings from a vendor who explicitly uses the phrase "e-business."

Business-to-consumer (B2C): e-Commerce services that link a business with consumers (e.g., current customers and prospects).

Business-to-business (B2B): e-Commerce services that link businesses with one another.

Consumer-to-consumer (C2C): e-Commerce services that link consumers with one another (e.g., online auction services); a subset of B2C e-commerce.

Consumer-to-business (C2B): e-Commerce services that link consumers with one another and, subsequently, to one or more businesses; another subset of B2C e-commerce.

Discussion: We introduced the terms B2C and B2B earlier in this chapter. As we'll discuss in Chapter 2, though, we believe that data warehousing services and environments in support of e-commerce need to vary slightly between those needed for traditional B2C companies (e.g., an online retailer, or "e-retailer"[7]) and those needed for the less common—but still real—C2C and C2B subcategories of B2C.

e-Marketplace: An Internet-based environment in which buyers and sellers "meet," exchange information, and buy and sell products.

Discussion: Three points are worth noting. First, e-marketplaces are more commonly thought of in a B2B context (e.g., vertical, industry-specific marketplaces, as we'll discuss in Chapter 4), though arguably e-marketplaces first gained a foothold in the C2C subset of the B2C marketplace: online auction sites such as eBay (*www.ebay.com*).

Second, adding an *e* in front of a commonly used word to create a term such as "e-marketplace" is extremely common in the world of e-commerce (yet another term created the same way). Rather than list and define all the commonly used terms such as "e-supply chain," "e-procurement," "e-marketing," "e-selling," and dozens (or more likely hundreds) of others, we will as necessary define other "e" terms as we introduce them; most, however, are self-explanatory.

The third point is that even though "e" terms are commonplace in the world of the Internet and e-commerce, so too are "i" terms (e.g., preceding a commonly used word with an *i* instead of an *e*, with *i* usually standing for "Internet"); this is particularly common in company names (e.g., iVillage—*www.ivillage.com*). Unless there is a very precisely defined "i" term that we need to use, we will avoid the confusion of intermixing "e" and "i" terms in subsequent chapters.

Opportunity

So far we've discussed the background and terminology of the various pieces of this book's subject matter. What is the significance?

Simply stated, the opportunity facing nearly every company is to apply various forms of business intelligence, as instantiated through a combination of classical and next-generation data warehousing, to their e-commerce efforts in an increasingly competitive marketplace. Or, as we put it earlier, combining data warehousing and business intelligence with CRM, selected ERP functionality (e.g., those related to business-to-business, cross-enterprise transactions) and e-commerce with "1 + 1 + 1 + 1 = 1,000" synergy.

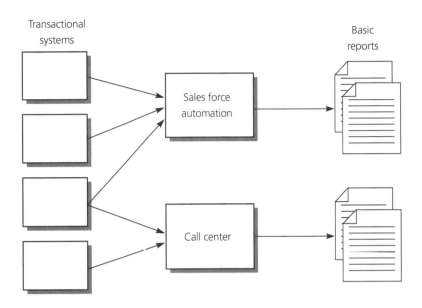

Figure 1.1 Phase 1: initial deployment of CRM core systems.

Let's look at the CRM space as an illustration of how that discipline has been slowly—but steadily—evolving to include aspects of data warehousing. Figure 1.1 illustrates an organization with two first-generation CRM core systems, one each for SFA and call center support.

Note that in Figure 1.1 there is extremely limited reporting functionality available for each of the CRM core systems: basically, a few rudimentary package-produced reports that show weekly and monthly counts for new sales staff contacts (from the SFA package) and inbound customer calls (from the call center package). No advanced analytical capabilities (e.g., drill-down analysis) or data mining was supported. In effect, the CRM core systems were early 1990s incarnations of old-fashioned mainframe-based legacy systems: they captured data from transactions and then "locked the data away" rather than use that information for business intelligence purposes.

As illustrated in Figure 1.2, the next step taken by most organizations was to extend (or at least attempt to extend) the basic reporting capabilities of the packages through custom coding. As reporting functionality increased, though, many of the systems-based reasons for data warehousing (e.g., reports using large volumes of data adversely impacting the performance of the transactional database) began impacting the SFA and call center applications.

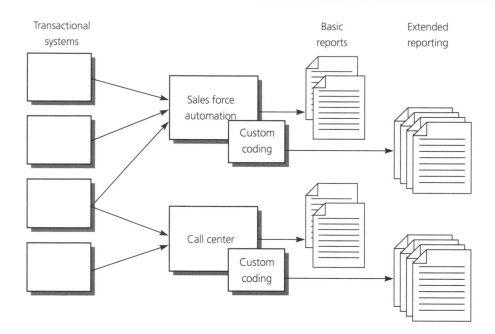

Transactional systems   Basic reports   Extended reporting

Sales force automation

Custom coding

Call center

Custom coding

Figure 1.2 Phase 2: extending CRM core systems' reports through custom coding.

Attempting to overcome performance problems, the next step taken by most organizations was to extract data from their SFA and call center packages' databases, copy that content into a separate database, and move the reporting capabilities from the core systems to the new copy of the data. Basically, even though the term wasn't commonly used, these organizations were creating functionality-specific data marts (see Figure 1.3).

Note that the evolution to CRM data marts typically was problematic, for several reasons. Most organizations found themselves facing a mix of reporting capabilities, with some remaining against the CRM core systems due to difficulty of migration and with newer reports and, finally, some advanced analytics (e.g., OLAP functionality) applied against the CRM data mart.

A more significant problem, though, was that many larger organizations typically found themselves by the mid-1990s with *multiple* call center and SFA systems. Whether due to corporate mergers or organizations within a corporation simply choosing to pursue their own, nonintegrated CRM initiatives, most companies found themselves faced with an environment like that shown in Figure 1.4.

Faced with the desire to obtain a "whole customer view" (i.e., a comprehensive picture of customer interactions and behavior), the next step taken by

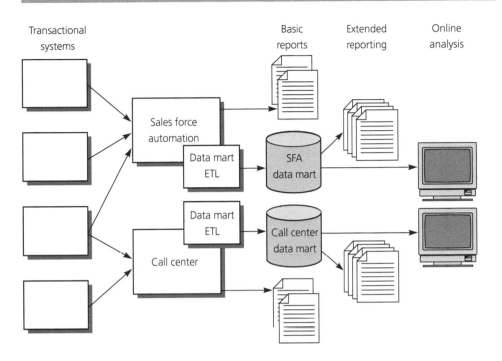

Figure 1.3 Phase 3: creating functionality-specific data marts for CRM support.

forward-looking (some would say "courageous," others might use the phrase "foolishly optimistic") organizations was to evolve from their hodgepodge of CRM data marts to a single integrated customer data warehouse. Two different approaches were popular, as illustrated in Figure 1.5. Some organizations chose to create a new customer-oriented data warehouse with the sole mission of supporting CRM analytics—not only basic reporting and analysis, but also customer segmentation, profiling, and so on. Alternatively, other organizations chose to extend an existing data warehouse that already contained customer data with content from the various CRM core systems.

Though both of the approaches illustrated in Figure 1.5 appear to be a straightforward, desirable state of integrating CRM-produced data for reporting and analytical purposes, it should be noted that most organizations' experiences with this step along the evolutionary path are usually only partially successful—not for reasons of technology, but because of organizational issues such as system ownership and lack of incentive to move from an environment in which "subenterprise" organizations control their own systems with a minimum of necessary cooperation with other organizations. The reason it's important to note these difficulties is that, as shown in

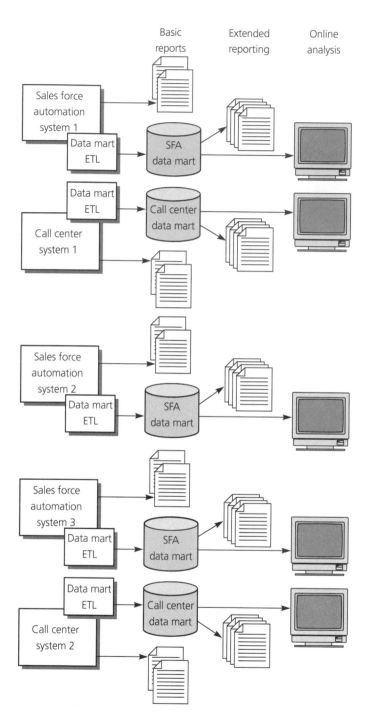

Figure 1.4 Phase 4: multiple CRM core systems and nonintegrated data marts.

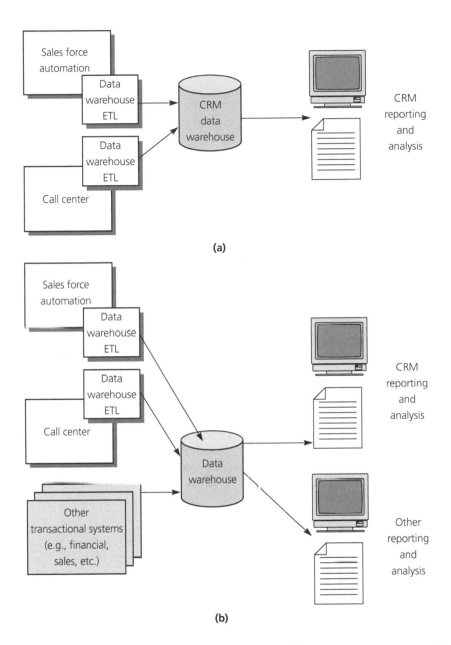

Figure 1.5 Phase 5: two approaches to integrated CRM-focused data warehousing: (a) CRM-specific data warehouse and (b) CRM data added to a general-purpose data warehouse.

Figure 1.6, along comes the Internet and e-commerce . . . and an entirely new set of CRM integration problems.

Figure 1.6 represents the current state of affairs with regard to most click-and-mortar corporations' CRM systems. Whereas an Internet pure-play company such as an online B2C retailer might have an environment like that shown in Figure 1.5(b), a click-and-mortar company typically finds itself backing away from whatever successes it was able to attain in building integrated whole-customer views with a data warehouse for the purpose of supporting CRM analytics. Why? The frenzied pace at which "old economy" companies (e.g., those that existed before the late 1990s and that contain non-Internet sales channels) rushed to get onto the Internet was often accomplished by either (1) chartering an internal e-commerce organization to build and deploy e-commerce capabilities as quickly as possible and deferring plans for integrating their e-CRM capabilities with already existing CRM core systems and CRM analytics until "some time in the future," or (2) spinning off an entirely separate company (as was common during 1999 and early 2000, when dot-com divestitures were all the rage). In the latter case, integration between e-commerce and existing non-Internet channels wasn't deferred; they weren't part of the business model.

And now we come to the critical juncture that provides the foundation for this book's subject matter. It would be natural for a company to take a step back, look at an environment such as that shown in Figure 1.6, and initiate a program to integrate their e-CRM information (e.g., online customer contacts, requests made through an online customer support system, etc.) with corresponding content from traditional CRM core systems into a single, consolidated *traditional* data warehouse. By "traditional" we mean a data warehouse that is stocked in a batch-oriented manner using traditional ETL processes, and whose primary purpose is supporting the various types of business intelligence discussed earlier in this chapter (e.g., basic reporting, OLAP, EIS, and data mining). Figure 1.7 illustrates this approach.

While success with the approach shown in Figure 1.7 would certainly provide high levels of integration across e-commerce and traditional channels, that integration would typically be limited to *after-the-fact* business intelligence. This is an important distinction to make. As illustrated in Figure 1.8, a "diversion" on the CRM analytics evolutionary path shown in the previous figures is using customer data not only for after-the-fact analytics but also applying the results of those analytics to "quasi-transactional" business processes such as targeted marketing and campaign management.

The step-by-step, loosely coupled, and typically batch-oriented business processes illustrated in Figure 1.8 may be satisfactory for traditional customer interaction channels, but at the "Internet speed" of e-commerce, they are woefully

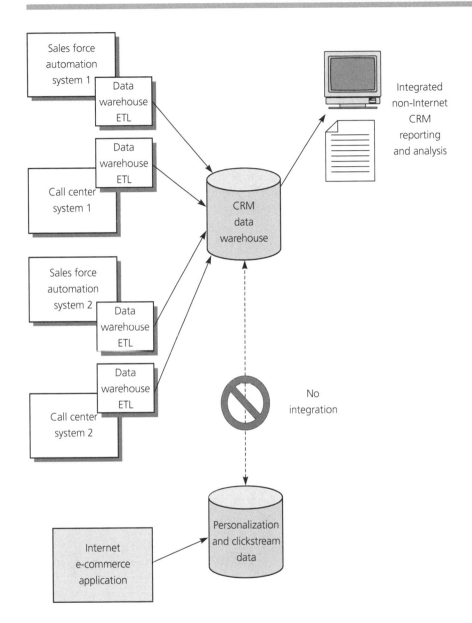

Figure 1.6 Phase 6 (current state): CRM-specific data warehouse with nonintegrated e-commerce and traditional CRM analytics.

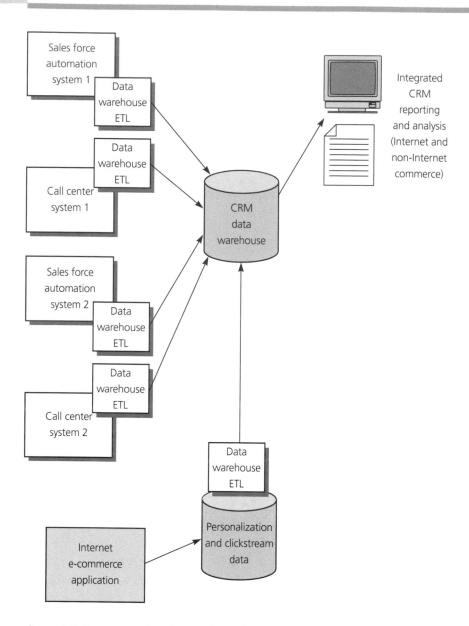

Figure 1.7 One approach to integrating e-CRM and traditional CRM data content.

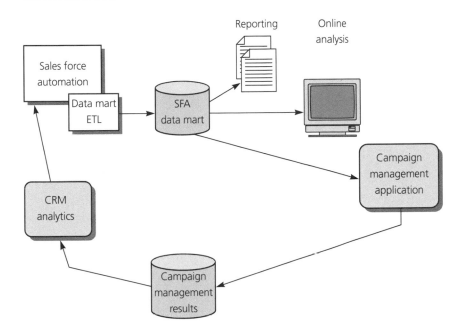

Figure 1.8 Using content provided by CRM analytics in customer-facing transactional processes.

inadequate. *And this presents the opportunity:* rather than simply graft "old economy" business processes onto Internet-produced customer data, organizations are taking a fresh look at innovative ways of applying business intelligence to various aspects of e-commerce (in this thread of examples, CRM-focused processes and systems). We'll take an in-depth look in subsequent chapters at many examples. As a transition to that subsequent discussion and as a conclusion to this section, one next-generation example of applying business intelligence to e-commerce in a B2C scenario is using a "whole-customer profile" created from online and offline channels and, in real time, combining that static business intelligence content with a customer's online shopping activity—what he or she is putting into the online shopping cart, what items are being removed from the shopping cart, what items are being browsed and not selected for purchase, and so on—and making shopping-time recommendations for complementary products, alternative products, as well as other shopping-time suggestions. Figure 1.9 illustrates this type of environment.

As will be discussed in subsequent chapters, traditional, batch-oriented data warehousing products and capabilities are *not* adequate to completely support an

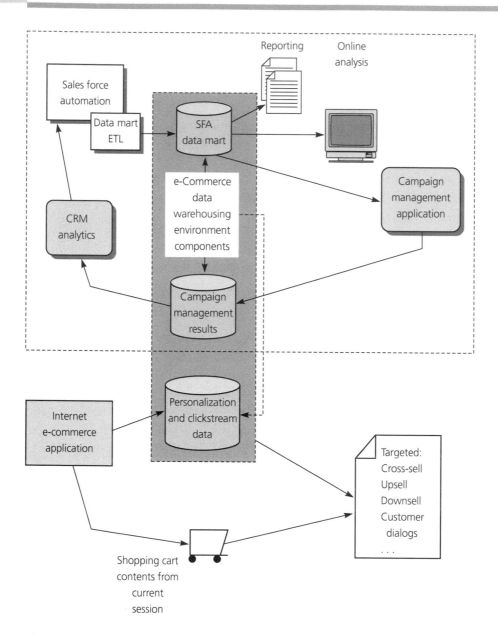

Figure 1.9 An example of combining traditional data warehouse content with other e-commerce data.

environment like that shown in Figure 1.9. Real-time access to various types of data is needed; bidirectional flows of data are required; and robust applications logic, far more complex than that required for traditional after-the-fact business intelligence or even offline campaign management, is a necessity.

Summarizing the opportunity: instead of just letting the natural CRM evolution proceed to include e-commerce, an organization should jump-start its approach to using customer data in business processes, both on the Internet as well as through traditional non-Internet channels, if applicable (i.e., for a click-and-mortar company). Doing so extends far beyond the simple-to-understand B2C e-retailing example illustrated above; innovative ways of applying current and next-generation data warehousing and business intelligence to e-commerce are applicable to B2B environments (see Chapter 4), as well as the C2C and C2B variations of B2C that we'll discuss in Chapter 3.

And, as we'll discuss later, it's essential to ensure that business processes are modernized and kept in concert with their underlying technology. Therefore, implementing the models and architectures we'll discuss throughout this book *must* be done as part of an overall end-to-end business strategy that encompasses both e-commerce and traditional channels and the necessary touch points throughout those respective sets of processes.

Challenges

There are demonstrable and self-evident business advantages to making data warehousing and business intelligence capabilities an integral part of an organization's e-commerce efforts. However, it needs to be noted that there are three primary challenges in doing so, as will be discussed in this section:

- "Discipline-centric" views among corporate strategists, consultants and systems integrators, and product vendors

- "Dot-com" spin-offs as separate companies

- The need to deliver products and solutions in "Internet time"

Discipline-Centric Views

Simply stated, there exists an artificial, unnatural, and unhealthy demarcation between the discipline of data warehousing and that of e-commerce. Refer back to the sequence of evolutionary steps in the CRM space throughout the 1990s that was described and illustrated in the previous section. Looking back, it's natural to wonder why, back when organizations were first embracing and deploying SFA and call center capabilities, they didn't recognize that implementing CRM core systems without a close integration with corresponding CRM analytics wasn't desirable. Why didn't they implement both sides of CRM—transactional and informational—together, or at least in lockstep with one another?

Many reasons exist, such as companies' budgets and tight development schedules that typically permitted implementation of CRM transactional capabilities. Additionally, CRM product vendors faced intense pressure to focus their development energies on their primary products—initially, the CRM core systems—in an ever-competitive marketplace and to defer analytical extensions to "some future release."

The above reasons are understandable. The same marketplace, time, and budgetary pressures were evident in the ERP arena, and it wasn't until the latter part of the 1990s that ERP vendors began providing data warehousing extensions to their core products (e.g., SAP's Business Information Warehouse—BIW, also known as Business Warehouse or BW).

A more ominous part of the problem, though, is that many consultants and systems integrators who specialized in CRM dismissed data warehousing and business intelligence as irrelevant to the management and use of customer data. Even when clients and prospective clients expressed an interest in coupling their SFA or call center functionality with robust reporting and analytical capabilities, many CRM-centric consultants proposed and attempted to implement solutions such as those illustrated in Figures 1.2 or 1.4—solutions that were problematic for reasons of performance, lack of necessary data integration, or both.

Correspondingly, many data-warehousing-oriented consultants and integrators were unfamiliar with emerging product-provided CRM analytical capabilities, and instead implemented custom-built and often error-prone solutions using general-purpose querying and reporting tools rather than integrating a CRM analytics package with an underlying data warehouse.

While the barriers between CRM and data warehousing have finally crumbled with the introduction and acceptance of CRM analytically focused products from vendors such as E.piphany (*www.epiphany.com*) that contain an underlying data mart to support campaign management and other functionality, *history is repeating itself in the e-commerce world*. Many consultants and systems integrators who specialize in e-commerce have a lack of understanding of data warehousing, and instead see e-CRM as being all that's necessary for business intelligence purposes. While this may be true in pure-play Internet companies, click-and-mortar companies with a combination of traditional and e-commerce channels *need* a mixture of traditional data warehousing and business intelligence with the analytical capabilities provided by e-CRM. And, likewise, other consultants and systems integrators who specialize in data warehousing still see their discipline in an early-1990s context, based solely on batch processing and simplistic after-the-fact reporting and analysis.

Dot-com Spin-Offs

A second complication is that organizations themselves are inadvertently contributing to the problem through their e-commerce spin-off activities, as discussed earlier in this chapter. While a dot-com spin-off may provide (at least temporarily) high returns through stock market valuation of the separate company, integration of "new economy" and "old economy" channels then becomes extremely problematic. As a separate company, an e-commerce spin-off's technology and business strategists often have little or no incentive to integrate their online customer data with that of their offline cousin's systems. For example, a company embracing the trend toward mixed-channel customer processes—for example, ordering a product online but picking it up at the local mall rather than having that product shipped to the customer's home—will face many problems trying to retroactively "reintegrate" e-commerce and non-Internet customer activity data to report on and analyze mixed-channel activity (e.g., tracking the relationship between additional purchases in a store when picking up a product ordered online and the relationship between complementary in-store product sales and subsequent online purchases).

Operating at "Internet Time"

The third challenge is the need for every entity involved in e-commerce—companies selling products to the general public (i.e., B2C companies); companies frantically trying to build online marketplaces with one another (i.e., B2B companies); the venture capital and investment community; consultants and systems integrators; and product vendors—to deliver functioning results (systems, products, online customer interactions, etc.) as quickly as possible . . . that is, in what has become known as "Internet time."

A direct relationship exists between time-to-results and amount of functionality. That is, the need to deliver results extremely quickly *will* result in reduced functionality (or at least less functionality than if more time had been available). The consequence of "Internet time" driving functionality has been the challenges discussed above: demarcation between e-commerce and data warehousing, as well as the lack of an up-front consolidated strategy covering integration between Internet and non-Internet channels.

Overcoming the Challenges

Throughout this book we'll present solutions that take the challenges discussed above into consideration. That is, we won't make recommendations and present architectures for overwhelmingly complex three-year "Big Bang" business-to-consumer projects in which a team locks itself away for two or three years, performs requirements analysis and then design and development, and then finally delivers its initial comprehensive functionality long after the window of business opportunity has closed. Rather, we'll focus on iterative and incremental approaches in which up-front strategy and architecture needs to be comprehensive to prevent architectural dead ends, yet at the same time components of functionality can be delivered in 90–120-day increments, with each component building on what has already been delivered.

This approach, however, does require an awareness of the challenges discussed above and a conscious effort by all those involved to overcome them. Of particular note is the first challenge discussed, the artificial demarcation between data warehousing and e-commerce. It is imperative that whoever is driving an initiative within a particular setting—whether internal person or outside consultant—acknowledges up front the necessity of making data warehousing and business intelligence an integral part of an e-commerce initiative.

Summary

In this initial chapter, we have provided the foundations and framework for the material in the chapters that follow. The background material and terminology presented for the various disciplines such as CRM, ERP, and data warehousing that are now converging is, we believe, very important to understand to ensure that past missteps of insufficient integration (which in turn results in less-than-optimal solutions) aren't repeated in the e-commerce arena.

By way of transitioning from this introductory material to concepts and architecture, we'll next discuss applying data warehousing to business-to-consumer settings in Chapter 2, since most readers are likely to have had personal experiences with various B2C companies through product browsing, purchasing, and customer service.

Endnotes

1. A more detailed—and somewhat irreverent—discussion of how DDBMS failure evolved into 1990s-style data warehousing can be found in A. Simon, *Data Warehousing for Dummies,* IDG/Dummies Press, 1997, Chapter 1.

2. Most data warehousing professionals recognize Bill Inmon as having first coined the phrase "data warehouse," though IBM's DDBMS effort that was still under way at the time was called their "Information Warehouse."

3. Of course, nearly everyone has had experiences with call centers, both on the inbound side (e.g., calling for customer support) and on the outbound side (e.g., receiving one of

those aggravating trying-to-sell-you-something calls, usually at the most inconvenient time possible).

4. There is no *official* definition of a data warehouse, that is, a standard definition supported by a standards committee such as the American National Standards Institute (ANSI).

5. More information about data mart architecture can be found in A. Simon, *90 Days to the Data Mart,* John Wiley & Sons, 1998.

6. Another less frequently used term is "clicks and bricks."

7. Also referred to as "e-tailer."

2

Business-to-Consumer Data Warehousing

In this chapter we'll discuss how data warehousing can best be applied to business-to-consumer settings. We focus on B2C before discussing B2B and other e-commerce variations for a couple of reasons:

- B2C—the "dot-com" world of selling goods and services to the general public—is the oldest form of e-commerce (relatively speaking, that is; nothing in e-commerce is really that old), having preceded the more complex B2B environments that we'll discuss in Chapter 4.

- Of all the e-commerce combinations—including C2C and C2B (see Chapter 3) as well as emerging areas of e-government and business-to-employee (B2E) that we'll discuss in Chapters 5 and 6—B2C business models are the most straightforward to understand and, therefore, to kick off our discussions about applying data warehousing to various e-commerce business models. (Though, as we'll discuss, there are a number of different types of B2C business models, some more complex than others.) In many ways, B2C data warehousing and business intelligence is a direct descendant and next step of non-Internet CRM analytics that we briefly discussed in Chapter 1.

As we noted in Chapter 1, the C2C and C2B business models that we'll discuss in Chapter 3 can be considered subsets of the B2C world. However, we segregate our discussion of those two settings in a separate chapter because B2C, C2C, and C2B differ from one another in the transactional side of their business models as well as the informational and analytical sides.

In this chapter, we'll cover the following:

- Various types of B2C business models

- Applying "after-the-fact" data warehousing and business intelligence to B2C (e.g., the customer analytics)

- Extending the after-the-fact customer analytics to transactional business activities such as campaign management

- Further extending the transactional usage of customer analytics into real-time transactions such as knowledge-driven shopping-time suggestions

- Building a bidirectional data warehousing environment in which services are provided to customers and prospects, the objective being to help overcome consumer backlash to collection and sale of data

B2C Business Models

It's tempting to think of B2C as simply "selling things over the Internet"—basically an online, Internet-based version of a television shopping channel or a product catalog you would receive in your mailbox (your "offline" one at your home or another location, not your e-mailbox)—but in reality, there are a variety of B2C business models. Depending on the complexity—or lack thereof—of a particular B2C business model, different approaches to the underlying data warehousing capabilities will be required to best provide the necessary business intelligence services. Figure 2.1 illustrates the range of B2C models that are discussed below.

Basic Product Selling

Many e-tailers are simply Internet-based versions of a catalog retailer or a brick-and-mortar retail location: "retailing in cyberspace." They publish a list of goods available to the general consuming public over the Internet, and their site is fully available through a Web browser for consumers to research and select products and pay for them.

There are actually several factors that differentiate product-selling e-tailers from one another. Some are pure-play e-tailers such as amazon.com (*www.amazon.com*)—they exist on the Internet alone with no corollary non-Internet channels—while others are click-and-mortar businesses with physical stores as well as Internet (and perhaps other) sales channels (see Figure 2.2).

Another factor is a company's position in the "value chain" from goods production to the eventual consuming public. Consider Wal-Mart (*www.walmart.com*) as compared to Levi Strauss (*www.levistrauss.com*) (see Figure 2.3). Wal-Mart would

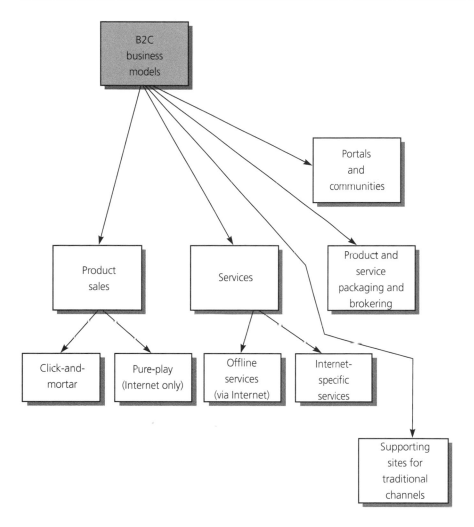

Figure 2.1 Various forms of B2C business models.

be considered a click-and-mortar e-business: the company's roots are in retail outlets that of course still exist and are a major channel for reaching consumers, but at the same time their online services provide Internet users access to products Wal-Mart sells via their PCs and Web browsers.

Within Wal-Mart's inventory of clothing for sale are a mixture of their own labels as well as other clothing manufacturers' products. Over time, an equilibrium has developed within that world whereby clothing manufacturers relate to Wal-Mart as

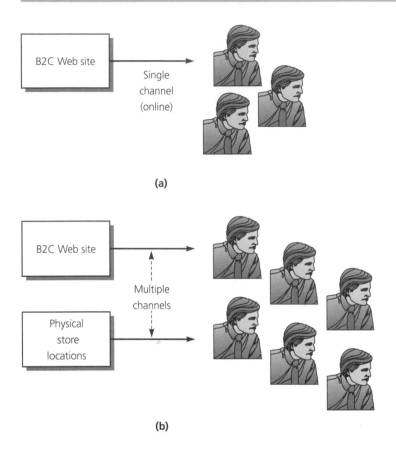

Figure 2.2 (a) Pure-play versus (b) click-and-mortar B2C e-tailers.

a key retail outlet for their products, even though that same retailer might also be a competitor in specific product lines. And, at the same time, Wal-Mart realizes that clothing manufacturers whose products they sell also wholesale goods to other retailers who are Wal-Mart's competitors.

Levi Strauss, however, has primarily been a manufacturer and wholesaler who has relied on retail outlets as the channels through which their jeans and other products would be made available for purchase by the consuming public. Now, by considering the Internet as a channel to *directly* reach the consuming public, there would be the potential for channel conflict that has not previously existed.

So with regard to selling products over the Internet, the underlying click-and-mortar business models need to take into consideration whether the Internet channel is

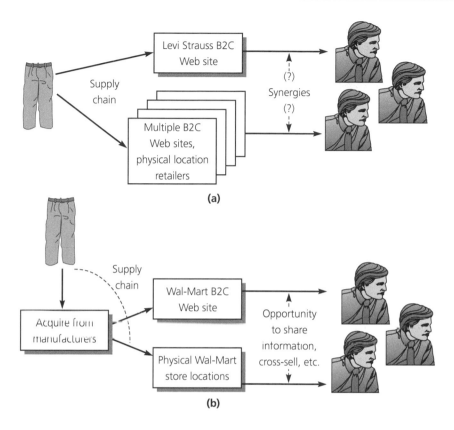

Figure 2.3 Different e-commerce value chains: (a) Levi Strauss and (b) Wal-Mart.

- a "peer" to the company's existing non-Internet channels (e.g., the company's roots were always in retailing of others' products and, perhaps, their own as well), or

- a deviance from the company's pre-Internet relationships with other companies and the consuming public, usually by attempting to "eliminate the middleman" and sell products directly to the public.

Note that in the latter case a precedent already exists in the form of outlet stores. Retail goods manufacturers or labelers such as Ralph Lauren, Bass Shoes, and numerous others have their own single-company retail locations in outlet malls and shopping centers, and over time an equilibrium has evolved between those companies and their traditional retailers. Though initial forays into Internet-based direct selling were sometimes met with resistance from retailers such as department stores, there is really nothing new about the potential for channel conflicts. Perhaps, over time, that channel conflict (as in the Levi Strauss example) in the Internet world will dissipate.

In all cases of basic product selling over the Internet—pure-play versus click-and-mortar, manufacturer versus retailer—it should be realized that basic business intelligence services have long been part of the e-tailing business approach. Click-stream data, personalization information, and CRM analytics have been used (to varying degrees of success, of course) in both acquiring customers as well as attempting to develop the highest levels of customer intimacy and loyalty possible. In this department alone, business intelligence and rudimentary data warehousing capabilities have been a key part of e-tailers' business models from the very beginning of B2C e-commerce.

Selling Services

A second B2C business model is offering and selling services—rather than physical goods—to the general consuming public. The primary distinction between the two: no physical, tangible goods are moving to the customer as a result of his or her purchasing behavior.

B2C e-commerce services can be further categorized (see Figure 2.4) into either

- "offline" services, that is, selling airline flight reservations, insurance policies, banking and investing services, or anything else that has been and continues to be sold through non-Internet channels; or

- Internet-specific services, that is, "content" available only online, such as intraday financial and investment research and commentary, books in electronic format (e-books), online magazines and periodicals, and so on.

Drawing a parallel with various forms of e-commerce product sales, the first form of selling "offline" services can be considered to be click-and-mortar e-commerce models, while the latter online-only content would be classified as pure-play service-oriented e-commerce.

In many cases, a click-and-mortar e-commerce service model is significantly more complex to build, deploy, and manage than a pure-play counterpart. The reason for this complexity isn't due to the existence of the multiple channels (Internet and non-Internet) through which consumers are reached (though the multiple-channel situation does factor into the complexity), but rather that in click-and-mortar services there tends to be a significant back-end infrastructure that is key to successful execution of a business model. For example:

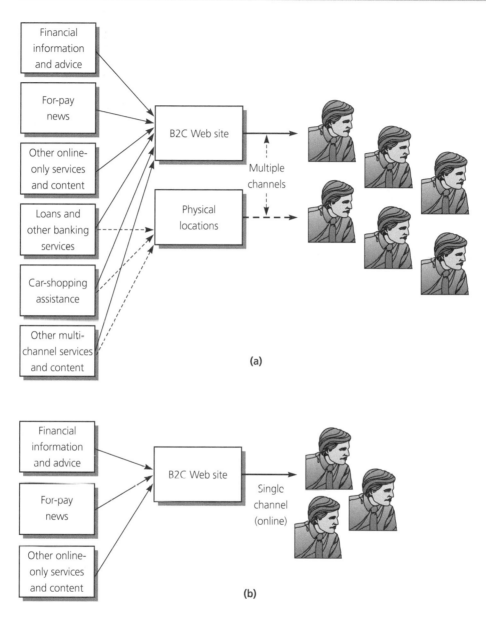

Figure 2.4 Different B2C service models: (a) "offline" services and (b) online-only services and content.

- If a customer purchases an online ticket from American Airlines, that trans-action needs to be turned into an actual reservation on an actual flight.

- If a customer researches and then purchases automobile insurance on the Internet, that commitment needs to be turned into an actual insurance pol-icy with all of the accompanying insurance company transactions needed to make that policy a reality.

In contrast, an online magazine or for-fee investment research Web site posts content on a regular basis, and when customers access or download that content, little or no back-end business processes need to accompany the customer-side transaction.

There are exceptions to the above guidelines, of course. For example, an Internet-only brokerage would arguably be considered to be a pure-play B2C e-commerce company, yet that company would still need to have all of the back-end services necessary to turn customer stock purchases and sales into real-world securi-ties transactions.

It's also not uncommon to see combinations of offline and online services: a sin-gle financial site that offers brokerage services along with online-only research.

Product and Service Packaging and Brokering

A common factor to both click-and-mortar and pure-play B2C services, though, is that in their basic business models, a single B2C company is interacting with the consuming public on behalf of its own services. Many companies have made the leap to the next generation of B2C services: packaging and/or brokering transac-tions between consumers and other companies.

For example, a Web site in the mortgage loan business may, instead of find-ing and qualifying customers for loans they themselves would underwrite, collect information from customers and gather quotes from direct mortgage lenders who are willing to bid on lending business for one or more of those prospective customers.

Likewise, another site might collect basic information from a prospect and then synthesize a number of packages for several types of services sought by the customer. One example might be automobile financing from one company and automobile in-surance from another company; another example would be comprehensive insur-ance packages (life, health, automobile, home, etc.) in the form of mix-and-match policies from a variety of companies.

There is nothing revolutionary about the basic service brokering business model, of course; insurance agents, travel agents, mortgage brokers, and many other traditional businesses have executed similar "old economy" business models for years. Nor, for that matter, is the e-commerce brokering business model only applicable to services. Consider priceline.com (*www.priceline.com*), in which that site brokers price negotiations for (referencing their commercials) product goods such as groceries and gasoline, in addition to their original travel-focused business model (airline tickets, hotel reservations, etc.). Or consider any one of the many online automobile services, in which the sites link up prospective car buyers with dealers or, in the emerging model, the automobile manufacturers themselves.

The packaging model is particularly suited to combining products and services. For instance, the example discussed earlier about packaged automobile financing and insurance can be naturally combined with online automobile purchasing services, resulting in complete "everything you need" offerings.

Another variation of e-commerce product and service brokering is a site that acts as a "shop-bot" (for "shopping robot") and instead of the prospective customer needing to manually surf among numerous online e-tailers to compare prices and find out about product availability, the shop-bot site performs those tasks and presents a consolidated results set to the person. (Shop-bot buying services were all the rage during the 1999 holiday shopping season, yet at the same time many industry observers were publicly critical of some sites, noting that in some cases e-tailers were paying shop-bot sites for preferential placement in the results set.) Again, as with travel and insurance agents, the basic concept of behind-the-scenes packaging and brokering isn't new, but there are some twists and complications in the e-commerce version. The Internet world in general, and B2C e-commerce in particular, is highly dynamic: sites pop up and disappear every day, requiring B2C brokers and packagers to factor those dynamics into their business models.

The important thing to note is that the more complex a company's B2C business model is, the greater the need for underlying robust data warehousing capabilities to combine and synthesize data from all points in the end-to-end business flows and then to turn that synthesized data into key intelligence to effectively manage and grow the business.

Portals and Communities

So far, all of the B2C e-commerce models we've discussed have one common factor: the *direct* exchange of products and/or services for a customer's payment. Whether product, service, or both; whether click-and-mortar or pure-play; whether direct sales or packaged or brokered—in all of these scenarios, B2C equals "selling something."

As most information technology professionals—as well as a large part of the general populace—know, B2C business models often involve something other than "selling something." This characteristic (some might say "silliness") became readily apparent in the spring of 2000 during the meltdown in technology stocks, particularly those related to the Internet. In fact, B2C companies had been out of favor with the investment community for a while before the general stock price downturn.

Many analysts and commentators from both the technology community as well as the investment world had seemed to initially view B2C e-commerce in the context of broadcast television or radio: the public wouldn't directly pay for what they were receiving. Instead of television programs or classic rock over the radio, the Internet as an entity would be the channel from which many different types of content would be made available to the public without charge. The economics of this world would be very much as they were in the broadcasting world: the real money was in the advertising that could be sold by a wildly popular site. And the key to the advertising dollars was the "eyeballs," or popularity of a site as measured by the number of visits. The revenue would flow to the company from other companies, *not* from consumers themselves.

The concept of the *portal* evolved to the point where the major players in the Internet space—Microsoft, Netscape, America Online, Yahoo!, and numerous others—competed to be *the* gateway to the Internet. The portal concept was echoed through numerous other corners of the Internet world: news sites (e.g., *www.cnn.com*, *www.abcnews.com*, *www.usatoday.com*, and others), or Web sites that served as *communities* (e.g., *www.ivillage.com* for women). The portal and community concept even converged with online-only B2C services in some cases: free online greeting cards, for example.

Another key contributor to many portals' and communities' revenue models was from selling consolidated data to others. Again, the more "eyeballs" the better, given that richer data sets would directly relate to higher earnings from data sales. But increasingly there are some pitfalls to the whole selling-data business in terms of privacy issues and consumer backlash.

Some observers would classify portals and communities not necessarily as B2C companies but rather as infrastructure companies—"infrastructure" not in the hardware and networking sense, but rather in the software and service sense. For the sake of completeness, we chose to include these e-commerce variations in this chapter, given that both are targeted toward the general public, meaning that some of the core data warehousing services applicable to B2C companies selling products or services also apply to these types of sites as well.

Supporting Site for Traditional Channels

Consider a traditional fast-food restaurant chain such as Burger King or Arby's. "Every business must have a net presence," the e-commerce mantra goes, and every business attempts to do so. But will Burger King sell Whoppers and french fries over the Internet? Probably not. The B2C strategy for a fast-food restaurant in this particular segment is likely to be focused on driving customer traffic in existing brick-and-mortar locations through tie-ins with current promotions, online coupons, focused marketing aimed toward certain user population segments (e.g., teenagers), and otherwise promoting brand awareness.

In some click-and-mortar business models, the Internet portion of the business strategy serves primarily as a complementary marketing channel for the overall selling of products through traditional physical retail outlets. Customer loyalty initiatives might be instituted through special Internet-based programs. For example, specially encoded numbers on cash register receipts could be entered via a Web interface and tracked in a consumer's online account, with rewards in the form of specially encoded coupons, discounts on promotional goods, and so on. Whatever the B2C business model, data warehousing services will be needed underneath to track and analyze customer activity—something usually not done in the anonymous world of high-traffic restaurants (fast food or otherwise) where, at best, paper-based (with special stamps or punches) frequent-purchaser programs were instituted for a limited time.

Classifying a B2C Business

Aside from serving as a general introduction to B2C e-commerce, the discussion in the preceding sections is extremely useful in helping us to classify a particular B2C business according to certain key characteristics. These characteristics in turn are used to help specify, architect, and deploy the correct type of data warehousing capabilities that are aligned with *that particular business*. Just as a data warehousing environment suitable for a B2B company might be an ill fit for a particular B2C company, so too would a particular B2C's data warehousing environment be just as unsuitable for some other B2C's business.

Table 2.1 illustrates a simple classification model against which a B2C company's business model should be analyzed and characterized. The attributes and their values are explained below.

Table 2.1 B2C business model classification.

Pure-Play or Click-and-Mortar	Physical Supply Chain	Service Supply Chain	Packager and/or Broker	Direct Customer Selling Opportunities	"Traffic Driver" or Other Supporting Role
P = pure-play	Y = yes	Y = yes	Y = yes	Y = yes	Y = yes
CM = click-and-mortar	N = no	N = no	N = no	N = no	N = no

Pure-Play vs. Click-and-Mortar

As was discussed in several sections above, click-and-mortar businesses are inherently more complex than their pure-play counterparts simply because of the multiple channels through which customer interactions occur. This means that your underlying data warehouse will need to

- collect and synthesize customer activity data from multiple channels, which likely means from different back-end applications and platforms

- ensure that a "whole customer view" profile can be built that includes behavioral and other data from each channel, built around correct matching of multiple identifiers for customers from the various channels and correctly handling discrepancies

- construct valid analytical models and underlying database structures to account for data gaps from traditional channels (e.g., store customers who pay cash and aren't identifiable)

- provide support for specific CRM analytics with regard to the multiple channels: static analysis such as how many customers are using each channel, how many customers use multiple channels within a given month, and so on, coupled with dynamic analysis such as channel migration, or how many customers who formerly shopped in physical retail outlets now only shop online

Physical Supply Chain

The presence of a physical supply chain (i.e., when goods are being ordered and sold) requires that aspects of the supply chain be considered in the data warehousing environment. Details about shipments (fulfillment times, number of lost shipments, etc.), canceled sales transactions due to delayed product availability or product defects, warehousing costs and other data—all of these items provide valuable content for analytical purposes.

Service Supply Chain

When a service supply chain is present (e.g., online selling of airline seats or insurance policies), data about the suppliers of those services needs to be included in the data warehouse: customer satisfaction, pricing trends, volume and revenue trends, results of test marketing programs or campaign management, and so on.

Packager and/or Broker

Building on the data needed for physical and/or service supply chains, it is important to track items such as relative frequency of particular types of packages (e.g., trends in customers wanting loans and insurance along with automobile purchases vs. just loans). For brokers with intratransaction pricing negotiations occurring (e.g., name-your-own-price models with companies accepting or declining offers), it is critical to collect and be able to analyze data such as average number of consumer price offers before acceptance, statistical variances from official pricing, trends among companies supplying goods or services with regard to accepting or declining offers, and so on.

Direct Customer Selling Opportunities

For most e-tailers, it's important to collect data about types and amounts of transactions (e.g., traditional credit card, Internet credit card, various forms of electronic currency, etc.). Conversely, portals and communities who don't directly sell products or services would not be collecting or analyzing this type of information.

"Traffic Driver" or Other Supporting Role

As noted above, the concept of using the Internet primarily to drive retail outlet traffic applies to businesses such as fast-food chains. It's critical to institute customer-oriented data warehousing structures in which customer profiles are built, maintained, and analyzed—something rudimentary within other environments (e.g., banking) but very foreign to business models in which customer anonymity was assumed. Correspondingly, it's important to build structures and establish relationships that analyze growth in cross-channel traffic (e.g., how many in-store clients show up with Web-produced coupons, and how does that number compare with last month?), which geographical markets are most "Internet-ready," and so on.

Note that the factors shown in Table 2.1 and described above represent a model for classifying a B2C business itself, rather than being a framework for the contents of that business's data warehousing environment. The primary purpose of this information is to present some early, high-level guidance about what is—and what isn't—important to any given B2C company in terms of what to concentrate on when building a data warehouse. As we'll discuss in the next section, the results of this high-level analysis will guide which parts of the generic e-commerce data warehousing framework are most applicable to a particular business's situation.

Finally, it's important to ensure that as a company's business model evolves, its underlying data warehousing services—not just its "face to the market"—change as well. Consider this straight-from-the-headlines example. In June 2000, Hollywood Entertainment halted sales of videos on its Reel.com site (*www.reel.com*), shifting instead to referring prospective purchasers to Buy.com (*www.buy.com*). Hollywood's CEO noted that "Reel.com still exists as a content-only site, partly to encourage customers to rent movies from Hollywood Video stores." Further, at some point in the future the site "could let consumers electronically download movies."[1]

The shift of this particular e-tailer from physical product seller to traffic driver, and possibly in the future to selling electronic nonphysical content, will require not only the transactional side of the Web site to evolve in step with the changes in business model, but, to most effectively understand business operations and customer dynamics, so too must their data warehousing capabilities evolve. Data that might be critical to capture when selling physical products becomes irrelevant when the site's purpose shifts to traffic driver . . . but then might once again become important should they shift to selling electronic content. Or, perhaps data important to the new traffic driving function might not have been collected and made available for analysis in the former product e-tailing model, and now the underlying data warehouse needs to evolve to manage data structures with this information.

A Data Warehousing Content Framework for e-Commerce

Just as there are a variety of B2C e-commerce business models, there are correspondingly a variety of different data warehousing environments that will provide the highest degree of business intelligence.

Before introducing a general framework of data warehousing contents, let's take a quick look at a high-level methodology through which you can determine how that framework should be tailored to a particular e-commerce situation. Figure 2.5 illustrates the sequence of phases, beginning with your e-commerce business strategy and culminating in the successful deployment of a supporting data warehouse.

There is, as you might guess, nothing that is particularly e-commerce specific about the methodology shown in Figure 2.5, or for that matter nothing that is even data warehousing specific. The idea of linking the eventual building and deployment of an automated environment back to a business strategy goes back to the structured programming days of the 1970s, if not earlier.

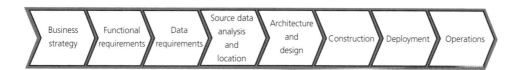

Figure 2.5 An e-commerce data warehousing methodology.

But in the context of the challenges we discussed in Chapter 1—specifically the need to deliver capabilities extremely rapidly (i.e., in "Internet time"), but also the artificial demarcation between data warehousing and other disciplines as well as the trend toward dot-com spin-offs as separate companies—it is *extremely* easy to lose focus and try to simply graft rudimentary reporting and analysis features onto an existing or in-progress B2C transactional environment . . . with the results often being less than satisfactory in terms of achieving high-value business intelligence.

Recall our discussion in the previous section in which we described a variety of different B2C business models, each with its own unique characteristics. The business strategy phase of the methodology shown in Figure 2.5 must draw *directly* from the company's business model and the characteristics described in Table 2.1 so the next phases in which requirements are collected can be most effectively focused on those that are directly in alignment with the business model. It will be of little value, for example, to architect, design, and build data warehousing structures suited for pure-play online product sales if your business model is for click-and-mortar packaging and brokering of offline and online services and content.

Another point worth noting is that there is a specific activity phase dedicated toward collecting functional requirements that precedes collecting data requirements. Many 1990s-era data warehousing environments were seemingly successfully deployed yet failed to deliver expected business intelligence capabilities because their builders focused primarily on data during analysis and design activities without regard to how the data would be used (i.e., for customer segmentation analysis, for targeted marketing, etc.). Instead, data warehouses were often built with the philosophy of "put lots of data in there that will probably be useful," and the end result was usually a data warehouse that was rarely used.

Because a data warehouse built in support of e-commerce—B2C as well as the subject of Chapter 4, B2B—needs to be tightly aligned with the business strategy, it is *imperative* that architects and strategists don't skip a step and proceed directly toward data requirements and design. The time spent on mapping the e-commerce business strategy into specific functional requirements will provide the necessary guidance needed to focus on which data is needed, where that data can be found (both Internet-based as well as in non-Internet applications), and (in a critical step that *cannot* be overlooked) what data gaps and inconsistencies exist that must be handled.

But since the foundation of a data warehouse is its contents, it is useful to have a general framework to guide the contents of the "typical" e-commerce data warehouse. Figure 2.6 shows this framework.

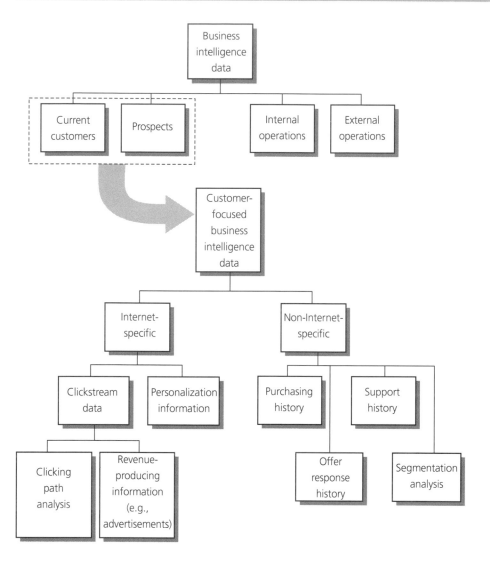

Figure 2.6 The e-commerce data warehousing framework.

The first model indicates the four major categories in which data necessary for business intelligence can be categorized:

1. Current customer data - "deep" data about current customers (transaction history, buying and browsing behavior, etc.) as discussed below with regard to the second part of the framework

2. Prospective customer data - similarly "deep" data about prospective customers, also as discussed below

3. Internal operations - anything to do with internal operations (e.g., purchasing, accounting, inventory management—all the "back-office" functions) that is essential to understand with regard to overall business effectiveness

4. External operations - anything to do with external relationships (e.g., a B2B supply chain) that supports the primary B2C business model

The second model (different types of customer-focused business intelligence information) applies to the first two categories above: current and prospective customers. One principle is that traditional pieces of customer-focused data (past purchases, history of support requests and their resolution, etc.) are important in *both* click-and-mortar and pure-play situations, and that in click-and-mortar B2C companies it's essential to have an integrated cross-channel environment to synthesize the Internet and non-Internet data (e.g., an integrated picture for a customer of purchases he or she has made in a physical location *and* online). This data includes the following:

1. Purchasing history

2. Support history - Including both online mechanisms and traditional call centers.

3. Offer response history - Is the customer or prospect someone who responds to e-mail offers? To online banner ads? To offline advertising directing him or her to a Web site? If the person is responsive and goes to a Web site, does he or she then make purchases? If so, does the person purchase the targeted merchandise, other items, or both?

4. Segmentation and customer valuation analysis - All of the "old-fashioned" CRM analytics through which customers are segmented according to the company's business model into categories that are then specifically managed.

In addition to the general-purpose customer data, it is important to also allow for Internet-specific data that helps understand customers' and prospects' behavior and thought patterns. This data would include the following:

1. Clickstream data - Available through cookies (see Chapter 7) or other mechanisms, an individual's browsing patterns, where he or she has been on the company's Web site and elsewhere, and other online tracking data can be collected and made available for analysis. Note that portions of this clickstream data (e.g., responsiveness to online advertisements) can be fed

into other customer analytical capabilities to help segment and value customers.

2. Personalization data - Taking information a customer chooses to enter about himself or herself—areas of interest, tailored product news requests, and so on—and feeding that information into the overall customer analytics models.

In Chapters 9 and 10, we'll discuss potential pitfalls in areas of data quality, privacy, and security with regard to all types of customer data, particularly Internet-specific data such as clickstreams. By way of introduction to that discussion, though, we will note here that the overly simplistic approach many dot-com e-tailers have taken with regard to their customer analytics—capture as much data as possible from tracking online behavior as well as through purchased data, the goal being to build up a whole-person view of customers *and prospects*—is very often (if not always) a faulty one that is likely to be extremely expensive *and* of little business value.

It's important to understand that a mix-and-match approach must be applied to both portions of the framework shown in Figure 2.6. For example, a B2C company that sells physical products online should, ideally, manage detailed information in all four categories: current customers, prospects, internal operations, and external operations (e.g., the supply chain). If that company is a pure-play online-only e-tailer, then their data integration challenges are significantly less than for a click-and-mortar counterpart.

Alternatively, consider a second B2C company that only sells electronic online content . . . no physical goods at all. Chances are that external operations, at least those dealing with a supply chain, aren't applicable at all to their business model nor to their underlying data warehouse.

Therefore, it's essential to follow the process shown in Figure 2.5 with regard to driving data warehousing requirements from analytical and informational functional requirements, which in turn are directly aligned with the company's business strategy. This way, the folly of "just put lots of data into the data warehouse so we can create reports" won't result in a failed B2C data warehousing environment.

B2C Data Warehousing Needs

In this section, we'll further discuss—in a business context—*how* data warehousing should be used as part of B2C business operations. There are two main categories of data warehouse usage:

- Customer-focused business intelligence
- Operationally focused business intelligence

Note that these usage models directly align with the different types of data discussed in the previous section and illustrated in Figure 2.6. But rather than simply view data warehousing as little more than supplying reports containing data from these respective areas, the following sections discuss different models of how functionally rich business intelligence services can be created from the underlying portions of the data warehousing content . . . again, in direct support of a company's business model.

Customer-Focused Data Warehousing and Business Intelligence

Unlike traditional customer-focused data warehousing (e.g., the CRM analytics discussed in Chapter 1) the Internet side of a B2C company's business operations presents the opportunity for not only after-the-fact analysis but also proactive, "shopping-time" customer interaction. The following sections discuss different forms of customer-focused business intelligence built on top of the B2C data warehouse.

Basic Customer Intelligence Services

In Chapter 1, we briefly discussed CRM analytics as belated "companion" functionality to CRM core systems (sales force automation applications and call centers). B2C basic customer intelligence services are, for the most part, functionally identical to the same CRM analytics used in brick-and-mortar (i.e., non-Internet) businesses.

As illustrated in Figure 2.7, data about customer and prospect activity (see Figure 2.6) is brought into the data warehousing environment from transactional systems, synthesized, and made available for reporting and analysis.

There are two primary forms of customer intelligence functionality:

- Rules engine

- Statistical modeling

A rules engine uses the synthesized data stored in the data warehouse and, basically, processes that data through a complicated set of if-then-else logic to determine customer segmentation, customer valuation, or whatever CRM analytical function is being instituted. For example:

```
IF customer_purchases_in_last_quarter > 5

AND time_as_customer > 18  -- months

AND average_purchase_amount > 100.00

AND customer_shops_competitive_sites is FALSE

THEN
```

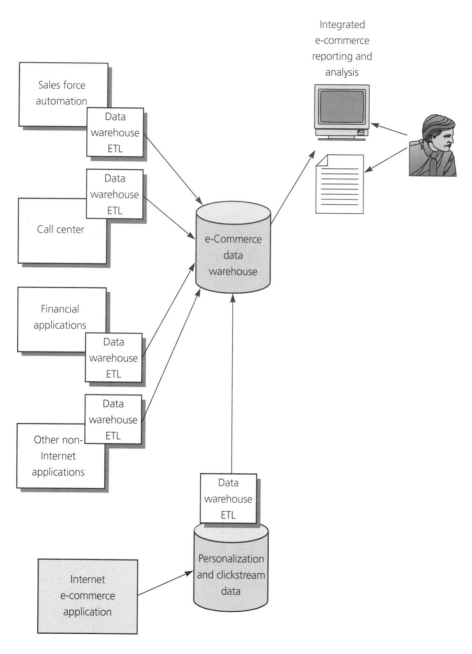

Figure 2.7 Basic customer intelligence in click-and-mortar and pure-play B2C environments.

```
set customer_class = "longterm_highvalue_loyal"

ELSE

. . .
```

The second variation of basic customer intelligence uses statistical modeling (association, classification, pattern matching, etc.) as the foundation for its analytical functionality. For example, a model might be built that processes large volumes of customer data (purchase transactions, clickstream data, personal profile information, etc.) with the purpose of identifying characteristics and data items that frequently occur together. From this information, promotions and campaigns can be created that specifically target customers and prospects in a focused manner.

In most business settings, the primary foundation upon which basic customer intelligence is provided is through the development of a whole-customer picture with a comprehensive view of customers' (and, ideally, prospects') buying patterns, personal data, and so on. In a pure-play B2C setting, developing a whole-customer picture is challenging, but often achievable in a straightforward manner—because typically a single e-commerce transactional environment is the business's foundation. Extracting customer activity and profile data from that single environment is often a matter of copying the data to a separate data warehousing platform and performing some minor restructuring and other data warehousing processes.

Click-and-mortar situations, however, are significantly more complex, simply because of the presence of multiple transactional systems for the various channels through which customer interactions occur. (And, of course, there is usually more than one transactional system, including legacy applications, that contain customer data). Different customer numbers . . . different product codes . . . different ways of designating and handling inactive customers . . . data quality issues . . . all of these application-specific features and quirks create your typical data warehousing problematic situation with regard to data integration.

But even in pure-play B2C businesses, building the whole-customer portion of the data warehouse is often not quite a slam dunk. Consider the consolidation among e-tailers that has increasingly occurred starting in early 2000, with stronger e-tailers buying weaker ones. Suddenly, the same merger-and-acquisition concerns of brick-and-mortar enterprises with regard to data warehousing integration begin to apply to B2C e-commerce businesses.

Beyond the basic set of traditional customer data (payments, personal data, etc.), B2C businesses are increasingly incorporating data from other online environments to augment their data warehousing environments. For example, data might be drawn from company-sponsored product support chat rooms and matched with other contents in the data warehouse: customers, products, and so on (see Figure 2.8).

To be blunt, though, basic customer intelligence provides very little "value add" in the context of an overall B2C business model, even when successfully accomplished. The after-the-fact nature of the analytics, coupled with the manually intensive business processes with the results of those analytics, typically results in a business process cycle in which it is very difficult to act upon the results of those analytics "in Internet time" (i.e., in time to make a substantial positive impact on operations).

As discussed in the next two sections, B2C businesses are best served by extending their basic customer intelligence services beyond reporting and analysis as an end point in the chain of automated functionality into feeding directly into critical business operations.

Before proceeding, though, we present a brief side discussion with regard to operational usage of data warehousing content. Many data warehousing strategists and technologists classify an integrated data environment as a data warehouse only if the contents are used for after-the-fact reporting and analysis. Their view is that if the contents are used for operational purposes, the environment should be called an operational data store (ODS). Our view is that you can use any term you wish—data warehouse, data mart, ODS, customer information system, the name of an application, or anything else—because the terminology is secondary to the business usage of the environment. A more important aspect than the data environment itself is how it is used—the business intelligence side. Some business intelligence (or customer intelligence, in this particular context) involves after-the-fact functionality, for example, generating reports. Other business intelligence is more operational in nature, for example, providing the foundation for targeted marketing and campaign management (the subject of the next section).

Extending Customer Intelligence Services: Part 1

Figure 2.9 depicts how rudimentary "extended" capabilities can augment the basic customer intelligence functionality discussed above. (Contrast the automated flows in Figure 2.9 with those shown in Figure 2.8.)

As with basic customer intelligence, extended capabilities such as campaign management transcend B2C e-commerce, and in fact have been available through some CRM products for a while. In a B2C environment, however, these data flows are very tightly integrated with the transactional environment with which customers and prospects interact (e.g., the Web site to which they connect with their browsers). Additionally, these interapplication data flows are augmented by other means of communicating with customers and prospects: e-mail, online banner

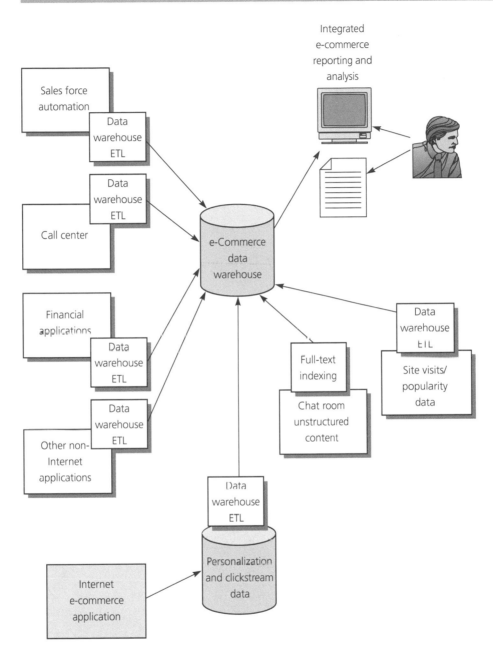

Figure 2.8 Incorporating other forms of Internet data into a B2C data warehouse.

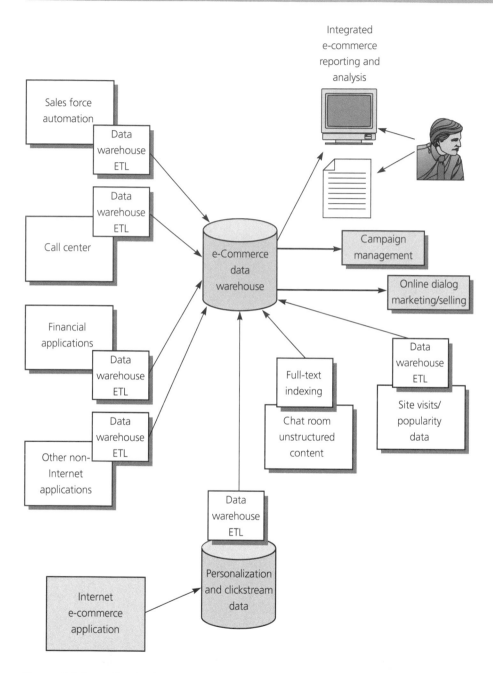

Figure 2.9 Extending basic customer intelligence capabilities with automated B2C campaign management.

advertisements, faxes (both paper-based and online faxes delivered to e-mailboxes), and so on.

The primary objective of extended customer intelligence services is to dramatically reduce the elapsed time between the business and technical processes that use information in the data warehouse to provide insight into customers' behavior—past behavior as well as likely future behavior—and other business processes that make use of that insight to tailor interactions and dialogs so that they are likely to be more productive and profitable. The inherent connectivity between the B2C business and its customer base provided through the openness of the Internet provides the mechanism for evolving from the data flows and business processes of Figure 2.8 to those shown in Figure 2.9.

Extending Customer Intelligence Services: Part 2

Even extended B2C customer intelligence such as highly automated campaign management doesn't fully take advantage of (as we noted above) the inherent Internet-provided connectivity between the business and its customer base. Specifically, the customer intelligence is still "too after-the-fact"—the contents of the data warehouse used for customer intelligence purposes is historical in nature. *Past* purchases, *past* support requests, clickstream data representing *past* Internet usage patterns—building a customer intelligence infrastructure based on the batch-oriented processes of classical data warehousing is often insufficient for what an online business needs.

Consider the interaction between a human salesperson and a customer to whom he or she has sold merchandise in the past. A good salesperson knows what the customer has previously purchased and when, knows what the person's likes and dislikes are, knows the customer's sensitivity to merchandise pricing, and knows what new products are in stock that might be of interest to that customer. More importantly, though, the salesperson can also process data points from the in-progress customer interaction such as what the customer says, nonverbal clues (e.g., a male customer having a gleam in his eye when looking at a suit but then wincing when reading the price tag), and other real-time information. It is the combination of (1) historical information and (2) the real-time data points that provides far greater shopping-time customer intelligence than available through either by itself.

Many pure-play B2C e-tailers have long provided some variation of this integrated customer intelligence—for example, an online bookseller suggesting specific titles based on a customer's past purchases together with browsing patterns of the current session. It is essential, though, for click-and-mortar B2C companies to implement similar capabilities *including data from across all of their channels*, though doing so is far more complex than for their pure-play counterparts. All of the issues we discussed earlier—multiple applications and platforms that process customer purchase transactions, different sets of customer numbers, and so on—serve to complicate the processes necessary to provide shopping-time intelligence.

An emerging form of shopping-time intelligence is called *dialog marketing*. It is discussed in Chapter 8 as part of our overview of vendor-provided business intelligence capabilities for e-commerce.

Bidirectional Data Warehousing Services

No one can argue that Internet technologies enable B2C companies to build far more comprehensive pictures of customers and prospects than ever before. The convergence of traditional forms of data warehousing content with data about online behavior (refer back to Figure 2.6) enables companies to know more and more about people with whom they deal.

Not surprisingly, there is a growing backlash within the general populace against what is increasingly viewed as invasion of privacy. The general, business, and technical press has been filled with stories in recent years about this topic that we'll address in more detail in Chapter 10.

One way a B2C company can quell some of the uneasiness among its base of customers and prospects with regard to how it uses its data warehouse for customer intelligence is to offer data warehousing services of its own to customers, prospects, or both—basically, a bidirectional approach to both CRM and data warehousing.

For example, an online packager of automobile purchasing services (including insurance and financing) can make available portions of its own data warehouse about vehicles (including often-too-elusive defect and recall data); financial institutions and their products; insurance companies and their ratings; and perhaps external market data that it purchases that details customer satisfaction ratings with companies in each of these categories.

Or perhaps an online grocer might make reports of product popularity and evaluations available to its customer base—for example, what healthy products are rated as being best tasting. Examples abound in all forms of online B2C businesses. The data made available to the public must of course be subject to contractual and legal guidelines. Some externally purchased data might not be able to be resold or republished, for example, and it certainly wouldn't be prudent to publish the names and addresses of the company's highest-volume customers for all to see.

In reality, the information provided to customers and/or prospects is likely to be of marginal value. The primary business strategy in providing bidirectional CRM and data warehousing capabilities is to soften consumer concerns about a company's own data collection policies by offering the results of other data collection to the public.

Operationally Focused Data Warehousing and Business Intelligence

There are two major types of operationally focused data warehousing that apply to B2C companies. The first—providing information about internal operations—is, for all intents and purposes, "plain old data warehousing and business intelligence." Each company's business operations model will drive how data can best be used for business intelligence purposes. With regard to the second type of operationally focused data warehousing—that focused on external operations—this is actually the same as B2B data warehousing and business intelligence, the subject of Chapter 4.

The key point to remember is that all companies—pure-play B2C companies as well as click-and-mortar or even "old economy" brick-and-mortar companies—need to have insight into their internal operations and, if applicable, cross-enterprise relationships with other companies (e.g., a supply chain). Coupling a rich set of capabilities in these areas with the customer intelligence functions discussed earlier often means the difference between survival or demise in the increasingly brutal B2C marketplace.

Summary

During the B2C euphoria as the 1990s drew to a close, conventional wisdom often held that all a company had to do was have a decent business idea, a slick Web site, and adequately performing online transaction management facilities for customer orders and payments . . . and success was just about guaranteed.

Now, however, rational thought has overtaken euphoria in the B2C place. Consider the following quote: "e-Retailers were the guinea pigs for bricks-and-mortar retailers waiting to let someone else figure out online selling, he [an Internet fund manager] says. To win, all retailers, online or not, will have to have both a Web and physical storefront."[2]

No doubt click-and-mortar B2C companies aren't the laggard dinosaurs futilely struggling to catch up as they had been portrayed by many observers during the euphoric years. Even though we believe that there *is* a place for pure-play B2C companies, one lesson from the B2C meltdown should not be lost on any firm, whether pure-play or click-and-mortar: it takes more than just (as we mentioned above) a slick Web site to succeed in B2C e-commerce. It takes a solid business strategy and solid business intelligence about *all* parts of the company's operations—those that are customer-facing as well as those related to operations. And delivering that solid business intelligence requires a sound data warehousing strategy that is closely aligned with the company's current business operations and future direction.

Endnotes

1. D. Kong, "Dot-coms struggle with e-retailing, close online stores," *USA Today,* June 28, 2000, page B1.

2. Matt Krantz and Adam Shell, "Amazon dive deepens dot-com gloom," *USA Today,* June 26, 2000, page B1.

3

Data Warehousing for Consumer-to-Consumer and Consumer-to-Business Models

In this chapter we'll look at two "derivatives" of B2C e-commerce: consumer-to-consumer (C2C) and consumer-to-business (C2B). We'll first discuss why we make the distinction, then look at examples of each of these two e-commerce models. Finally, we'll take a closer, more in-depth look at how data-warehousing-enabled business intelligence can be applied to these business models to dramatically enhance their core transactional aspects with analytical and informational capabilities.

Why the Distinction?

By now, you're probably scratching your head wondering just why in the world these authors are using the terms "C2C" and "C2B." The multitude of press—business, technical, and general—about e-commerce is dominated by discussions of the merits and shortcomings of B2C and B2B, as well as other related categories such as Internet infrastructure services and companies. For the most part, the e-commerce models that we term C2C and C2B are typically grouped with the many other B2C business models we discussed in Chapter 2.

There is, however, a fundamental distinction within this overall B2C umbrella that makes it desirable and useful to separate out the two variants discussed in this chapter. As illustrated in Figure 3.1, the many different varieties of B2C e-commerce that we previously discussed share a common characteristic: consumers

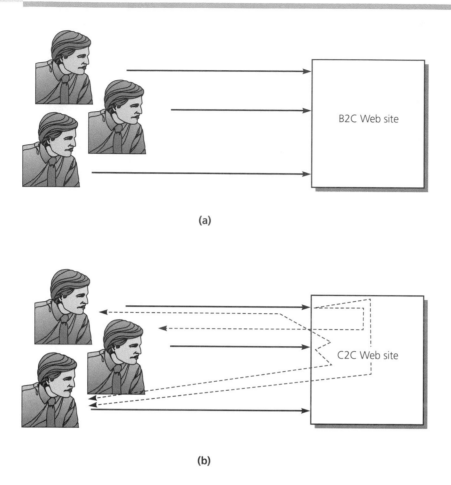

(a)

(b)

Figure 3.1 Contrasting (a) B2C and (b) C2C business models.

interact with an e-commerce provider but not with each other. This lack of cross-consumer interaction is true even when the e-commerce provider is acting as a broker for services provided by other behind-the-scenes businesses (e.g., as an online agency). Even then, the path that any given e-commerce exchange will take flows to and from a *single* consumer at a time.

But as illustrated in Figure 3.1(b), the most commonly found C2C business model—the auction Web site—has consumers interacting *with each other* throughout a given e-commerce transaction, as you might expect given the moniker of "consumer-to-consumer" to describe the category. Likewise, as we'll discuss later in this chapter, C2B e-commerce also has a foundation through which consumers interact with each other.

In addition to this key distinction in the transactional aspects of these e-commerce business models, there needs to be a corresponding distinction in the business intelligence side of the picture as well. On the one hand, the underlying data warehousing capabilities needed to provide analytical and informational capabilities are likely to be less complex with regard to integrating data from an organization's information systems than many B2C businesses. Why? Because unlike a click-and-mortar e-tailer (discussed in Chapter 2), where optimal business intelligence requires that data warehouses be built from a mixture of Internet and non-Internet transactional applications, C2C and C2B business models are inherently Internet dominated; in most cases, a single transactional application—or a closely related family of transactional applications—will provide the contents for the data warehouse (though, as we'll discuss later in this chapter with regard to eBay and half.com, dot-com mergers are complicating the data integration picture).

But this relative simplicity of source applications for the data warehouse is countered by the need for a rich set of business intelligence functionality that provides insight into how consumers relate to one another—capabilities typically not applicable to B2C business models.

The following sections discuss C2C and C2B e-commerce in more detail, focusing on both the transactional and analytical/informational sides of these business models.

C2C Business Models

Most readers are likely to be familiar with online auction sites. eBay (*www.ebay .com*) is arguably the best known, though a number of others do exist, including those that are part of larger B2C companies such as Yahoo! (*www.yahoo.com*) and amazon.com (*www.amazon.com*). We classify an auction site as a primary example of a C2C business model.

Online Auction Sites

At an auction site, the e-commerce company serves primarily as a broker and facilitator for online commerce between sellers and customers, both of whom are categorized in the "C" (consumer) arena in the context of e-commerce. The e-commerce company provides the infrastructure; sets up the rules; provides value-added services such as resolving disputes and maintaining the privacy of personal information about buyers and sellers; and provides hyperlinks to related online services and sites.

But unlike a B2C site with a relatively stable list of goods and services for sale, the "inventory" of available goods and services at an auction site is solely dependent on what is offered by sellers who choose to use that site at any given point. And, unlike most (but not all) B2C sites that sell physical goods, where those physical goods are typically brand-new and not previously owned or used by anyone, much of what is sold at an auction site would be categorized as used or previously owned.

Consider, then, that in the simplest sense B2C business success often has a direct correlation to a company's ability to (1) attract prospective customers to a Web site, and (2) turn those prospective customers into actual customers who purchase adequate amounts of goods and services and who then become repeat customers. In the C2C auction world, however, the need to attract and retain customers is only part of the equation for success; just as important is to attract sellers who offer adequate amounts of desirable goods of "sufficient" quality to generate and sustain demand on the part of those on the buyer side of the equation.

At the same time, B2C business models are often predicated on undercutting prices offered for the same or comparable goods in competitive physical brick-and-mortar locations, while in the C2C auction world, price is a nonfixed property of a particular product or service, established not by the seller but by the portfolio of candidate buyers who choose to attempt to purchase (i.e., bid for) a given item. (At most auction sites, sellers do have some input on pricing by specifying a starting bid and establishing a minimum final bid at which an item will be sold. But the ultimate price paid is determined by those on the buyer side, not the seller side.) Table 3.1 summarizes some of these key distinctions between B2C and C2C business models.

In Figure 2.6, we illustrated different groups of data that should be included in a B2C e-commerce company's underlying data warehousing environment. These same families of items are *part of* the foundation upon which a C2C data warehouse can be built, but it would be a serious mistake to attempt to "plug in" a B2C data warehouse model for C2C use. Specifically, a C2C company such as an auction site

Table 3.1 Comparing key properties of B2C and C2C business models.

Comparison Item	B2C	C2C
Products and services	Typically fixed list	Highly variable list
Pricing	Seller-specified; typically fixed	Buyer-specified (with seller constraints); marketplace-driven
Goods	Typically new	Typically "preowned"
Quantities available	Retailer-driven, subject to supply chain and other constraints	Constrained by number of sellers attracted; usually small numbers (often one) of each distinct item

would need to collect, consolidate, and make available for analysis the following data items in addition to those applicable to a B2C company:

- Additional customer attributes - Whether a customer is a seller, buyer, or both.

- Categories in which a customer participates - For example, sports trading cards, antiques, equestrian goods, nonantique collectibles, and so on. And, for each category, whether a customer is a seller, buyer, or both.

- Details about individual auctions that are summarized and aggregated by category, time, and other dimensions - For example, duration; total number of bidding customers; total number of incremental bids per customer; whether an auction goes into a "fly-off" with two or three bidders remaining long after all others have dropped out, continually outbidding each other until only one remains; and so on.

- Pricing history for similar or identical goods - For example, all of the final winning bid prices for same-quality Sandy Koufax 1960 Topps baseball cards, to be analyzed according to statistical measures (e.g., looking for outlying low or high prices vs. the norm), seasonality (e.g., if winning bid prices are higher during baseball season than during the winter), and other factors.

- Details about listings - For example, whether or not a picture is provided. (We'll use this particular attribute in the business intelligence presented later in this chapter.)

- Information about fraud and disputes - For both sellers and buyers, keeping detailed records of who is involved in disputes and/or fraudulent transactions, what the resolution was, and other related information . . . and possibly feeding that information back into the transaction management engines to prevent certain customers from participating as buyers and/or sellers.

Note that the above list is certainly not all-encompassing, but rather should present the reader with an understanding of how certain data attributes are applicable to one e-commerce business model but perhaps not to another, and how those attributes can be not only collected at transaction time but also aggregated and made available for analysis and other business intelligence purposes.

Finally, it's important to note that key subsets of the C2C data warehouse might be made available to the e-commerce company's customers—buyers, sellers, or both—as a means of building brand loyalty and providing value-added services. Some information may be in the form of rudimentary reports and queries, such as

- all selling and/or buying activity performed by a particular customer, including auctions in which the customer was not the successful high bidder

- lists such as those provided on eBay where a user can filter and review recently completed auctions and order the results according to date, price (ascending or descending), and other attributes

C2B Business Models

In the C2C business model discussed above, customers actively interact with each other based on highly dynamic supply-and-demand issues driven by the goods available at any given moment (e.g., those provided by the sellers) and the demand for each of those items (e.g., the number of potential buyers and their individual price thresholds for that given item). For all intents and purposes, there is no "B" (i.e., business) within these scenarios other than the value-added—and mostly behind-the-scenes—services provided by the auction site itself (security, privacy, infrastructure, etc.).

The C2B business model is in many ways a hybrid of B2C and C2C e-commerce. Rather than a highly dynamic, unpredictable supply of goods for sale as provided by selling customers, C2B sites make available packaged goods from "real businesses" such as electronics manufacturers, goods that are usually factory-new. But, unlike B2C e-commerce with its single-threaded flow to one customer at a time, C2B e-commerce features the collaborative flavor among customers that is found in C2C, such as in an online group buying service.

A C2B business model shares several of the same characteristics found in C2C e-commerce but not in many of the B2C variants, such as the following:

- Interaction among geographically dispersed consumers who most likely don't know each other.

- Prolonged—but fixed-time—periods during which those consumers come together, interact, dynamically establish a price according to market forces, and then complete the transaction. (Note though that in C2C e-commerce such as auction sites, prices go higher during the fixed-time period, while in C2B prices drop.)

Consequently, many of the same data warehousing needs applicable to C2C businesses also apply to C2B: for example, the need to collect data about how customers interact with one another (number of customers participating in each transaction, how prices change, etc.).

A Closer Look at Integrating Business Intelligence into a C2C Business Model

In this section, we'll take a closer look at how an organization can augment its core transaction-side e-commerce services with closely integrated business intelligence capabilities, built on top of an underlying data warehouse.

Consider an online auction site, the classical example of C2C e-commerce. Back in Figure 2.5 in Chapter 2, we noted that the recommended phasing for developing an e-commerce data warehousing capability should follow a "best practices" sequence of steps:

- Develop a business strategy.

- Collect and validate functional requirements.

- Identify data requirements.

- Identify data sources and potential data gaps and issues.

- Create the data warehousing architecture and design.

- Build (construct) the data warehouse.

- Deploy the data warehouse.

- Manage ongoing operations.

Let's take this sequence of steps from the top. The first phase—developing a business strategy—should ideally be done *not* in a data-warehousing-centric (or business-intelligence-centric) manner, but rather in conjunction with the company's overall business strategy. Too often in classical, after-the-fact data warehousing, organizations would myopically document a data-warehousing-focused strategy that would be oriented around report creation or other lower-level business functionality . . . and the resulting "strategy" (to use the term loosely) would usually be viewed by key business executives as nonstrategic and not worthy of business sponsorship or support.

Therefore, for our auction example, we'll denote a hypothetical business strategy as the following:

> . . . to build the leading online auction site covering a wide range of categories of physical goods and services. Our auction site must be seen by the online public as a 100% safe place to sell and/or to purchase goods. Fraudulent transactions will not be tolerated, and we will attempt to flag individual auctions that have a high likelihood of being fraudulent. Additionally, we will quickly resolve all seller-buyer

disputes over claimed product quality, and we will also attempt to flag individual auctions that exhibit characteristics of other disputed auctions. We will also . . .

Again, note that the above business strategy is exactly that: an overall business strategy rather than a data warehousing or business intelligence strategy. We then need to identify key aspects of the business strategy that will be built and managed not through transactionally focused technology (e.g., the software that runs the auctions themselves) but rather through closely related data warehousing and business intelligence. Looking at the business strategy, we identify the following portions:

- we will attempt to flag individual auctions that have a high likelihood of being fraudulent

- we will also attempt to flag individual auctions that exhibit characteristics of other disputed auctions

(In a real-world situation, there will be a number of other portions of the business strategy that would fall within the data warehousing realm, but for purposes of this chapter we'll focus on the two items listed above that are closely related.)

The next step is to identify and validate specific analytical and informational functionality that would be directly related to the identified business strategy portions. At the highest level, the functionality items are often simple rewordings of what was stated in the business strategy:

- Detect and attempt to prevent potential fraud.

- Detect and attempt to prevent potential disputes over product quality.

Next, each high-level functionality item is decomposed into more detailed functionality:

- Detect and attempt to prevent potential fraud.

  - Analyze past transactions—fraudulent and legitimate—and attempt to identify common characteristics for each category.

  - Analyze all new auction postings and flag those auctions that exhibit "potential fraud characteristics."

  - Determine whether or not to prevent auction from being posted.

- Detect and attempt to prevent potential disputes over product quality.

  - Analyze past transactions that involved quality-related disputes and attempt to identify common characteristics.

- Analyze all new auction postings and flag those auctions that exhibit "potential dispute characteristics."

- Determine whether or not to prevent auction from being posted.

Two things should be noted about the functionality requirements listed above. First, note that each item begins with an action verb—in this example, *analyze, detect,* and *determine.* We strongly recommend that identified functionality be action oriented to ensure that data-warehousing-provided capabilities don't degenerate into simple report generation that is hopelessly detached from an organization's primary business mission and strategy.[1]

Second, we see a high degree of similarity between the two functionality groups we've identified—fraud detection and dispute management—and as such, we decide that a common set of business intelligence capabilities, with common underlying data warehousing content, can be built for both of these functional requirements.

We next identify the types of data needed to enable the desired functionality, and come up with a list that includes the following:[2]

- Seller's information (name, e-mail address, customer number at our auction site, if the seller has sold goods on our site before, etc.)

- Details about the product being sold (product category, product subcategory, actual product, etc.)

- Details about the listing (whether a picture is included or not; seller-specified duration of the auction; reserve—minimum amount for a winning bid—specified by the seller; wording used in the listing; payment method(s) specified; etc.)

Next, we need to identify where the required data can be found so it can be extracted and loaded into the data warehouse. In our example, we actually have a quite easy task, as compared to the typical data warehouse: everything is located in a single source application, the one that manages the online auction process. Keep in mind, though, that perhaps another auction company could have a more complex source data environment, such as either of the following:

- Our online auction company had, one year earlier, purchased another online auction site, and the respective transactional systems hadn't been integrated until three months ago; therefore, access to historical data requires access to the acquired company's archived databases.

- Our online auction company had begun operations three years ago with auction management software that was replaced six months ago with a completely rewritten, more functional system; therefore, access to historical data requires access to no-longer-used transactional databases that are stored on offline tape.

The key point is not to overlook potential complexity as you transition from identifying required data to the next steps of architecting and designing the data warehouse. Even in a pure-play dot-com C2C company with no non-Internet operations, data integration as part of constructing a data warehouse may very well be as complex as it would be for a click-and-mortar B2C company.

Next comes the data warehouse architecture and design. It's important to note that we're not simply referring to rudimentary database structures and design, nor even to the "extended" data warehousing services such as extraction, transformation, and loading (ETL) capabilities to move data from source applications into the data warehouse's database. In the context of "advanced" data warehousing for e-commerce, we must also architect and design how the data will be used in the course of analytically focused e-commerce business processes.

For example, the first item under the decomposed functionality for both fraud detection and potential dispute detection notes that past transactions need to be analyzed with the goal of identifying common characteristics that can help predict fraud and/or disputes. In data warehousing terminology, this would be considered *data mining:* sifting through large amounts of data but not under the guidance of specific queries or reports; instead, statistical or artificial intelligence-related models are built through which data is examined and certain items of interest are discovered and noted. In the statistical world, modeling techniques such as association and classification are used; from the artificial intelligence world, neural networking technology is often applied to data mining problems.

The next requirement—to screen all new auctions to see if they exhibit characteristics common to past fraud or customer disputes—likely means that the transactional services of entering a new auction will need to be augmented with filters through which applicable attributes can be analyzed. It then becomes a matter of business policy rather than technology to determine what to do when a new auction is flagged for potential problems. The auction site may choose to automatically reject the listing (unlikely, unless there is a "showstopper" item such as the name and e-mail address of a known problem customer who has been barred from selling goods on the site). Or perhaps flagged new entries are routed to a specialist within the company who contacts the poster and then makes a human-intervention determination whether or not to permit the new posting.

Finally, the architecture and design needs to take maintenance and upkeep into consideration. For example, it may be decided that since our auction site handles hundreds of thousands of auctions every month, it's imperative that the data mining capabilities be frequently rerun (let's say once a week). Therefore, there would need to be not only a mechanism to bring in the latest rounds of transactional data (basically, the standard ETL "restocking" processes found in most data warehousing environments) but also a means to translate the new results into updated filters and ensure that those new filters are put into place to scan all new auctions.

How would this all work? Let's say that the "analyze past transactions" process comes up with the following information:

- Past fraud has occurred in the categories of "antiques" and "art."

- Past customer disputes over quality are most commonly found in "sports trading cards," and within that overall category commonly within "baseball cards" and even further decomposed into a high degree of disputes for baseball cards between 1960 and 1975.

- With regard to fraud in antiques and art, the number of incidents has been small, and other than "known problem people" there are no statistically valid common characteristics to those incidents; therefore, a "fraud filter" for new auction postings is *not* pertinent, at least at present.

- With regard to baseball card quality disputes, the data mining functionality did discover that a "statistical majority" of disputed items exhibited at least three of the following characteristics:

  - Were not accompanied by a picture

  - Only accepted payment by check, not credit card nor through payment services provided by the auction site

  - Had no reserve (minimum acceptable bid) specified by the seller

  - Had a seller-specified auction duration of three days or less

  - Used language in the description that gave a sense of urgency (e.g., "your only chance ever to own this . . .")

Using the above information, the auction site can build a filter that flags baseball card auctions with the "warning characteristics" and, as noted earlier, devise and enforce business policies for how that information will be used (automatic rejection, human intervention, etc.).

Data warehousing can be applied to many different aspects of a C2C auction site's business operations. For example, suppose the auction site was originally organized around high-level categories, and subsequently a decision is made to introduce subcategories to further filter the listings. The company can analyze auction patterns from before the subcategorization and after: bid prices, numbers of bids, duration of auctions, tendency for sellers to offer new merchandise, and so on.

Finally, changes over time in business operations will require a company to revisit its data warehousing environment and business intelligence capabilities. For example, in early 2000 eBay purchased half.com *(www.half.com)*, a similar company except that half.com is an online consignment service with fixed prices rather than the auctions. eBay may very well wish to build a consolidated customer database across its various online companies, with much of the same information as we detailed earlier in this chapter (e.g., product categories in which a customer participates; within each category, whether the customer is a seller, buyer, or both; etc.). If either company has a fraud and potential dispute detection engine similar to that of our example, they may wish to extend that engine to encompass operations from both Web sites. Additionally, they may wish to perform cross-site campaign management and targeted marketing; analyze pricing trends for similar products under the auction and consignment sale business models; look at comparative profitability between both sides of business operations; and other functionality. All of this would require any existing data warehousing capabilities to be extended to accurately reflect the combined companies' business strategy. (Disclaimer: The above discussion about eBay and half.com is only an example; neither author has done consulting work with either company nor is familiar with their internal operations, integration plans, or data warehousing capabilities.)

Summary

The key take-away from this chapter is that e-commerce data warehousing must reflect a company's business strategy. Whether that company is a click-and-mortar B2C site, a C2C or C2B variant of B2C, or a B2B company (discussed next in Chapter 4), there is no such thing as a one-size-fits-all approach to data warehousing and business intelligence in e-commerce. Additionally, the steps we worked through in this chapter's example would be just as applicable to any other type of e-commerce business model (or, for that matter, *any* business model in which business intelligence becomes an integral part of operations).

Endnotes

1. More information about how to collect and prioritize data-warehousing-related functionality can be found in A. Simon, *90 Days to the Data Mart,* John Wiley & Sons, 1998, in the "Week 1" chapter.

2. In a real-world setting, the mapping of functionality to data would occur at the lowest levels of identified functional requirements. In our example, we would note that the requirement for "Analyze past transactions . . ." would require certain data elements, while the next requirement of "Analyze all new auction postings . . ." would require another set of data elements, some of which might be the same as those already identified but possibly augmented with new ones. In the interest of space and readability, we skip the one-by-one discovery of each set of data elements, instead proceeding to the aggregated set. Readers interested in learning more about how to use matrices to organize and consolidate individual sets of data elements as part of the requirements collection process are referred to *90 Days to the Data Mart,* referenced above.

4

Business-to-Business Data Warehousing

During several months in late 1999 and early 2000, the e-commerce universe underwent a major shake-up, at least in the investment community. Suddenly, business-to-consumer (B2C) business models and companies were out of favor, a "relic of Internet past." What was now in favor? Business-to-business (B2B) companies—those e-commerce business models that focused not on selling goods and services over the Internet to the general public, but rather facilitated companies doing business with each other through Internet technologies.

Alas, it was only a few short months before B2B went out of favor—again, with the investing public and financial advisors—in favor of yet another subcategory of Internet technologies, those companies that dealt with infrastructure (e.g., networking products). Farewell, B2B . . . we hardly knew you.

Wait a moment . . . not so fast. The fact of the matter is that B2B e-commerce is very much alive and well, stock prices and investor sentiment at any given moment notwithstanding. (For that matter, so is B2C e-commerce, though as we discussed in Chapter 2, there is a fundamental shift under way toward more hybrid click-and-mortar business models and away from pure-play, Internet-only e-tailers.) Indeed, B2B e-commerce is very much at its infancy, meaning that unlike the B2C world, there is still time to ensure that business intelligence and data warehousing become integral parts of companies' business-to-business initiatives.

However, there is another parallel between B2C and B2B that needs to be considered and that we'll discuss in this chapter. To most of the general and business public, the term "B2B" is a not-easily-understood, sort-of-fuzzy categorization for e-commerce that is . . . well, it's something different than B2C, but that's about as precise as many people get. Just as we discussed several varieties of B2C business models in Chapter 2 to establish a context before discussing B2C business intelligence, we'll begin this chapter by looking at several different varieties of B2B e-commerce. We'll then further discuss how data-warehouse-enabled business intelligence can best be coupled with the transactional side of B2B.

B2B Business Models

There are two primary categories of B2B e-commerce:

- Supply-chain-oriented B2B
- Marketplace-centric B2B

Both are discussed below.

Supply-Chain-Oriented B2B

Supply chain automation has been a goal—an elusive goal, at that—of businesses (mostly large, Fortune 1000–sized ones) since the early 1980s. As illustrated in Figure 4.1, supply chain automation has evolved from proprietary attempts (that usually failed) to quasi-open interfaces based on electronic data interchange (EDI) standards to, by the mid-1990s, private cross-company interfaces based on Internet technologies that were usually termed *extranets*.

As Internet-provided capabilities and services exploded in the late 1990s, providers of supply chain software such as I2 *(www.i2.com)* shifted their focus toward using the public Internet as the channel over which supply-chain-related services

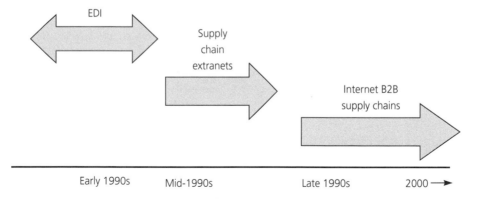

Figure 4.1 Evolution of supply chain automation.

would be made available to businesses. New vendors such as Ariba (*www.ariba.com*) emerged, also competing in this space.

In essence, supply-chain-related B2B e-commerce permits companies to build and manage highly open interfaces among one another, all in the interest of moving physical goods from an originating source to a final destination (and usually some number of other stops in between) as efficiently as possible. A supply chain is made up of much more than ordering, moving, and accepting delivery of physical goods, of course; therefore, a number of services are usually part of the B2B environment, including the following:

- Procurement - the actual process of ordering goods, processing the order, and sending appropriate confirmations to all applicable parties

- Order fulfillment - the set of business processes that "make an order real"—managing the picking and packing processes, shipping and transportation, and so on

- Payment - all services associated with the transfer of funds from the party or parties who are paying to the party or parties who are to receive part or all of the payment

Of course, as with most things in the world of the Internet, the above services—when spoken about in the context of B2B e-commerce—are termed

- e-procurement

- e-fulfillment

- e-payment

A distinguishing characteristic of this B2B variety is the relatively stable nature of the parties involved in the supply chain. For example, a manufacturer of watercraft may have several companies from which it purchases marine-quality lumber, several other companies that supply hardware, perhaps only one company that provides navigational equipment, and so on. While new trading partners may come and go on occasion, the end-to-end flows of materials and funds tend to involve most of the same companies with only minor evolution over time.

Likewise, prices in the supply chain tend to be fairly stable. Even when different price points are available, it's usually through a fairly orderly quantity-discount process: for example, a 5% discount for one quantity, an 8% discount for a higher quantity, and so on. Prices will change over time but usually through formally announced changes to the price list.

Some providers of supply-chain-oriented B2B services provide entire end-to-end packages upon which most or all of a given company's cross-enterprise operations can be based. Other B2B providers concentrate on only one or two specific services that are intended to be integrated with other supply chain capabilities obtained elsewhere. For example, a company called Submitorder (*www.submitorder .com*) specializes in e-fulfillment. According to its Web site:[1]

> If it involves e-fulfillment we do it. By bringing together core competencies in information technology, small package distribution, customer service and marketing, we provide the e-fulfillment services your business needs to get an e-tail site up and running quickly, while keeping your customers happy and sales growing steadily. We'll work with your site designers, or ours, to ensure your site is shopper-friendly and seamlessly integrated with our flexible distribution management system. We'll work with you to streamline the supply chain, determine inventory levels, train our service specialists on your products . . .

A point worth noting in the above description is the reference to "provid[ing] the e-fulfillment services your business needs to get *an e-tail site* up and running. . . ." An often overlooked point in the ongoing debate over the relative merits of B2C and B2B e-commerce is that the two are often irrevocably linked together in a company's business operations . . . even if the company's transactional and—more likely—informational and analytical systems don't reflect the proper degree of integration. Back in Chapter 2 we mentioned that the highest degree of business intelligence can and should be obtained through synergistically building integrated analytical systems that combine data from *both* the customer-facing (B2C) and back-end operational (B2B) sides of a business (see Figure 2.6). Later in this chapter we'll look at some B2B-focused examples of how data from customer-facing and back-end operational processes should be consolidated and synthesized.

Marketplace-Centric B2B

Whereas supply-chain-oriented B2B features a relatively stable set of participants and prices, marketplace-centric B2B is a highly dynamic environment in which buyers and sellers come and go, and prices are set in an auctionlike manner. Basically, marketplace-centric B2B can be seen in the same light as an auction site (see C2C e-commerce in Chapter 3), but instead of sellers offering antiques and baseball cards and other forms of collectibles to prospective buyers, B2B sellers offer building materials, machinery, automotive parts, or any one of thousands of other types of goods.

Marketplace-centric B2B is still very much at an infancy stage. Major, high-profile announcements in late 1999 and early 2000 appeared in which, for example, automotive manufacturers were planning to band together and build an automotive manufacturing exchange through which parts and components could be purchased from potential suppliers. But while the largest B2B exchanges were just beginning to be built in 2000, smaller exchanges have already begun to appear and are changing B2B commerce in their respective vertical markets. For example, farmers might use the Farmbid.com exchange *(www.farmbid.com)* as "a one-stop shop for everything they need, like heavy equipment, market information, seeds, chemicals, or weather reports."[2] In the case of Farmbid.com, there not only is an exchange with auctions and classifieds, but also an "Ag Superstore" with fixed prices—sort of a cross between a B2C e-tailer (the farmer as the consumer, in this case) and supply-chain-oriented B2B services (with the farm being considered as a business).

In the context of the Big 3 automobile manufacturers or aircraft manufacturers or other gigantic companies with enormous, highly complex cross-business trading needs, an area such as farming might seem a bit . . . well, more B2C than B2B. However, Goldman Sachs estimates the marketplace for the 1.9 million U.S. farms will top $1 trillion by 2004,[3] certainly sizable enough not only for transactional B2B e-commerce to be applied but also (as we'll show in examples later in this chapter) for business intelligence and data warehousing to be part of the picture as well.

Another example is Rightscenter.com *(www.rightscenter.com)*, an exchange for intellectual property related to books and publications. As noted on the site's home page, Rightscenter.com is a "marketplace where agents, sub-agents, scouts and publishers meet to buy and sell rights."[4] Elsewhere on the site, specific Rightscenter.com services and capabilities are described:

> Rightscenter.com users can instantly exchange multipage proposals, manuscripts, galleys, covers, author photos, illustrations, press releases, and other materials—all without mailing costs or bulky email attachments. And rightscenter.com makes it easy to send manuscripts or catalogs to any number of contacts, in any number of countries, in less time than it would take to send a single submission using conventional methods.[5]

Unlike Farmbid.com and other types of exchanges, physical goods are not being bought and sold; instead, intellectual property is, meaning that there aren't the same types of supply-chain-related issues behind the B2B e-commerce found at Rightscenter.com.

A common theme to marketplace-centric B2B is that the exchanges tend to be vertical market oriented: automotive manufacturing, farming, writing and publishing, and so on. The premise is that companies in a given line of business are best served by very focused, targeted e-commerce services oriented toward their particular business needs—and, importantly, are more likely to participate in marketplace-centric B2B e-commerce as buyers, sellers, or both.

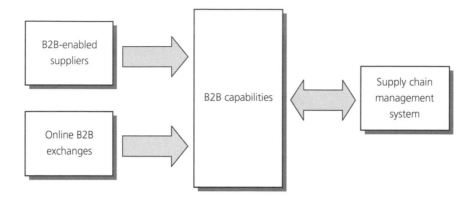

Figure 4.2 Hybrid B2B e-commerce approaches.

Hybrid B2B Models

As B2B e-commerce continues to take hold, most organizations will likely adapt a mixture of services containing both supply-chain-oriented and marketplace-centric capabilities (see Figure 4.2).

For companies pursuing a hybrid approach to B2B e-commerce, augmenting core transactional services with business intelligence becomes a necessity (see Figure 4.3). Consider a manufacturing company that purchases some portion of its raw materials and components from other companies through an Internet-enabled supply chain, but is also dabbling in online marketplace exchanges.

An organization needs to be able to answer questions such as

- Over the past six months, what savings have resulted from shifting part of the e-procurement process away from regular trading partners to a dynamic set of suppliers through a vertical market B2B exchange?

- Has there been any drop-off in overall quality of procured components, and if so, is that attributable to using new suppliers through the exchange?

- Have there been any price reductions from regular supply chain trading partners, and if so, are they attributable to the shift toward using the exchange?

- Should all e-procurement occur using an exchange?

- If more than one exchange is being used, which is more cost-effective? Which has more reliable suppliers?

Being able to answer critical questions such as those posed above—and hundreds, maybe thousands of others—requires that applicable data be drawn from all

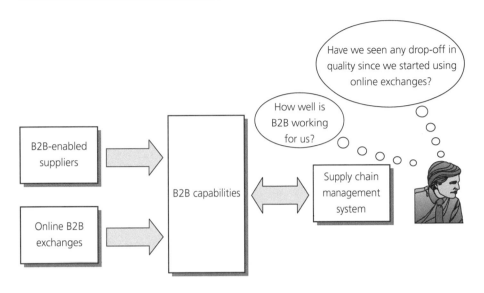

Figure 4.3 Adding business intelligence to hybrid B2B business models.

applicable transactional systems into a data warehousing environment (see Figure 4.4).

More about Business Intelligence Models for B2B

The previous section presents an example of data warehousing being applied to a fairly complex, multifaceted B2B environment. Even for less complex B2B situations, data warehousing and the resultant business intelligence are still an essential part of the picture. This section presents several different facets of the B2B business intelligence arena and how data warehousing capabilities can best be deployed.

Basic Customer Intelligence

In Chapter 2, we discussed "basic customer intelligence"—in the form of CRM analytics—as an integral part of B2C business intelligence and data warehousing. The same principles apply to the B2B world as well . . . we're still talking about customers and trying to learn as much as possible about them, right?

Well, sort of. The core aspects of basic customer intelligence, such as performing customer segmentation by marrying purchasing behavior with clickstream data, do apply to B2B. Statistical modeling, rules engines, or perhaps a combination of both are the same in B2B as in B2C.

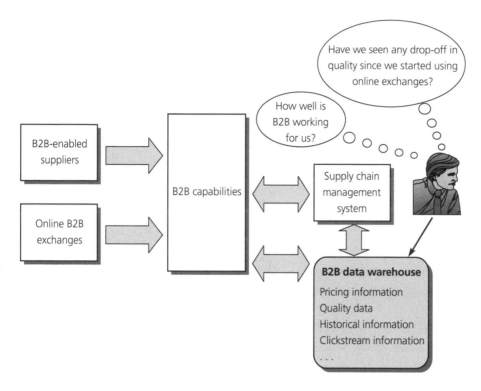

Figure 4.4 Providing highly integrated B2B intelligence through an underlying data warehouse.

But it's important to understand that there are some key differences between the B2C and B2B worlds, and just popping in a generic solution for customer analytics is often a recipe for disaster. Consider the following four significant distinctions:

1. Size of customer base - A B2C company has a customer base that could range into the millions (or at least they hope that's the size of their customer base!). Even though most B2C companies are "quasi-vertical" in nature—that is, they focus on a narrow topical area such as real estate, gardening, automobiles, and so on—the general public at large represents their target market. In the B2B world, however, customer bases are smaller—usually much, much smaller. Consider a B2B company that sells supplies and equipment for commercial restaurants. Their target market may range into the tens or hundreds of thousands, and their actual customer base may be in the hundreds or thousands, but this is nowhere near the millions of customers that an online bank might have or the millions of book purchasers from an online bookstore.

On the one hand, the smaller B2B customer base can be advantageous. Less disk storage might be needed to manage basic customer data, including detailed transaction history. Data quality issues (see Chapter 9) are likely to be less of a problem than in a B2C environment.

At the same time, however, more is at stake with regard to the effectiveness of applying business intelligence. Monetary values of each transaction are usually larger, often much larger, than with B2C purchases. Even though transactions might occur less frequently in B2B settings than in B2C, customers are likely to be more demanding and less forgiving should shipping delays, incorrect e-fulfillment (e.g., wrong contents of the order), or defective products occur.

2. Customer ≠ Person - In a B2C setting, a "customer" is usually associated with a single individual or, should *householding* (e.g., grouping individuals who live together into a single household for reporting and analysis that supplements basic single-customer business intelligence) be part of the B2C company's business model, a small, usually fixed number of rarely changing individual customers. However, in a B2B setting a customer equates to a company, even if that company might actually be a single-person enterprise. But for customer companies larger than single-person or small family enterprises, there is usually a procurement person—or maybe more than one—who factors into the seller-buyer equation. Therefore, B2C analytical models that segment customer (read: person or household) behavior are likely to inaccurately analyze B2B customer behavior should, for example, different procurement specialists make purchases in unpredictable patterns (e.g., one person one time, maybe—or maybe not—a different procurement person the next time).

For that matter, even just the basic "record keeping" (e.g., determining the data warehouse's contents) is more complex in the B2B setting than in B2C—recording not only customer attributes (again, those about the company) but also attributes about the various people involved.

3. Different segmentation models - As we discussed in Chapter 2, there are a variety of ways in which customers might be segmented. However, a B2C-oriented segmentation model might provide value for targeted consumer marketing but be unsuitable for a B2B environment.

4. How about "seller intelligence?" - In a B2C setting, the business intelligence picture is overwhelmingly weighted toward the "B" side of the equation. Businesses build data warehouses (or they should do so, anyway); people (the "C"

side) don't. But in B2B, *both* sides of the equation are businesses. Therefore, not only should businesses build data warehouses to provide intelligence about their customers, but other businesses should also build data warehouses to provide intelligence about their suppliers. And, for that matter, it's not just "other" businesses, but businesses in general. That is, a business that purchases materials and/or services from other companies and, at the same time, sells goods and/or services to other companies should build a *unified* data warehousing environment including data about *all* of its trading partners, sellers and customers. And since a given company may be both a supplier and a customer of another company, that needs to be considered also in the data warehouse's contents and resultant business intelligence (reports, online screens, etc.).

As we noted in Chapter 2, B2C customer intelligence can also take on an operational flavor in addition to after-the-fact reports and other forms of intelligence; the chief example is campaign management. Consider the following example, then, from the B2B world of how B2B data warehousing can be operationalized. Earlier, we discussed Farmbid.com as an example of an auction exchange and an online fixed-price marketplace. (Disclaimer: Neither author has performed consulting services for, nor is familiar with, Farmbid.com operations or capabilities; the example below is purely hypothetical and could apply to any farming-oriented B2B site or exchange.)

In addition to the exchange and marketplace, Farmbid.com also offers online weather reports. Farming is a highly weather-dependent activity, and one of the most frustrating occurrences to a farmer is making specific plans (e.g., cutting hay or harvesting oats) based on a weather forecast only to find a totally different weather outlook later the same day or the next day. Therefore, farmers often check a provider of weather information (e.g., the Weather Channel or a local forecast) frequently each day.

Farmbid.com might build a data warehouse that contains the types of data content we've been discussing—customer purchasing history for the fixed-price marketplace, auction activity, and clickstream data. In analyzing the clickstream data, they might notice that a large portion of their regular customer base checks the weather report several times a day during peak seasons of farming activity. Looking for new sources of revenue, they might begin a targeted marketing effort for a new service in which owners of farming businesses who are "heavy users" of weather reports can subscribe to a multichannel weather alert service. For example, whenever there is a significant change in the local weather (e.g., tomorrow's rain will actually

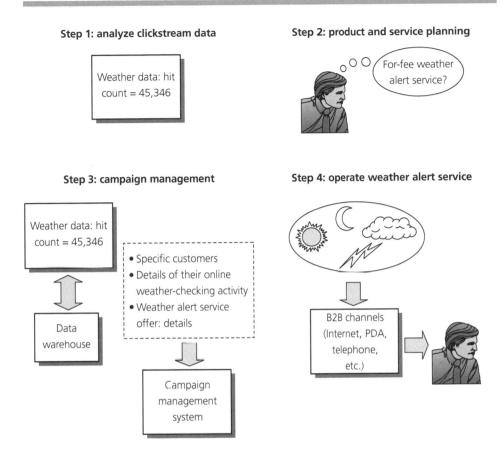

Figure 4.5 Extended B2B customer intelligence and new business operations.

be showing up this afternoon), the farmer will receive immediate notification via one or more of several different communication channels: e-mail, automated telephone message, pager, fax, and so on (see Figure 4.5). This way, farmers who are out in their fields might wear a pager or carry a mobile phone, and even away from their computers, they can receive alerts of impending changes to what had been anticipated for weather activity.

e-Marketplace Intelligence

In Chapter 3, we presented a hypothetical situation of how an auction site such as eBay might use data warehousing for key business functions such as fraud detection and reducing the number of customer disputes. In a C2C environment such as an auction site, data warehousing isn't really applicable to either "C" side—only to the exchange itself.

Now consider a B2B e-marketplace. Not only does the exchange itself need to build data warehousing capabilities for the same reasons as a C2C marketplace (e.g., fraud detection and dispute management; marketing; seller and buyer activity analysis; etc.), but so too should companies on either "B" side of the e-marketplace build data warehousing functionality (see Figure 4.6).

Value Chain Intelligence

Earlier, we discussed how a typical online business would likely participate in both supply-chain-oriented and marketplace-centric B2B services . . . and would build a data warehousing environment in which data from both channels is synthesized. While there is certainly great value to be gained from the consolidated procurement and supply intelligence, focusing on various supply chain models is only part of the overall business intelligence picture.

One of the overused terms in the management and technology consulting world during the past few years is "value chain," a phrase typically used to refer to end-to-end creation of value as a result of whatever a business happens to do (e.g., builds and sells automobiles; provides banking and financial services; etc.).

As illustrated in Figure 4.7, a driving factor for building an enterprise-wide data warehouse may very well be to optimize that company's end-to-end value chain. For example, building in a mix of B2B and B2C data may enable business intelligence such as is shown in Table 4.1 (value chain "extensions" highlighted in bold).

Summary

The world of B2B e-commerce is, as we noted at the outset of this chapter, just beginning to take form. For the most part, B2B is a "brave new world," and companies can define their business models in whatever way they see fit.

It is, therefore, *imperative* that business intelligence services be defined as critical, highly integrated aspects of those B2B business models, with business intelligence enabled by the appropriate forms of data warehousing underneath. The material in this chapter is merely a starting point for B2B companies. By following the approach we've discussed several times in this book so far, where the data warehousing capabilities track directly back to the company's business strategy, building a business-intelligence-enabled enterprise can be a straightforward proposition with universal support and buy-in.

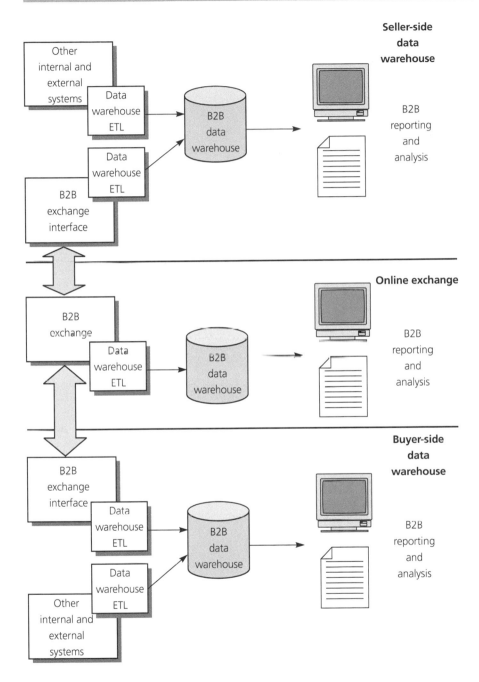

Figure 4.6 Data warehousing and e-marketplace exchanges.

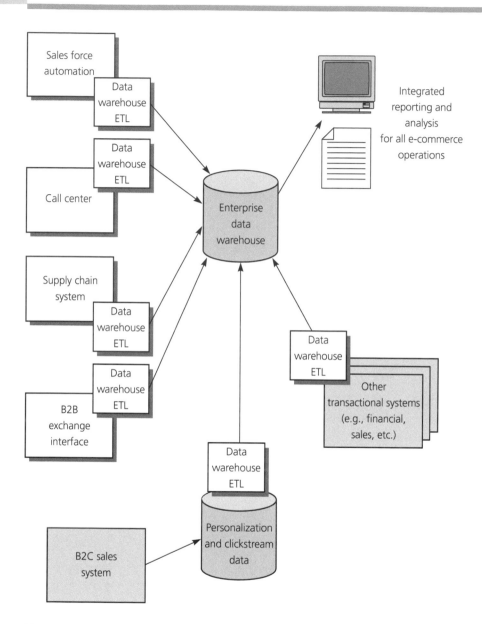

Figure 4.7 An enterprise-wide "value-chain-focused" data warehouse.

Table 4.1 Value chain analytical questions.

B2B-focused analytical question (from earlier in the chapter)	Value-chain-focused analytical question
Over the past six months, what savings have resulted from shifting part of the e-procurement process away from regular trading partners to a dynamic set of suppliers through a vertical market B2B exchange?	Over the past six months, **how has customer satisfaction been affected** after shifting part of the e-procurement process away from regular trading partners to a dynamic set of suppliers through a vertical market B2B exchange?
Has there been any drop-off in overall quality of procured components, and if so, is that attributable to using new suppliers through the exchange?	Has there been any drop-off in overall quality of procured components attributable to using new suppliers through the exchange, **and if so, how has that affected key customer retention measures?**
Have there been any price reductions from regular supply chain trading partners, and if so, are they attributable to the shift toward using the exchange?	Have there been any price reductions from regular supply chain trading partners, and if so, are they attributable to the shift toward using the exchange? **If we're dynamically lowering prices to mass market consumers by keeping our gross margins at a fixed amount, how has that affected new customer acquisition and customer reordering?**
Should all e-procurement occur using an exchange?	**If we shift all e-procurement to an exchange, what statistical models do we need to build to predict the likely effect on revenue, earnings, and customer satisfaction ratings?**
If more than one exchange is being used, which is more cost-effective? Which has more reliable suppliers?	**Are any of the exchanges we use selling products directly to consumers, and if so, how is that affecting our revenue and earnings?**

Endnotes

1. As of August 7, 2000.
2. M. Santosus, "A growing business: Farmbid.com tries to give farmers everything they need," *WebBusiness Magazine,* March 2000, referenced from the *CIO Magazine* Web site (*www.cio.com*).
3. M. Santosus, op. cit.
4. From *www.rightscenter.com,* August 2000.
5. Ibid.

5

e-Government and Data Warehousing

During the late 1990s and into 2000, most attention in the world of e-commerce was focused on

- business-to-consumer
- the B2C offshoots of consumer-to-consumer and consumer-to-business (typically auction sites and group buying sites, respectively, as discussed in Chapter 3)
- business-to-business

There are other e-commerce models that exist, however, and that began grabbing attention by mid-2000 and will continue to grow in lockstep with their more well-known predecessors. In this chapter, we'll discuss two forms of *e-government*—government-to-citizen (G2C), which might also be termed government-to-public (G2P), and business-to-government (B2G).

Just as had occurred with B2C and B2B e-commerce, the transactional sides of these newer e-commerce models typically began to take hold without adequate levels of accompanying analytical and business intelligence capabilities. In this chapter we'll discuss not only the business models themselves and where they're expected to go, but also the need for accompanying data warehousing environments, as well as unique properties of each that make simple adaptation of B2C and B2B data warehousing capabilities to the governmental e-commerce spaces all but impossible.

In the simplest sense, e-government means bringing Internet technology into the governmental realm. Governmental organizations are no strangers to computing, of course; from the earliest days of computing the U.S. federal government has been one of the primary adopters of computer and communications technology for defense and civil needs, accompanied by widespread usage by each U.S. state as well as all but the smallest municipalities. The same is true in countries all around the world.

What has been and continues to be unique about governmental usage of information technology, however, is the rigid and often highly confusing set of procurement rules that dictates the processes by which technology may be sought, put out for bid, and purchased by governmental organizations at all levels. In fact, it is this uniqueness in the procurement process that is increasingly providing the foundation for business-to-government e-commerce environments that we'll discuss shortly.

First, however, let's discuss government-to-citizen and how data warehousing technology and architecture will increasingly be applied.

Government-to-Citizen e-Commerce Models

Think of all the ways in which money flows between you and various governmental organizations. Almost always, of course, the money is flowing *from* you toward these governmental organizations, as you pay income and property taxes, municipal fees (e.g., garbage collection, sewer use fees, etc.), driver's license renewal fees, fees for a boating or snowmobile license, and so on.

Occasionally, funds may flow from a governmental organization to you instead of the other way around: income tax refunds; payments that result from unfortunate circumstances such as unemployment, injury, or death; payments from funds collected elsewhere by a state, such as those received by Alaska residents as a result of that state's oil-related businesses; and so on.

Most everyone is aware of the processes typically associated with both sides of the exchange of funds between government and the public—not only the actual payment and receipt of money, but also all the accompanying forms and paperwork. The premise behind G2C e-commerce is to build as much Internet-based capability as possible to support these types of transactions. Note that there is a *huge* distinction between nonmonetary e-government functions and those that involve monetary exchange. In essence, the same paradigm shift that occurred in the B2C world where the "billboardware" of the mid-1990s gave way to online commerce (see Chapter 2) is occurring within the e-government realm. For example, the Internet technology and resulting architecture that is needed for a state to simply post information about its income tax procedures—online copies of forms and instructions, frequently asked questions (FAQs), historical copies of forms and instructions, public records statistics, and so on—is less complex than when electronic filing and payments are added to the e-government model.

Increasingly, "passive" e-government (the analog to B2C billboardware) will fade away, replaced by active transactions in which information posting is universally accompanied by actual commerce (tax and license payments, etc.).

What is missing as part of the picture circa 2000–2001, however, is the accompanying business intelligence functions to create highly efficient, productive environments in which transactional and analytical e-government functions operate cooperatively—and efficiently—for the good of the affected population. There are several reasons for the lack of widespread data warehousing in this realm:

1. Limited government computing budgets - Most government computing environments are constrained by somewhat limited available funds. Even though the late 1990s into 2000 has seen something many of us never thought we'd see in our lifetime in the United States—many governmental entities at all levels flush with budget surpluses year after year—nearly every governmental organization finds itself needing to review its technology wish list and lopping off those projects that are deemed less critical—or less politically desirable—than others. (To be fair, the same financial constraints exist in most corporations as well, which is part of the reason why data warehousing and business intelligence has lagged corresponding e-commerce transactional environments.)

   The result: as interest in G2C e-government technology snowballs post-Y2K, the overwhelming majority of initiatives are exclusively transactional in nature—implementing online driver's license renewals, extending existing online tax filing capabilities, and so on. Analytical functions are typically mentioned in strategy and planning documents, yet funding is slated for "sometime later."

2. A lack of governmental familiarity with data warehousing - Governmental organizations, particularly those at the subfederal level (i.e., states and municipalities), have been notoriously late adopters of data warehousing technology and business intelligence models. Consultancies with public sector practices are finding a highly lucrative marketplace for first-time implementations of rudimentary reporting and OLAP capabilities that began appearing in corporations a decade earlier, in the early 1990s. This lack of familiarity with data warehousing has resulted in the same unnatural and unhealthy demarcation between e-commerce and business intelligence that hallmarked most corporations' first attempts at B2C and B2B environments.

3. The lack of a "must increase productivity" imperative - Most governmental organizations do not face an imperative for increased productivity . . . or, at least, not anywhere near the extent that for-profit private sector companies do. Except for

rare occasions—such as the recession in the United States during the early 1990s—governmental organizations don't find themselves forced to reduce headcount while still maintaining precutback productivity, customer satisfaction levels, or other metrics. Even when cutbacks do occur, most governmental organizations warn of longer lines and elongated response times, rather than attempt to reengineer their work processes to do more with less. Given that a key purpose of pursuing data warehousing of any type—e-commerce-related or not—is to provide business intelligence for purposes such as customer satisfaction and retention, the lack of any such imperative on the part of governmental organizations usually means that the actual benefits gained from constructing and deploying data warehousing capabilities are marginal at best . . . at least when viewed from the government's perspective (though the general populace would usually disagree . . .).

So is data warehousing a nonplayer in the world of G2C e-government? Not at all. Rather, the time lag between the implementation of G2C transactional capabilities and correspondingly analytical capabilities will likely be a bit longer than what had occurred in the B2C world.

G2C Data Warehousing Implications

Going on the assumption, then, that data warehousing will eventually become an integral part of G2C e-commerce, what needs to be considered?

Click-and-Mortar Environments

The most critical architectural issue is the same one faced by click-and-mortar B2C companies: the integration of data from Internet-based transactional applications with that from the governmental organization's traditional non-Internet transactional systems. In fact, there is no such thing as the equivalent of a pure-play Internet-only B2C retailer; all governmental organizations engaging in e-government are, at present, click-and-mortar. While it's possible that sometime in the future specific functions, such as tax filing or purchasing certain licenses, may evolve toward an online-only environment, the likelihood of that happening before we see the year 2010 is slim at best—not for reasons of technology, but rather because of the lack of *universal* computer access on the part of the constituency of a particular level of government (e.g., all the people that live in a particular city, county, or state).

Therefore, *any* G2C data warehousing environment must be architected from the very beginning to serve a click-and-mortar way of doing business: Internet-based

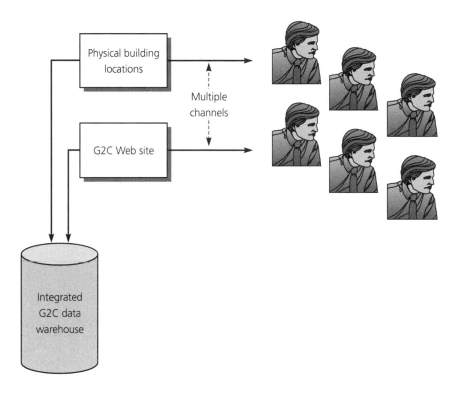

Figure 5.1 A typical click-and-mortar G2C environment.

as well as office walk-in, telephone, and other channels through which the public interacts with that particular governmental organization (see Figure 5.1).

Necessity of a Complete "Customer Database"

There exists a fundamental distinction between the contents of a private company's comprehensive customer database (whether part of a data warehousing environment or not; whether part of a B2C environment or not) and the corresponding customer database in a G2C environment.

In the private sector, customers come and go *according to their own free will*. Whether someone chooses to go to a company's Web site or not is his or her choice; a company may attempt to influence a visit via advertising, targeted marketing, or some other means, but that individual may decline all overtures if he or she desires. Correspondingly, if that person does choose to visit a particular company's Web site but chooses not to make any purchases, that also is a matter of choice. The company may follow up with those prospects who visit but who don't make a purchase, or perhaps identify those who began shopping but then "dumped their shopping cart" and left the site without completing a purchase, but the consumer is under no obligation to either make a purchase on an initial visit nor to respond to the "please come back and buy something" pleadings.

Consider, though, the types of transactions that would occur through various forms of G2C e-commerce. Some are very much like those discussed above with regard to B2C: purchasing a boating license, for example. If an individual is browsing his or her state's Web site to find out the requirements for, or the cost of, obtaining a boating license, that person may not even have a boat . . . so there is no requirement for the individual to "make a purchase" (i.e., buy a boating license) at that particular time or at any time afterwards.

Think about annual state income tax filings in most states in the United States, however. *Every* person who meets the criteria for having to file a return—typically, the majority of the population in that state—might be considered as a "mandatory customer." The same is true for driver's licenses: the majority of the population will inevitably be over the legal age at which you can drive a car, and therefore a very large group of customers needs to be considered.

There are four key items that must be considered with regard to the consolidated list of "customers":

1. Initial population of transactional and analytical environments

2. Rigid "membership" rules

3. Inherent exchange of customer data

4. Reactive work processes when "a purchase isn't made"

Let's consider each of these in turn.

Initial Population of Transactional and Analytical Environments

Before commencing operations, the customer data within the transactional side of a G2C environment must be preloaded in a data-warehousing-like manner from one or more other applications within that governmental organization's domain. For example, an online driver's license renewal G2C site needs to begin operations with a comprehensive list of all drivers registered in that state within the various classes (general automobile, motorcycle, commercial, etc.) with pertinent attributes about each person: name, address, driver's license number, driving record, expiration date of current license, and so on (see Figure 5.2). It would be wholly inadequate and unacceptable for a driver's license renewal Web site to begin operations with an empty list of customers and require every person to enter information that the state already has when that individual logs on for the first time.

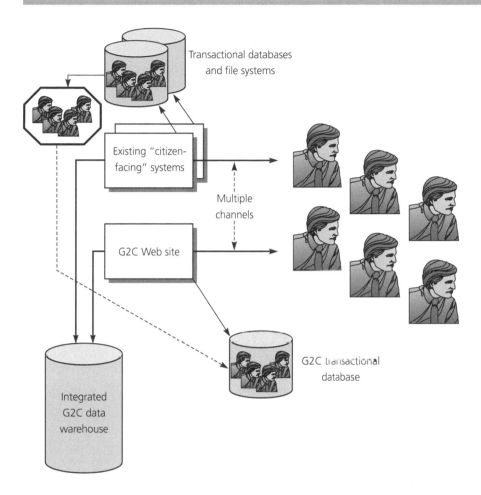

Figure 5.2 Mandatory initial population of a G2C transactional database and data warehouse.

It makes sense, then, that when initially populating customer data into the transactional side of a G2C environment an equivalent initial population should occur into the analytical side, that is, the data warehousing environment (see Figure 5.3).

Rigid "Membership" Rules

One of the hallmarks of B2C e-commerce is that an organization can use the power and reach of the Internet to acquire and service customers beyond its traditional boundaries. A small "mom and pop" retailer based in a rural Illinois location, far

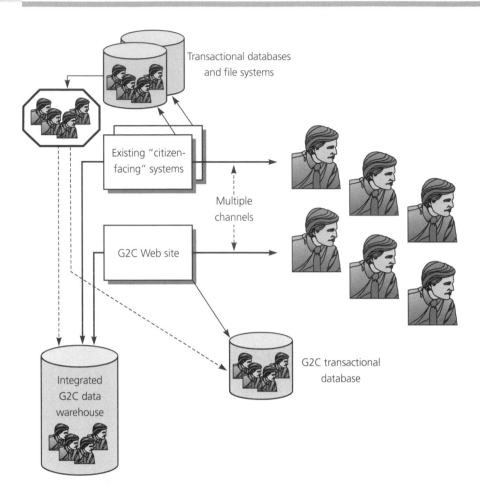

Figure 5.3 Parallel initial customer data populations for G2C transactional and data warehousing environments.

from any major population center, can build a Web site and (in theory, at least) acquire customers from around the United States and even around the world.

The reverse is true also. A person who lives in that same rural Illinois location can use the Internet to purchase goods and services from providers who may be physically located anywhere else in the United States or the world.

But consider a G2C environment. Whether or not you're pleased with the service you receive from the organization that manages your state's driver's license processes, you can't simply find another provider (e.g., another state) courtesy of the

Internet from which to purchase a driver's license. Dissatisfied with high property taxes in your municipality? You might be able to pay those taxes via a G2C site, but you can't elect to switch to a lower-cost provider such as a neighboring municipality or, say, one in a state where property taxes are extraordinarily low.

The key point to remember is that unlike the freewheeling, obliterate-all-barriers nature of B2C e-commerce, G2C e-commerce features a much more rigid set of rules governing the relationship between the "G" and "C" sides. Consumers are limited, in most cases, to interaction with their respective legally binding governmental organizations. And (with a few exceptions, as will be discussed later under "Rigid Geographic Boundaries") governmental organizations have no authority to conduct commerce with consumers who don't fall under their jurisdiction.

Inherent Exchange of Customer Data

Consider our driver's license renewal example from above. Some people may embrace online renewal as a time-saver; others may not, because of technophobia, lack of computer access, or some other reason. Though not desirable, a click-and-mortar B2C company may be able to get by with separate customer databases for Internet-based commerce and physical location transactions, forcing long-term physical location customers to enter personal information that may have already been collected when they first experience the "click" side.

In a G2C environment, however, a separation of Internet-based and non-Internet customer-related data is unacceptable: there is no such thing as a "dot-com spin-off" (see Chapter 1) equivalent in G2C e-commerce. Rather, Internet-based and traditional channels must be seen by the public as nothing other than "pipes" leading to the same underlying set of data (see Figure 5.4).

If possible, a single common transactional database would underlie *all* channels applicable to a given G2C function such as driver's license renewal, as shown in Figure 5.4. Correspondingly, this single source of information would become the provider of content to the G2C data warehouse for analytical purposes (see Figure 5.5).

In reality, though, it is just as likely that separate physical databases may exist for each channel because of the existence of legacy applications that won't be replaced solely because the governmental organization begins to provide G2C e-commerce (see Figure 5.6). In these multiple-database settings, it is imperative that a regular exchange of data occur between all applicable channels—Internet, telephone, physical locations, and so on—to ensure that all database content is consistent across the governmental enterprise.

For example, a person may log onto a state's Web site to renew his or her driver's license. After completing all the applicable online forms and paying the renewal fee online via credit card, the typical process then is to take a unique identifying

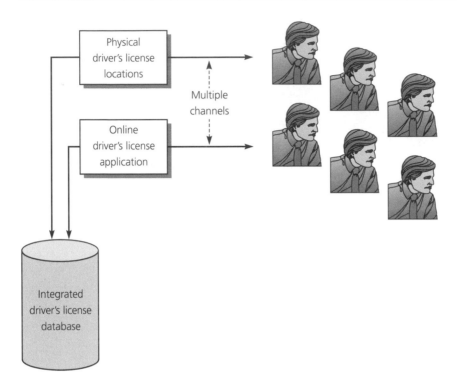

Figure 5.4 The necessity of parallel customer access channels in G2C.

number that indicates payment to a photo-only driver's license location where those who renew online don't have to wait in long lines while other applicants go through the entire renewal and payment process or apply for the first time for a license, as occurs in that state's regular motor vehicle bureau locations.

Suppose, though, that after renewing the license online but before having a picture taken and the driver's license card printed and laminated, that person moves, necessitating a change of address, and the state's procedures require the person to then go to a regular motor vehicle bureau location rather than a photo-only location. It is essential that when being served at the motor vehicle bureau, all applicable facts about that person's renewal—the fact that he or she *did* complete an online renewal, that payment was made and processed against a credit card, and so on—need to be available at that time.

In a multiple-channel, single-database environment such as that shown in Figure 5.4, data integrity is essentially guaranteed since there is only one record for that person, and updates are processed against that record regardless of the channel that

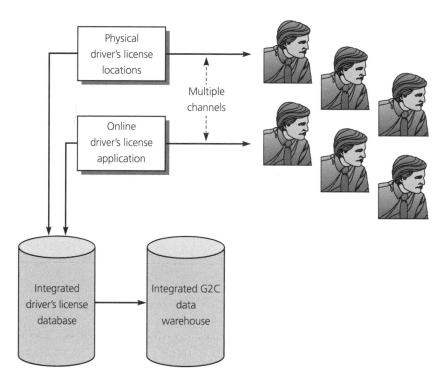

Figure 5.5 A single G2C database as the source for a G2C data warehouse.

person uses and the application that underlies that channel. In a multiple-channel, multiple-database environment, however, such data integrity is *not* guaranteed because that individual likely has a record in each channel application's database or file system. The state doesn't know, nor can it dictate, which channel the person will use to renew a driver's license (or to file taxes or apply for a boating license, or for any other G2C e-commerce function). Rather, it needs to be prepared so that whatever channel the consumer chooses to use, he or she will be adequately served in a transactional sense.

However, G2C multiple-database situations require a regular exchange of information among all applicable databases (Figure 5.6). In the example noted above, online renewal information for that person stored in the e-commerce application's database needs to be "quickly" available in the database of the application that supports the physical location renewal processes. What does "quickly" imply? The answer: it all depends. In most G2C settings, it's unlikely that real-time availability of data in an alternative channel will occur, so real-time messaging of the data from

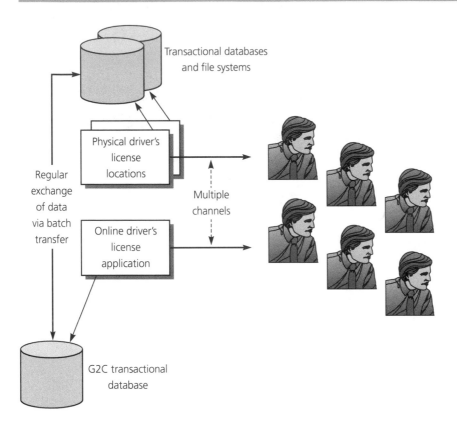

Figure 5.6 A G2C environment with different databases for each channel.

one database to one or more other databases isn't likely to be necessary. It's typically sufficient to build behind-the-scenes data synchronization processes that are run on a daily basis.

It's important that these data synchronization processes operate upon *all* affected databases. In situations with two channel-specific databases—one for Internet commerce, the other for all non-Internet commerce—a bidirectional exchange of data is required. When more than two channel-specific databases exist—for example, one for Internet commerce, one for telephone transactions, and one for physical location transactions—the synchronization processes need to support the additional complexity to ensure that each database reflects the activity from all other databases following the completion of the synchronization.

With regard to G2C data warehousing, there are several different approaches that can be taken to the restocking/maintenance procedures (see Figure 5.7).

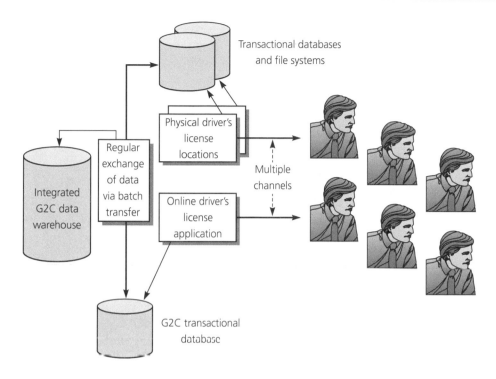

Figure 5.7 Two approaches to building a G2C data warehouse from multiple source databases.

Assuming that the governmental organization's cross-database synchronization processes work as expected, it might be sufficient to simply take one of the databases as the exclusive data source for the data warehouse, the rationale being that all e-commerce transactions are also reflected in that database.

Alternatively, the restocking of the data warehouse can be integrated into the data synchronization processes themselves, as also shown in Figure 5.7. Given that many of the data consolidation and transformation processes inherent in data warehousing also need to be part of the processes that synchronize the transactional databases, it makes sense to couple these processes together rather than perpetuate an artificial demarcation between the transactional and analytical sides of the G2C environment.

Reactive Work Processes When "a Purchase Isn't Made"

As noted earlier, in a B2C environment, consumers are under no obligation to purchase goods or services. In a G2C environment, however, certain obligations *do* exist: renewing a driver's license or car registration, filing taxes, and so on. Some percentage of that governmental organization's constituency will have a valid reason for not "purchasing," such as having sold a car and no longer needing to register it, or not having to pay income taxes because income earned that year was under the filing threshold and no refund is needed because nothing had been withheld.

But aside from these exemption-related situations, the G2C e-commerce environment can play a role in enforcing rules about licenses and taxes. e-Mail reminders can be sent at various intervals; warnings can be sent, via e-mail or via other channels, when deadlines have passed; and so on.

Data about the reactive work processes should propagate into the G2C data warehouse, collecting and reporting information such as

- In each month, of the people who missed a filing deadline, how many of them finally completed their transaction online?

- How many of the late online filings/renewals had never used the online service before?

- What percentage of just-in-time online filings/renewals had to be rejected because of faulty data entry by the consumer, and what percentage of those rejections were resolved in the same online session as compared to a subsequent session?

Geographic Boundaries

Earlier, we discussed how G2C environments have rigid "membership rules" typically governed by residence and citizenship, as contrasted with the B2C principle of breaking down geographic boundaries. The G2C transactional and data warehousing environments must, however, support a concept of "extended membership" that takes into consideration nonresidents who are under obligation to transmit funds to that governmental organization.

Taxes are a good example. Many states enforce a policy of requiring nonresidents to pay state income taxes on the portion of their annual income that is earned within that state's boundaries (e.g., during a business trip). The state's income tax collection system, then, cannot be limited to full-time and part-time residents of the state—a rigid membership list that can be predetermined from other governmental records and loaded into the G2C data warehousing and transactional environments—but must also have considerations for nonresidents subject to their taxation policies—a highly volatile membership list that will vary from year to year. Further, it is likely that the volatile nonresident list will be created "just in time" from W-2 forms prepared and submitted by those persons' employers.

The implications are that, perhaps, nonresidents may not be given the opportunity to use certain G2C transactional facilities, such as online income tax filing, being forced instead into paper submissions. However, the data warehouse that underlies the overall G2C environment—and that governmental organization's environment as a whole—*does* need to take this data into consideration for consolidated revenue reporting, filing statistics, and so on.

Point Solution vs. Enterprise Data Warehousing

The data warehousing sides of all of the G2C examples we've used so far—income tax filing, driver's license and vehicle registration renewals, boating license renewals, and so on—have all had the characteristics of being a point solution: that is, a single environment to analyze driver's license renewals; another environment, probably unrelated to driver's license renewals, for analyzing state income tax filings and receipts; and so on.

In reality, governmental organizations will find themselves facing the same decision point that private sector data warehouse planners have been facing since the mid-1990s: What is the most appropriate scope and breadth of the data warehouse that needs to be built?

Logically, it makes sense to combine similar functional areas together for analytical purposes, even if separate transactional systems are used. A state's motor vehicle bureau may build a data warehousing environment that contains data about driver's licenses and vehicle registrations; that state's department of revenue might consolidate personal income tax data with business income tax information, even if online Internet capabilities are available only for personal tax filing; and so on.

But it may be desirable on the part of a governmental organization to want to see a consolidated set of *all* data relating to G2C e-commerce: taxes and license fees coming in; unemployment compensation, family assistance, and other payments going out; and so on. And in the spirit of classical data warehousing they'd like to do trending, looking at changes from one year to the next in the volume of commerce being conducted online, which areas are growing the fastest, which areas have the most complaints from the public, and so on.

It is *not* desirable to construct an all-encompassing "Big Bang" data warehousing environment for all of—or the majority of—the state's analytical and reporting functions. The sheer complexity and data volumes would likely prevent such an environment from ever being completed, and even if it were to be completed, it would be unmaintainable.

Rather, as illustrated in Figure 5.8, a more sensible approach is to construct and deploy a "G2C data mart" that draws all applicable data about that state's online commerce from a variety of functionally oriented data warehousing environments and, if necessary, transactional environments.

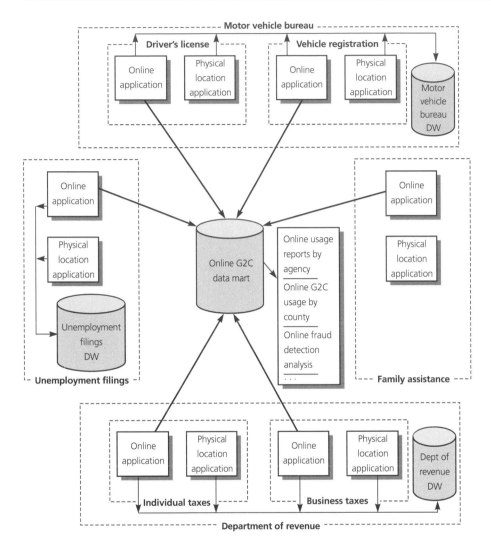

Figure 5.8 Recommended approach to building a cross-functional G2C data mart.

As illustrated in Figure 5.8, functionally focused analytical processes and business intelligence would typically occur within functionally organized data warehousing environments that map to different governmental organizations (motor vehicles bureau, department of revenue, etc.). However, providing a consolidated picture of current and historical G2C activity is *not* part of the responsibility of any one of those functionally organized data marts; rather, applicable data is extracted and sent "downstream" to the G2C data mart where the aforementioned analytical and reporting processes for that state's e-commerce activities can occur.

Government-Specific Business Intelligence Metrics

One final item to note with regard to G2C data warehousing is in the area of business intelligence. Many of the traditional business intelligence functions for which data warehousing has been used—simple after-the-fact reporting, online analysis, providing key performance indicators to the organization's leadership, and so on—map directly into the governmental world. However, many of the emerging customer-focused business intelligence functions that we discussed earlier in the book—customer retention and loyalty, for example—either don't map directly (some variation exists) or don't map at all.

Consider the topic of customer satisfaction. Does a state really care how satisfied its "customers" (i.e., general population) are? Perhaps they do. Certainly, there is likely to be an interest in capturing customer satisfaction metrics that specifically relate to online G2C commerce. Do people like the vehicle registration renewal Web site? Are they likely to continue using the site in the future? What other features would they like to see?

It's important to note, however, that in the context discussed above, customer satisfaction relates to the online, G2C aspect of the applicable process—vehicle registration in this example—but *not* to the vehicle registration process as a whole. Certainly, there is likely to be interest in offering good online customer experiences, but regardless of whether the person has a bad experience or not, he still must register his vehicle anyway, whether online or not. As we noted earlier, deciding to register a vehicle in another state with a better Web site or lower fees is not an option.

Therefore, it's important when designing the business intelligence side of a G2C data warehousing environment that the architects and planners don't simply drop in metrics and underlying data structures that have been used in B2C environments. Widely used or overly used CRM terms such as "customer retention," "customer loyalty," and "cost of customer acquisition" typically have a different meaning in the G2C world . . . if they apply at all.

Business-to-Government e-Commerce Models

We noted earlier that B2G e-commerce is analogous to Chapter 4's subject, B2B, with some key distinctions. Many of the functions that comprise B2B—e-procurement, e-payments, e-collections, e-fulfillment—also apply to B2G.

The key distinction, however, is that B2G e-commerce is governed not only by marketplace dynamics of logistics, supply and demand, and other factors, but equally as much by a myriad of rules and regulations that have long applied to government procurement. In the open marketplace, those responsible for their companies' procurement processes adhere to processes that take factors such as price, quality, availability, contractual business relationships, and other items into consideration as they make buy-or-not decisions. Further, these buy-or-not decisions are sometimes manually intensive, and in other cases may be semi- or fully automated, managed not only by information systems along the supply chain but also by formally encoding rules and regulations into the logic of those systems.

When constructed properly, the data warehousing environments accompanying private sector interbusiness commerce—both Internet-based B2B as well as traditional, pre-Internet supply chain processes—provide guidance and recommendations as to whether or not business relationships should be maintained. These recommendations take into consideration the raw data we mentioned above—pricing, quality of individual shipments, timeliness of individual shipments, and so on.

Finally, any given company is just as likely to be a B2B buyer as a B2B seller, depending on where their own products and services fit within an overall larger cross-enterprise value chain. For example, a manufacturer of automotive ignition systems may be a purchaser in a B2B supply chain with providers of the parts that comprise an ignition system, and then turn around and become a seller of those ignition systems to one or more automotive manufacturers or aftermarket parts channels.

In B2G, most of the flexibility and variability discussed above does *not* exist. Specifically:

- Most governmental organizations establish a fairly small threshold (e.g., a few thousand dollars) above which all purchases must adhere to a contractual relationship that has been formally put out for bid, competed for, and awarded to one or more suppliers. It is then prohibited for anyone in the affected government organization(s) to make purchases outside of the contractual boundaries (i.e., from another supplier) for the length of the contract award.

- Whereas a private sector purchasing agent could look at data-warehousing-produced reports and detect a disturbing rise in product defects from a single supplier—and consequently direct purchases to an alternative supplier with a slightly higher price but much higher overall quality—such freedom of choice is typically not permitted in B2G environments.

- In B2G environments, business is always—or almost always—the seller and government the buyer.

Given these distinctions, let's look at how B2G e-commerce impacts data warehousing.

B2G Data Warehousing Implications

There are several areas to discuss with regard to B2G data warehousing implications:

- Processes related to bidding and awarding contracts

- Ongoing supply chain operations

- Marketplaces and exchanges

Bids and Awards

The typical government contracting process begins with the issuance of a request for proposals (RFP), possibly preceded by a request for information (RFI) or request for quote (RFQ). Recipients of the RFP—those to whom the RFP has been specifically directed as well as those who become aware of the RFP through public information channels—decide whether or not to bid for the business. Those who decide to bid may decide to do so themselves, or possibly by partnering with one or more other companies.

The steps from that point are typically governed by the rules and regulations applicable to that particular governmental entity. Proposals are submitted; perhaps demonstrations are scheduled and delivered; revised proposals are resubmitted; pricing is adjusted; and then an award is made.

Entities involved in both sides of B2G e-commerce—the companies that provide goods and services to governmental organizations, as well as the governmental organizations themselves—need to build data warehousing capabilities focusing on the bid-and-award processes. Among the contents of a business's data warehouse is the following:

- Contact information for all governmental organizations with whom the company has done business in the past or may seek to do business in the future (names and titles, e-mail addresses, telephone and fax numbers, etc.).

- The rules and regulations that govern bid-and-award processes for each governmental organization with which they have done business or seek to do so. Wherever possible, structured (i.e., traditional) data should be used to store this information in a relational database as part of the data warehouse. Some items such as dates and intervals between dates (e.g., a fixed number of days past the submission of the final proposal that the final pricing sheet must be submitted) can be directly encoded into relational database content. Other content that is more "unstructured" in nature can be encoded by use of Boolean values and other relational constructs. For example, a particular state government agency's bid-and-award regulations may have a paragraph that reads "Failure to provide at least three in-state governmental references will result in automatic elimination of a vendor's proposal from further consideration." This might be encoded in the database as

```
REFERENCES_NEEDED BOOLEAN;

NUM_INSTATE_REFERENCES INTEGER;
```

A row would then be inserted into the data warehouse's database indicating a value of TRUE for REFERENCES_NEEDED and a value of 3 for NUM_INSTATE_REFERENCES.

- Information applicable to the goods or services that are likely to be part of its B2G business processes: product names and identifiers, results from in-house total quality management (TQM) programs, inventory quantities, and so on.

- Historical information about contracts with that particular governmental agency.

- Historical information about similar contracts with other governmental agencies.

On the other side of the B2G picture, a governmental organization should build its own data warehousing capabilities that include the following:

- Contact information from vendors with which it has dealt in the past or may deal in the future

- Its own encoded bid-and-award rules and regulations

- Historical information about its dealings with vendors in the past

- Historical information about the dealings of other governmental agencies (e.g., other agencies within the state) with vendors

So far, the contents of the two sides' respective data warehouses seem to have little to do with Internet-based B2G e-commerce; they could be just as applicable to non-Internet, traditional government bid-and-award processes. However, where the Internet enters the picture is when both sides enable access to selected portions of their respective data warehouses to the other side (see Figure 5.9).

For example, it makes sense that the governmental organization's own encoded rules and regulations be directly accessible to businesses wishing to bid on contracts,

Figure 5.9 B2G data warehouses and open access.

rather than those businesses having to build and maintain their own encoded versions. Doing so is a next logical step to publishing paper-based or online documents and manuals related to the procurement process, which will never disappear. However, key pieces of data that greatly aid the bid-and-award process can be encoded and made available, possibly in a bidirectional manner: vendors can submit databases back to the governmental organization indicating that they have provided three in-state references, who those references are, and other required pieces of data.

Likewise, other parts of the bid-and-award process can be automated by the exchange of information (usually from the business to the government). Detailed quality data—not just summarized statistics—from the TQM processes can be transmitted as part of the proposal; historical data showing adequate inventory levels to support the contractual volumes, should the company receive the award; product specifications; and many other pieces of information that typically are translated onto paper (via word processing and spreadsheet software) as part of a proposal effort can all be electronically transferred via the Internet.

Note that in the bid-and-award side of B2G e-commerce, there is little if any distinction between the transactional and analytical sides as would be found in traditional data warehousing. In fact, it is strongly recommended that a single database—call it a data warehouse or not—comprise a business's underlying store of B2G bid-and-award data, and likewise a single database should be used on the governmental side. The data volumes, throughput requirements, relatively low volatility, and relatively simple querying and reporting don't indicate a need to extract data and load it into a separate platform for performance reasons. Even if dimensionally oriented data structures are needed for rudimentary OLAP functionality, they can likely coexist with normalized or lightly denormalized data structures used for transactionally oriented purposes.

Ongoing Supply Chain Operations

After the awarding of purchasing-related contracts by a governmental organization to one or more businesses, the data warehousing environment should play a key role in the ongoing e-commerce supply chain operations, just as would occur in a B2B setting. From the business side, this would include the following:

- Building supply chain links back to inhouse and external suppliers of all components to ensure that adequate stock is available to meet contractual requirements.

- When no contractual purchase amounts exist (i.e., the contract is an open-ended one against which one or more governmental agencies may purchase any range of product quantities at any time . . . or none at all), "sales forecasting" needs to be built into the data warehouse's data structures and processing capabilities. Note that in the B2B world, the sales forecasting is usually provided from the CRM core transaction side of the business—specifically, sales force automation (SFA) applications—but typically no such CRM equivalent currently exists within the B2G world (Internet-based or not).

    Tracking historical purchases for longer-running contracts, and attempting to "mine" that purchase data by building statistical models to predict future purchasing patterns, should also be part of the B2G data warehouse's functionality.

- Quality and customer satisfaction metrics need to be monitored, stored in the data warehouse, and regularly analyzed against historical measures and other factors such as supply chain interruptions.

- Self-measurement of response time to orders should be included.

- Recording, storing, and analyzing government agencies' payment patterns is also important to help manage cash flow. When e-billing and e-payment functions are part of the B2G environment, associated data can be fed directly into the B2G data warehouse.

- When a customer service function is part of a contract (e.g., a call center, Internet-based assistance, or perhaps both), metrics from customer service such as call volumes, average call answer time, average time till problem resolution, number of situations requiring a follow-up customer inquiry, and many other types of customer-service-focused data should be included. And, ideally, this information should also be made available to the governmental agencies with which the company does business, not just created for internal use.

- All applicable regulations that govern the ongoing B2G e-commerce (transportation rules, payment guidelines, return policies, contract escape clauses, etc.) should also be part of the data warehouse. Actual operations should continually be measured against contractual parameters and thresholds to provide early warning of potential problems.

The governmental agency's B2G data warehouse would contain much of the same data, though likely slanted more toward reports and measures that are of interest to them as the side doing the purchasing rather than the selling.

Just as with B2C and B2B environments, it's important to realize that there is no such thing as a "standard B2G data model" or "standard B2G data warehousing architecture" that can simply be dropped into any given environment and automatically provide the desired levels of business intelligence. Rather, the approach introduced in Chapter 2—starting with an overall e-commerce strategy that eventually maps into a unique data warehousing architecture and corresponding business intelligence capabilities—needs to be followed.

Marketplaces and Exchanges

The role of marketplace-centric e-commerce in the form of exchanges is somewhat less clear (circa 2000–2001) in the B2G realm than in B2B. The primary reason has to do with all of our earlier discussion about the rigid set of rules that must be adhered to for government procurement and acquisition.

Consider that the fundamental premise of an online exchange is to create an Internet-based environment in which buyers and sellers dynamically come together, agree on the parameters of an exchange (including price, delivery details, etc.), and then close a deal. When the exchange is auction oriented, dynamic competition hallmarks the exchange. ("Dynamic" in this sense meaning rapid and unpredictable, not necessarily exciting.)

However, all of these characteristics are the antithesis of government procurement. Particularly constraining are the spending thresholds that control whether or not a formal bid-and-award process is necessary for certain types of purchases. Thus, for all but the smallest purchase amounts—office equipment, for example—B2G e-commerce is likely to reflect traditional government procurement, at least during the early B2G years (early 2000s), except with automated B2B-like supply chains (as discussed earlier).

Strategists and architects should, however, continually monitor trends in governmental procurement policies to detect future interest in exchanges becoming an integral part of the B2G landscape. This is not expected to occur before the 2003–2004 time frame, and even then, typically as part of governmental agencies' pilot programs rather than full-scale, wide-reaching B2G procurement.

Summary

Governmental organizations at all levels, from municipalities to the federal government, are striving with the same sort of customer/citizen service and support challenges that private business has tackled since the early 1990s. While it's certainly true that governmental organizations can be technology laggards at times, the almost universal and intense interest in both the citizen-facing and business-facing sides of e-commerce technology have made e-government a rapidly growing area all across the United States.

Further, as we've discussed in this chapter, business intelligence and data warehousing should be a from-the-beginning factor in both G2C and B2G e-commerce to avoid having to retrofit already-in-place business models with business intelligence capabilities, as has commonly occurred in the private sector.

6

Business-to-Employee Models and Data Warehousing

Employee-oriented Internet technology is nothing new, of course. From the first company-specific intranets in the mid-1990s, companies have been using Internet technology as a communications vehicle with their workforces. Just as other e-commerce models—B2C and G2C, in particular—began with "billboardware," so too did business-to-employee (B2E), though the term wasn't used at the time, in the form of postings of company rules and regulations, employee-specific information such as pay history and vacation time, and other information.

The B2E billboardware evolved into rudimentary applications by the later half of the 1990s for interactive functions such as registering for in-house courses or electing insurance options. For the most part, however, monetary exchange was not part of the B2E landscape at that time, except in a peripheral manner (e.g., electing an insurance option would ripple through and affect payroll withholdings).

But just as G2C e-commerce (Chapter 5) is evolving to move many different types of monetary-exchange-oriented transactions online, the same is occurring in the B2E space. Examples include the following:

- Directly paying for company-provided perks such as discounted movie tickets, day care, or discounted health club membership, not only via the traditional means of payroll deduction but alternatively through an employee's credit card or via some other type of e-payment service

- Performing online exchange of funds among, and redemptions from, company-provided investment vehicles such as stock purchase plans and retirement accounts

- Going online to sell unused vacation days back to the company, if the company's policy permits doing so

- Performing online banking services at the company's credit union through links provided by the company's B2E site

- Online payment of nonreimbursable medical expenses to your primary care physician following notification from your insurance company

- Access to the company's travel agency for your own personal trips, with accompanying e-payments following booking a reservation

- Registering and paying for online training provided by the company or an auxiliary organization such as a local university or technical school

- Purchasing company-logo items such as pens and sweatshirts from the online company store

- For manufacturing and consumer goods companies that have a company store, purchasing products made by your company (e.g., over-the-counter health and beauty products) at a discount via the Web and arranging for shipping to your office or home

Additionally, a number of other services are part of B2E environments that are financially oriented in nature, but don't necessarily involve at-that-point-in-time exchange of funds. These might include the following:

- Retirement planning that factors in the value of your retirement accounts and the parameters of your tenure with the company (position, salary history, longevity, etc.)

- Insurance planning assistance in which your personal health history and ongoing treatment is mapped against plans offered by the company and a recommendation is made as to what policy or policies are best for you

- Access to summarized historical human resources data that is of general interest to a company's employees (retention rates, job satisfaction ratings, etc.)

The ERP Link

B2E e-commerce is heavily dependent on a company's internal ERP system(s) to provide data. Whether an ERP package's human resources (HR) module is used, more than one HR module exists from different parts of the company, legacy nonpackaged HR software is used, or some combination of the above exists, the majority of the data needed for B2E transactional and data warehousing systems will come from the ERP realm in the company.

A key complication is evident from the way the preceding paragraph is worded: in all but the smallest companies it is unlikely that a single HR-oriented application exists. Even many medium-sized companies have different locations, each with their own HR applications, or have gone through a merger-and-acquisition process, with multiple systems being retained.

Consequently, the standard processes necessary to create an HR-oriented data warehouse comprise the starting point of not only the B2E data warehousing environment but also the B2E transactional application itself (see Figure 6.1).

In Chapter 5, we noted that G2C environments have a rigidly constrained "members list" that is dictated by factors such as where someone lives or if someone had done business within a particular jurisdiction. A similar type of restrictive membership criteria is true for B2E environments. Perhaps availability of services is available to all employees, or maybe only to full-time employees. Some companies may permit long-term contractors access to certain facets of the B2E environment (e.g., online ordering from the company store) but not to other employee-oriented services. Regardless of the specific policies any given company has with regard to its B2E environment, the roster of "customers" will be far less dynamic and open than a B2C environment, even when similar or identical online purchasing of goods and services occurs.

Matching Employees with Appropriate Services

Once a consolidated list of employees is built for the B2E transactional and data warehousing environments, companies cannot simply turn the employees loose and provide universal access to all available online services.

Consider the matter of health insurance. Most larger companies not only feature a wide range of insurance plans, but some of those plans are typically available only to employees who live and work in certain locations. For example, Massachusetts-based employees of a professional services firm may have access to certain insurance companies and plans that Michigan-based employees of the same company cannot use, or vice versa.

Just as with G2C environments in which the "rules of the game" need to be propagated into the transactional and data warehousing environments to provide necessary legal and policy-based access constraints, the same must be done with B2E environments. This means that the transactional database—and the data

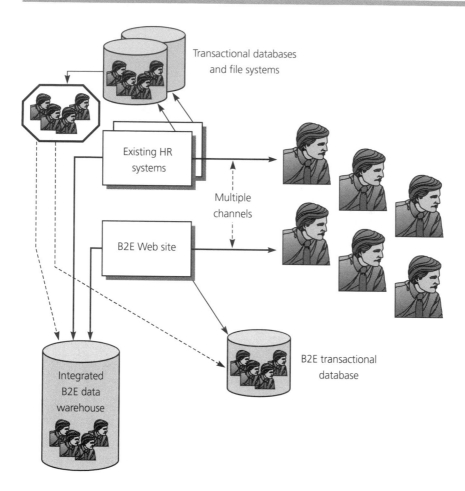

Transactional databases and file systems

Existing HR systems

Multiple channels

B2E Web site

B2E transactional database

Integrated B2E data warehouse

Figure 6.1 Initial loading of the B2E transactional and data warehousing environments.

warehouse—needs to contain data structures that, for example, record in what states particular insurance plans are available to employees. Then, at transaction time, only those plans permitted to the employee would be accessible for possible registration and payment.

Or perhaps in a multinational corporation, certain countries in which the company does business have a prohibition against online ordering of and receiving pharmaceutical products, even when those products are available without prescription. The transactional environment must prevent orders for cough medicine, aspirin, or other products from being ordered by employees based in that country.

Analyzing B2E Data

As with G2C environments, there is a close linkage between the database aspects and content of the B2E transactional and data warehousing environments. However, aside from the exact data structures and content, there are a number of analytically oriented functions that should occur within the data warehousing side of a B2E environment, including the following:

- Reporting on current B2E online usage—when given a choice between online and traditional methods for insurance registration and other services, how many employees are using the Internet capabilities? What does the usage trend look like? In what locations is online usage the highest? The lowest?

- Selection within a given product or service—what insurance plans are the most popular among online users? Is this the same percentage for those who register by paper form? If an insurance plan is only available within certain geographical locations, what percentage of employees select that plan? Would that hold true in other locations in which the plan isn't currently available?

- How many employees registered for online courses in the quarter just concluded? How does this number relate to the same quarter last year? Is there any correlation between online course availability and retention rates?

- Is there any correlation between the results of the annual employee satisfaction level and availability of online B2E services?

Click-and-Mortar Environments

One final note with regard to B2E e-commerce is that just as with G2C environments, there exists an inherent click-and-mortar nature. However, unlike with G2C, some companies may evolve toward an all-online B2E environment. Whether or not any given company does so will depend on its culture and workforce composition. For example, it's easy to envision how a software company or IT consulting firm would build and install an all-online B2E environment that would be used by everyone, given that every employee—even administrative and clerical staff—has access to a computer and is skilled in its use.

In contrast, an automotive parts manufacturing company with a heavily blue-collar workforce would likely retain the offline nature of its employee-facing commerce functions, even if online capabilities are put in place. Without stereotyping—it's likely that a large percentage of that blue-collar workforce is "Internet-capable"—that company's culture may be such that many of its employees view the Internet as something unrelated to work, and there is a high degree of preference that the status quo be retained for insurance registration, payroll and vacation forms, and so on.

When a click-and-mortar B2E transactional environment exists, it's essential that the accompanying data warehouse attempt to leverage any ongoing back-and-forth exchanges of employee data in a manner similar to that recommended for G2C environments, as discussed earlier in this chapter.

Summary

Expect to see rapidly increasing usage of B2E e-commerce by midsized and large companies. The question remains, however, how many of those companies will integrate business intelligence deeply into their B2E business models. Quite possibly, the "ERP syndrome" will repeat itself. That is, the transactional capabilities will be deployed first, and business intelligence will need to be done later in catch-up mode. As with all the other types of e-commerce models we've discussed in Part I, we strongly believe that companies that closely integrate transactional and business intelligence capabilities in their B2E services, built on top of a robust data warehouse with close links to the company's ERP system(s), will be well positioned to support their workforce.

Part II

Building Blocks, Challenges, and Solutions

The content of the chapters in Part I was, by design, very conceptual and business focused, the intention being to provide the reader with a solid grounding in the past, present, and future of e-commerce business models and accompanying business intelligence capabilities.

In Part II, we bring substance and real-world considerations to the subject of e-commerce data warehousing and business intelligence. Chapter 7 presents a comprehensive—perhaps even tedious—discussion of the many different technologies and building blocks that are likely to be part of any e-commerce data warehousing environment, if only through necessary interfaces to the accompanying transactional e-commerce facilities.

Chapter 8 presents a discussion of three different commercially available e-commerce business intelligence products to give the reader some idea of how vendors are addressing the issues and challenges presented in this book.

In Chapters 9 and 10, we address two real-world considerations that are particularly relevant to data warehousing in an e-commerce setting: data quality and integrity, and privacy and security.

Finally, in Chapter 11 we bring the many topics of the previous chapters together in a solutions architecture case study of a fictional company that desperately needs to implement B2C and B2B e-commerce capabilities.

7

Core Technologies and Building Blocks

Most of the major IT occurrences of the 1990s that we discussed in Chapter 1—data warehousing, CRM, and ERP in particular—have been, as the saying goes, a "mixed blessing." On the positive side, the ever-increasing availability of packaged software has brought about dramatic increases in productivity as compared to similar environments from the "prepackaged" era that were custom developed.

The downside, however, is that the availability of and reliance upon those packages has left many IT practitioners without adequate knowledge of the many pieces that must fit together to build a real-world, sustainable computer system. Consider the typical data warehousing "architecture diagram": A handful of rectangles are placed on the left side of the piece of paper and labeled "source applications." They are then connected via lines with a single arrow at the right to another larger rectangle that might be labeled "operational data store (ODS)" or "staging area." That ODS (or equivalent) rectangle is then connected to another equivalently sized rectangle labeled "data warehouse," which in turn has a handful of lines with arrows on the right side connected to a set of smaller rectangles, each labeled some variant of "Department XYZ Data Mart." Each data mart will have either (1) a stick person, (2) a better representation of a person courtesy of the clip art from a graphics package, or (3) a graphical representation of a desktop computer, indicating that users will access data from those particular components in the overall environment, but not any others.

Then, the lines between the source applications and the ODS will be instantiated through an extraction/transformation/loading (ETL) package; the ODS, data warehouse, and data marts will be hosted on some form of relational database management system; and one or more front-end tool packages (e.g., simple reporting, OLAP, EIS, etc.) will be the real-world instantiation of the stick person/clip art/PC screen. Then presto, the data warehousing architecture is complete; time for a long lunch.

The tongue-in-cheek cynicism of the preceding paragraphs aside, the reality is that the underlying technology behind the connect-the-blocks approach to putting together the packages that represent the ETL, data access, and database management aspects of a data warehousing environment is excruciatingly complex. The same issue has plagued the CRM core application space, where the typical first-round CRM architecture diagram shows an overly simplified data feed from one or more source applications of applicable customer data into the call center, sales force automation package, or both. ERP? The same holds true there as well; "architecture" diagrams indicating overly simplified one-time migration from the legacy systems to the magical ERP package, perhaps accompanied by ongoing refreshing of information during a prolonged implementation effort.

Adding the Internet to the gloomy picture painted above just complicates matters even further. Whereas most IT practitioners have at least a working familiarity with the Internet by way of their own Web surfing or use of the company intranet environment, an analogy can be drawn to your ability to drive an automobile versus knowing how to fix an engine or transmission: some small number of drivers might be able to make major repairs, but not many and certainly not as a result of simply knowing how to drive a car. The same holds true with Internet technology, and for that matter, distributed computing technology in general: those data warehousing practitioners (as well as those from other IT disciplines) whose backgrounds are dominated by packaged software and whose familiarity with the Internet is primarily as that of a user will no doubt be challenged when attempting to architect and design e-commerce data warehousing environments.

In this chapter, we attempt to bring technical reality to the subject of e-commerce data warehousing. We fully realize that not all practitioners need to have intimate familiarity with every topic we cover in this chapter, but in the interest of trying to be as complete as possible in a fairly short space, we present a comprehensive overview of many different core technologies and building blocks that are likely to be of importance at one time or another to those involved in e-commerce data warehousing.

We've categorized the topics in this chapter as follows:

1. Internet protocols and environment

2. Database technology

3. Application development and integration

4. Vendor Web development platforms (including product suites)

5. Networking and communications

6. "User-facing" technology

Looking through the above list, it's understandable that readers who are long-time data warehousing practitioners may think of many—perhaps most—of the topics as being much more applicable to transactional applications than to data warehousing and business intelligence. However, as we noted throughout the chapters in Part I, successful e-commerce requires that strategists and architects break through the artificial barriers between transactional and analytical processes and technology. The phrase *seamless integration* may be one of the most overused—and often ill-used—"hype terms" in all corners of technology, but in the case of e-commerce technology that phrase certainly represents an objective to strive to achieve as technology building blocks come together to build systems.

Internet Protocols and Environment

Most readers are likely to be familiar with the Internet, even if they've never developed applications using Internet technology, if only from the user "Web surfing" side. This section will present a brief overview of the major facets of Internet protocols and other aspects of the overall Internet environment that are important parts of any e-commerce environment.

HyperText Markup Language (HTML)

HyperText Markup Language, usually referred to by its acronym of HTML, defines the structure and layout of a Web document by using a variety of *tags* and *attributes*.

General Discussion

Tags in HTML use "<" and ">" surrounding a keyword, as in

```
<TITLE>Home Page</TITLE>.
```

In the above example, the slash (/) indicates the ending point for the construct being defined by its "companion" tag (TITLE, in this case). There are hundreds of standard tags used to format and lay out the information in a Web page. For instance, <P> is used to make paragraphs and <B> . . . </B>is used to create boldface fonts.

Tags are also used to specify hypertext links. These allow Web developers to direct users to other Web pages with only a click of the mouse on either an image or word.

Cascading style sheets (CSS) is a new feature added to HTML that gives Web site developers and users more control over how Web pages are displayed. With CSS, designers and users can create style sheets that define how different elements, such as font faces, font sizes, alignment, and other characteristics like headers and links, appear. These style sheets can then be applied to any Web page.

e-Commerce Data Warehousing Implications

In e-commerce environments, the primary means of implementing the "presentation layer" through which reports and query results are presented to users has been through HTML. Almost all front-end data warehousing tools (discussed later in this chapter) are "Web-enabled," meaning that HTML is an integral part of their products' presentation layers; no additional customized translation is needed.

An important concept in the data warehousing realm, however, is that of the "passive information consumer." The foundation of the passive information consumer premise is that in most data warehousing user communities, regardless of whether that community comprises 30 users or 3,000, 60 to 80% of those users do *not* want to be "active" desktop tool users to create and modify their own report and query formats as part of their regular work processes. Rather, these passive users want—and will only use—an on-screen equivalent of "green-bar reports" (i.e., old-style reports on large sprocket-holed computer paper with alternating green and white bars, from the mainframe and minicomputer days of computing). Traditionally, the means of satisfying the passive user community was to e-mail these reports to them. However, with the pervasiveness of Internet technology and accessibility, a more modern approach is to post system-generated "static" reports on the company's intranet or perhaps a secure portion of the company's Internet site. These reports—stored in HTML format—are then presented to users in the same way that any other Internet-style content (sports scores, stock prices, news, etc.) would be.

Consequently, a decision point for e-commerce data warehousing architects is determining exactly how support for passive users should occur. Many tools have a *portal* construct that is, essentially, a browser-based view into HTML-format reports and query results. However, an alternative to purchasing portal-like licenses from a vendor is to architect and build a data warehousing environment in which logic in the data warehouse itself has the responsibility for executing standardized reports and then translating the results of those reports into HTML format. In this case, the HTML translation capability must be built into the data warehousing environment along with applicable Web servers (discussed later).

As other protocols (XML, WAP, and WML, all of which are discussed later in this section) complement or subsume HTML, vendors and data warehousing strategists alike need to consider the impact of these new protocols and ensure that their environments are properly architected.

HyperText Transport Protocol (HTTP)

The Hypertext Transport Protocol is the network protocol used to deliver virtually all files and other data on the Internet or Web, including HTML files, image files, query results, and others.

General Discussion

HTTP by default utilizes port 80 through TCP/IP (discussed later). An HTTP client—often a Web browser—opens a connection on port 80 and sends a request message to the HTTP server, which is usually a Web server. The server then returns a response message, typically a Web page or HTML file. After delivering the response the server closes the connection. This action of closing the connection is what classifies HTTP as a *stateless protocol*; that is, it does not maintain any knowledge of multiple requests coming from the same user or server. We will discuss later how the issue of managing a user's state is often handled since it is desirable to maintain some knowledge across a user's multiple requests.

Two types of requests that are very commonly used in HTTP are *GET* and *POST*. (There are others; however, for our purposes we only cover GET and POST.)

The GET request is the most common type of HTTP request. As indicated by the term, it gets you the resource that you are requesting. For example, should you point your Web browser to *www.yahoo.com*, you are actually initiating a GET request that might look like GET / HTTP/1.0. This particular request is asking the Web server at *www.yahoo.com* to get for the requestor the default Web page (usually a page called index.html or something similar—if you were to type into your Web browser *www.yahoo.com/index.html*, you would likely receive the same Web page that you received when you excluded the reference to index.html).

The resulting HTTP GET request would look something like GET /index.html HTTP/1.0.

The POST request is used to send data to the server to be processed in some way. Most often anytime a user fills out a form on a Web page and then clicks on a "submit" type button, the resulting HTTP request is a POST. POST requests are different from a GET request in the following ways. First, there is a block of data sent with the request located in the message body. Second, the URL is not a resource to retrieve; it is usually a resource to handle data you are sending. Third, the HTTP response is normally program (i.e., query) output rather than a static file. Here is an example of what could be contained in an HTTP POST request that is used to send an e-mail to a user:

```
POST /cgi-bin/mail.cgi HTTP/1.0

From: johndoe@xyz.com

To: janedoe@abc.com

Subject: Sales Report

Body: Please take a look at the latest online sales report;
our B2C initiative is doing great!
```

e-Commerce Data Warehousing Implications

For the most part, HTTP operates totally behind the scenes in an Internet environment, meaning that data warehousing architects and designers usually don't have to worry about the mechanism by which HTML and other Internet content is transferred. However, it's important to realize that in situations where, say, the data warehouse generates certain information that does not arrive at its destination, or user queries seem to be "lost in cyberspace," the troubleshooting will likely require looking at all protocol layers—not just the lower-level protocols like TCP and IP that we discuss later, but also HTTP as well.

Extensible Markup Language (XML)

The Extensible Markup Language extends the concept of tags—as used in HTML (discussed earlier)—from display-oriented controls to the exchange of business metadata and data.

General Discussion

Both XML and HTML are actually derived from a 1980s-era tag-based language known as Standard Generalized Markup Language (SGML). Back in the days of text-oriented word processing software on personal computers (Wordstar, WordPerfect, etc.) and on first-generation workstations (e.g., Digital Equipment's VAX workstations), SGML was used as a way to specify desired formatting of text and graphics on the printed page, even when that representation wasn't available on-screen via the word processing software.

The display-oriented capabilities of SGML evolved into HTML as the Internet took hold, yet despite HTML's power as a means of delivering content that any compliant Web browser can display, there are shortcomings that have become more serious as e-commerce has taken hold. While HTML does a stellar job on the presentation layer side of exchanging Internet content, many other e-commerce functions aren't supported.

By definition, XML is extensible: one person or application can develop a set of tags that are oriented toward the exchange of environment-specific information, and those tags can be processed by a recipient in much the same way that a Web browser processes HTML as part of its display functions.

Just as HTML evolved from SGML, XML is also an offshoot—actually, an ISO-compliant subset. XML is not a single, predefined markup language; rather it is a metalanguage—a language for describing other languages. This allows the designers to create their own markup. In HTML, the designer is limited to the predefined markup constructs as defined in the standard. XML lets you define your own customized markup languages for different classes of documents.

The power of XML is only beginning to surface in the 2000–2001 time frame, and will likely have the biggest impact on the B2B side of e-commerce. This is because documents can be described at a higher (meta) level and then used to interface with systems that implement that definition. For example, the operators of an Internet-based home grocery delivery service and their suppliers would implement an XML standard interface for ordering products. This definition includes the attributes important to their business, such as product number, size, quantity, price, and so on.

Those who have access to this particular XML definition could implement a system that captures all order information and then build an XML document containing that order information. Next, using the Internet, the order information is posted to a supplier on one of their servers, and an order is placed.

Note that nowhere in a B2B transaction such as that described above is there a requirement for a Web browser or Web server; XML can be used "behind the scenes" in an interapplication manner. This type of B2B transaction is similar to Electronic Data Interchange (EDI) that has been used for years. The benefit of XML over EDI, however, is its flexibility and ease of implementation.

With regard to Web servers and browsers, however, XML is intended to replace HTML as the primary means of communicating information from a Web server to a browser (or, more accurately, HTML will be subsumed into XML). The result of the May 1998 World Wide Web Consortium workshop on the future of HTML resulted in the stated direction of the next generation becoming XHTML (Extensible HyperText Markup Language).[1]

e-Commerce Data Warehousing Implications

Understanding the significance of XML is essential to all aspects of e-commerce—B2B in particular—including the data warehousing domain and associated business intelligence. Though some overly eager XML proponents will occasionally claim that XML will sooner or later replace SQL as the primary interface to the content of a database, a more likely scenario is that SQL will remain the primary relational database language for the foreseeable future, but XML will become the primary means of cross-database communication of information.

Anyone who has dealt with cross-DBMS transfer of information in a transactional or data warehousing environment has dealt with many kinds of integration issues. XML's design as a language specifically intended to transfer information from one environment to another without having to undertake a laborious exercise to predevelop an inflexible cross-application protocol is of immense interest to all aspects of B2B e-commerce: e-procurement, e-payment, e-billing, e-fulfillment, and so on. Further, XML isn't only important for the transactional side but also for the business intelligence side, as trading partners "open up" portions of their data warehouse for accessibility by others outside their enterprise (see Chapter 4). In these scenarios, XML is likely to be the means by which cross-enterprise business intelligence occurs.

Cookies

Cookies are text files that contain small pieces of information sent by a Web server to be stored on the computer running a Web browser. Later, the cookie can be read back from that browser.

General Discussion

Some common uses for cookies include

- Personalization - When a person goes to a financial Web site that tracks stock information, that person could set up his or her own personal portfolio that filters the stocks to ones that he or she wants to track. From that point on—until the cookie expires or the profile is modified—that personalized view would be in effect. Cookie-based personalization is also useful for identifying start pages for particular users.

- Web site activity tracking - Site tracking shows the activity of users on a given Web site. It can provide accurate counts of how many people have been to pages on a site. An e-tailer, for example, could differentiate 50 unique people visiting the site from one person hitting the reload button 50 times.

- One-to-one marketing - Cookies can be used to build a profile of where site visitors go, what advertisements if any they click on, and other pertinent information, and then use this information to target promotions for visitors. Companies also use cookies to store which advertisements have been displayed so the flow of banner ads is managed according to business rules (e.g., perhaps the same advertisement is not displayed to a user twice if the person didn't click on that ad the first time).

- Tracking reporting and analysis usage and behavior - A unique usage of cookies is to track how data warehousing users access reports, issue queries, and otherwise use the business intelligence capabilities provided to them. Cookies can be used to show, for example, how frequently (or infrequently) particular reports are accessed to help the data warehousing administrators proactively provide a high degree of service to their user community.

e-Commerce Data Warehousing Implications

Cookies have long played a key role in B2C e-commerce business intelligence. Many of the e-CRM analytical capabilities such as customer segmentation, campaign management, dialog marketing, and others are built on a foundation of using cookie data as critical information in attempting to develop profiles of customers and prospects.

It's important to note, though, that cookies also have a key role in the B2B world as well. Consider that much of B2B e-commerce is not a "lights out" operation but rather does have a human element—purchasing managers who browse the B2B Web sites of their key suppliers as well as auction exchanges, for example. Collecting cookie data about the human side of B2B, storing the data in a data warehousing environment, and using that information as part of a company's B2B business intelligence functions should be an integral part of a company's e-commerce business model.

Often with the use of cookies the user is unknown. This does not limit, however, the amount and value of the data collected. In fact, data can be collected on the activities of the "anonymous" user and later be linked to an actual user or company when a purchase is made or some other activity that adequately identifies them. Populating such data in a data warehouse and analyzing it can shed light on particular "patterns" that users and buyers elicit, which in turn can influence how to market products and services.

Wireless Access Protocol (WAP) and Wireless Markup Language (WML)

Crucial to making the Internet accessible from mobile wireless devices is the Wireless Access Protocol. WAP is an open, global specification that enables mobile users with wireless devices to easily access and interact with information and services instantly. It works with most wireless transports and is intended to cover a wide range of wireless devices, including mobile phones, pagers, two-way radios, smart phones, and personal digital assistants (PDAs—discussed later in this chapter).

The Wireless Markup Language is based on the XML standard (discussed earlier in this chapter). WML is designed to optimize Internet text data for delivery over limited-bandwidth wireless networks and onto small device screens.

General Discussion

The key utility on WAP devices will be the microbrowser, which will allow access to any WAP-supporting Web site. Content providers are expected to support WAP enthusiastically since, for a minimum of effort, the technology will provide them access to a huge untapped market of mobile customers. Consequently, there should be no lack of such sites.

WML is specifically devised to support one-hand navigation without a keyboard. WAP is scalable from two-line text displays up through graphic screens found on items such as smart phones and communicators. It also supports WMLScript, which is similar to JavaScript but is designed to make minimal demands on system resources such as memory and CPU power. It is unlikely that WML will provide support for features such as color, audio, and video for a number of years.

With a WAP-compliant phone, an individual would use the built-in microbrowser to make a request—say, for yesterday's online sales figures—in WML. This request is passed to a WAP Gateway that then retrieves the information from an Internet server located at the company's headquarters or perhaps at an Application Service Provider (ASP) location (ASPs are discussed later in the chapter). The request is satisfied either in standard HTML format or, preferably, directly prepared for wireless terminals using WML. If the content being retrieved is in HTML format, a filter in the WAP Gateway needs to translate it into WML. The requested information is then sent from the WAP Gateway to the WAP client, using whatever mobile network bearer service is available and most appropriate.

The WAP Forum is the industry association responsible for driving the standard. Members represent over 90% of the global handset market, carriers with more than 100 million subscribers, leading infrastructure providers, software developers, and other organizations providing solutions to the wireless industry.

An important consideration is that content providers will need to reauthor their material into WML in order for a WAP microbrowser to use it. Today, this format is primarily text based. While somewhat limited, it is a mode of operation that works well for the delivery of news, stock quotes, and sports results.

e-Commerce Data Warehousing Implications

An increasingly mobile workforce in all parts of the world requires that wireless communications be actively considered as part of the architecture of nearly any application environment. Even when the transactional side of an application is "wire-bound" (e.g., the in-house accounting and finance system), it's likely that users of business intelligence produced from a data warehousing environment that draws content from that wire-bound application could be mobile users and, therefore, require access via WAP and WML rather than HTML.

As was noted earlier in the HTML discussion, WAP and WML need to be factored into architecture and implementation decisions. Certain forms of data-warehousing-provided business intelligence—operational alerts or delivery of key performance indicators (KPIs) to senior executives, for example—are particularly suited to wireless content delivery.

SSL

Secure Sockets Layer (SSL) is an important protocol for conducting business over the Internet. SSL was originally developed by Netscape and has been universally accepted on the Web for authenticated and encrypted communication between clients and servers.

General Discussion

The SSL allows an SSL-enabled server to authenticate with an SSL-enabled client to establish an encrypted connection. These capabilities are important in addressing concerns about security over the Internet. The default port for SSL communications is port 443.

SSL functionality includes the following:

- SSL server authentication - Server authentication allows a user to confirm a server's identity. SSL-enabled client software can use standard techniques to check that a server's certificate and public ID are valid and have been issued by a certificate authority, such as Verisign. This confirmation might be important if the user is sending a credit card number over the network and wants to check the receiving server's identity.

- SSL client authentication - Client authentication allows a server to confirm a user's identity. Using the same techniques as those used for server authentication the server software can check that a client's certificate and public ID are valid and have been issued by a certificate authority. This confirmation might be important if the server, for example, is a bank sending confidential financial information to a customer and wants to check the recipient's identity.

- Encrypted SSL connection - An encrypted SSL connection requires all information sent between a client and a server to be encrypted by the sending software and decrypted by the receiving software, thus providing a high degree of confidentiality. Confidentiality is important for both parties to any private transaction. In addition, all data sent over an encrypted SSL connection is protected with a mechanism for detecting tampering—in other words, for automatically determining whether the data has been altered in transit.

It is easy to see when SSL is being used while surfing the Web. When you see a URL preceded by HTTPS instead of HTTP, you are likely operating in SSL mode. Many Web browsers also display either a "lock" or a "key" symbol to further indicate you are operating in SSL mode. You should expect to see these indicators anytime you enter a credit card number, or any personal information, onto a Web form.

e-Commerce Data Warehousing Implications

Chapter 10 discusses the topics of privacy and security in detail. Aside from the obvious transactional security requirements of e-commerce, it's essential that related business processes—making B2B content from the data warehouse available to a supplier, for example—be secure and not become a weak link in an organization's entire e-commerce environment. Consequently, *all* e-commerce communications should be as secure as necessary, using not only the techniques and strategies we discuss in Chapter 10 but also, if appropriate, SSL.

Database Technology

The primary storage vehicle in almost any modern data warehousing environment is some form of a database. Typically, relational database management system (RDBMS) technology is used, though other data structures useful for data warehousing include

- proprietary multidimensional database structures (i.e., "data cubes")

- flat files (typically for inbound data staging areas or for feeding content to specialized software, such as certain data mining engine products)

- special-format files, such as vendor-specific (e.g., SAS) data sets

Relational Database Technology

Since the late 1970s and early 1980s, relational database technology has taken hold in all areas of computing and has become the dominant database model in use today. Interestingly, relational databases circa 2001 look very little like their research lab or first-generation ancestors. The once-rigid rules of the relational model (specified in 1970 by Dr. E. F. Codd of IBM) have given way to real-world considerations.

For example, the latest version of the SQL standard—SQL:1999—introduces an *array* data type that is, essentially, a deliberate violation of the first normal form of the relational model that prohibits repeating groups. SQL:1999 also represents the convergence of the relational database technology with object-oriented database technology that first began appearing in the mid-1980s. Object-oriented concepts such as user-defined data types, encapsulation, polymorphism, and others are all found in the formerly relational-only language standard.[2]

Nonrelational Database Technology

Not that long ago, in the mid-1990s, the major battleground in the data warehousing realm was whether or not relational technology could be used for data warehousing purposes. Some argued that the dimensional nature of business intelligence data was a mismatch for the way in which most relational products' query planning subsystems had been built, and therefore query performance on all but the smallest data volumes was bound to be abysmal. Instead, "data cube" products such as IRI's (and later Oracle's) Express and Arbor's Essbase were far more suited for business intelligence work.

As relational products evolved to include parallel database capabilities, "star joins" that made joining many tables together far more time-efficient than in the past, and other functionality, the database platform wars ended with a whimper as relational databases became the mainstay of data warehousing.

However, nonrelational technology, including multidimensional products, still does have a role in data warehousing. Often, a departmental data mart will be built using multidimensional structures that in turn are populated from a corporate relationally structured data warehouse. Or perhaps a small-scale data mart is created using a multidimensional product that a company already has in-house.

Likewise, SQL:1999's incorporation of object-oriented constructs into an "extended relational model" does not mean the end of "pure" object-oriented (i.e., no relational database foundation) databases. Applications such as computer-aided design (CAD) will still continue to make use of these types of products.

e-Commerce Data Warehousing Implications

Though e-commerce data warehousing planners can safely plan on using a relational DBMS product as the foundation of their environment, other technologies and models may still be applicable to different parts of the overall enterprise business intelligence environment: deploying multidimensionally structured stores of data to satisfy some subset of standard reporting needs, for example.

However, the nature of e-commerce data warehousing—particularly the real-time, back-and-forth flows of data into and out of the data warehouse, rather than only inbound data via bulk load—leads to the necessity of using a "real database" as the data management foundation. And, even though most leading relational products support extended data types for different types of Internet content (audio, video, images, etc.), the current Internet operations model of intermixing HTML-based text with other multimedia content from various files (e.g., JPEG files) will likely continue.

Within the data warehousing realm, the structured side of the data will continue to be dominated by relational technology. However, convergence between the structured data and, increasingly, unstructured content that is also part of the enterprise's e-commerce business intelligence picture leads to choices that must be made. Should the current model be propagated, using a mixture of a relational database and various file types, or should the extended relational capabilities be fully utilized and *everything* within the data warehousing realm be stored within the relational environment?

Factors such as product quality and stability, capacity, and, most importantly, the company's business model will guide the decision-making process with regard to database technology usage. It's expected that by the middle of the 2000–2010 decade, as the current (2000–2001) Internet protocols and architecture give way to a new generation, Internet strategists will revisit the data storage part of the picture. Given the state of extended relational technology by, say, 2005, an increasing number of environments containing all applicable enterprise data—transactional or business intelligence—within a single database instance will exist.

Application Development and Integration

Even though the 1990s saw distributed application architecture evolve from two-tier client/server environments at the beginning of the decade to three-tier and *n*-tier environments by the mid-1990s, and then to Web-based applications by the end of the decade, the data warehousing realm has been mostly stuck in the early 1990s. Even though "early adapter" organizations have built and deployed architecturally complex *n*-tier, Web-based data warehousing environments as their primary business intelligence delivery vehicle, many projects that are commencing even today (2000–2001) are still very much two-tier in nature.

As we discussed in Part I with regards to the various types of e-commerce business models, data warehousing needs to evolve from its early-1990s, tried-and-true foundation to become "real application environments" rather than just passive stores of data to be accessed by users via front-end tools. The topics in this section are among the most important that need to be considered when planning, architecting, and designing the business interoperability of an e-commerce data warehousing environment with other applications within the enterprise.

Extraction, Transformation, and Loading (ETL) Tools

ETL tools will continue to be an important part of data warehousing, whether for e-commerce purposes or in general. The earliest ETL tools such as Prism were built to generate COBOL code to handle the ETL processes, mostly because of the early-1990s dominance of IBM mainframe-based applications that were turning into information sources for data warehouses. That generation of tool has largely been supplanted in the marketplace by "codeless" tools from vendors such as Informatica and Ardent.

One common thread exists between the different ETL tool generations, though: the batch-oriented nature of the way in which bulk data flows from the sources to the data warehouse. Even as these tools evolve to provide designers and developers with alternative data transfer mechanisms (messaging, for example, as discussed next), the batch capabilities still remain the dominant part of their products.

Even in an e-commerce environment, some flows into and out of the data warehouse are still best deployed in a batch manner, such as

- bulk-loading large volumes of external data, such as credit bureau scores or market share statistics

- initial population of a data warehouse's content with the company's customers

- regular monthly loads of detailed financial transaction data into the warehouse

Therefore, the familiarity most data warehousing practitioners have with ETL tools will still be of value in the e-commerce realm.

Messaging-Oriented Middleware (MOM)

The preceding ETL discussion noted that *sometimes* batch-oriented flows of data are the preferred mechanism for an e-commerce data warehousing environment. In many situations, however, data must be transmitted to and from the data warehouse on a real-time or near-real-time basis. Many of the e-commerce-related data flows *cannot* be implemented with time-delayed batch transfers of data because of the business impact: lost online sales opportunities, lost B2B partnering opportunities, damaged customer and/or partner relationships, and so on.

Interapplication messaging—specifically, by using messaging-oriented middleware—has been around in various forms since the 1980s and is a primary means through which bursts of data can be transmitted from one application to another. The trigger for the transmission may be time based (e.g., number of Web site visits in the past hour, an important statistic to e-tailers during the all-important holiday shopping season), or event based (e.g., an existing customer has returned to the Web site; what were the last three purchases he or she made, and what competitors' sites has he or she visited in the past month?).

Messaging-oriented middleware (sometimes abbreviated as MOM) can be implemented in a number of different ways. "Low-level" messaging involves products like IBM's MQSeries family, in which applications send messages to and from various queues, including those of IBM's "legacy products" (e.g., the IMS hierarchical database management system). The messaging capability guarantees queue-to-queue delivery; the logic that governs when messages are triggered, what happens when they're received, and other higher-level functions needs to be coded in a programming language or development environment.

Application-oriented messaging uses products from vendors such as Active Software to create "business rules" that govern the circumstances for sending and receiving messages, as well as the surrounding logic. The concept of application-oriented messaging goes back to the late 1980s and early 1990s, though most early-generation products were only useful in small-scale, point-to-point environments.

And, with regard to point-to-point environments, system architects can implement messaging via either

- a set of point-to-point interfaces, one for each logical interapplication within the enterprise, or

- using the concept of a "message broker" to enable a publish-and-subscribe model (discussed next).

Publish-and-Subscribe

Data warehousing has traditionally been very "pull oriented," meaning that source applications have typically been passive participants in the overall architecture. They make available their data at regular intervals, but for the most part, the data warehouse could disappear tomorrow and its source applications would be totally unaffected.

Likewise, the Internet was traditionally based on the notion that users must "pull" content by visiting a Web site. The sites themselves have been passive in nature; no visitors, no content served.

In a "push" model, however, an Internet provider (i.e., a Web site) does not wait for visitors, and an application doesn't wait until the data warehouse comes knocking and requests new source data. The objective is to "push" content from one entity to another—or many others—based on business rules, time, or other factors.

Coupling the idea of push-based interaction with messaging-oriented middleware and message brokers (discussed above) leads to the architectural concept of publish-and-subscribe. In a publish-and-subscribe environment, an entity can

- "publish" its content, based on its own internal business rules (events, time, etc.)

- "subscribe" to content published by other entities, based on its "areas of interest"

- be both a publisher and subscriber, if supported by that entity's business model

With a message broker architecture, a publisher sends its content to the broker, rather than to 1 or 2 or 10 or 500 different applications, users, or other entities. The message broker contains a directory of what entities inside the enterprise as well as possibly outside the enterprise (B2B trading partners, for example) have "registered" their interest in that content. The message broker, upon receiving content "pushed" to itself, will in turn "push" the content to all registered subscribers.

Directory Services

Directory services are a network service that identifies all resources on a network and makes them accessible to users and applications. Traditionally, these resources might include e-mail addresses, computers (including Web servers), and other devices such as printers. However, the concept of directory services can also be extended to include resources such as applications (including data warehouses), metadata, XML files, and so on.

The primary goal of a directory service is to hide the physical architecture so users on a network can access any resource without knowing where or how it is physically connected.

The Lightweight Directory Access Protocol (LDAP) was derived from an older directory standard known as X.500. The X.500 standard is extremely complex and difficult to fully implement. LDAP can be thought of as "X.500 lite" and enables corporate directory information to be managed in a hierarchical structure that reflects geographic and organizational boundaries. Using LDAP, companies can map their corporate directories to actual business processes—e-commerce or otherwise—rather than arbitrary codes.

Intelligent Agents

Intelligent agents are software programs used to perform often-repetitive tasks such as retrieving and delivering information. Since the Internet is so highly dynamic in nature, made up of an ever-increasing number of interconnected Web servers, each with widely varying content, intelligent agent software is increasingly applied to methodical tasks. For example, Web search engines send out intelligent agents that "crawl" from one server to another, compiling the enormous lists of URLs that are at the heart of every search engine. These intelligent agents are often referred to as "crawlers" or "spiders."

Intelligent agents have great potential in data mining, specifically finding patterns in enormous amounts of data. Because data mining often requires a series of searches, intelligent agents can save labor as they persist in a search, refining it as they go along. They can make decisions based on past experiences, which will become an important tool for data miners trying to perfect complex searches that delve into billions of data points.

In an e-commerce environment, intelligent agents can "crawl" to applicable places within an enterprise or, using the Internet, outside the enterprise (subject to security restrictions). Armed with a "mission" they might

- gather competitors' prices for the same or similar goods sold on your company's Web site

- gather statistics from a B2B auction exchange for products or components of interest

- regularly visit the sites of trading partners and bring back lists of new products

- sift through large volumes of publicly available data on the Internet ("public data mining") to try and find patterns and relationships that may be of interest to a company's business operations

Web Servers

As indicated by the name, Web servers serve content over the Internet using HTML. The Web server listens for HTTP requests coming from Web browsers and then returns the appropriate HTML document. (HTTP and HTML were discussed earlier in this chapter.) A number of server-side technologies can be used to increase the power of the server beyond its ability to deliver standard HTML pages, including CGI scripts, SSL security, and application server functionality.

There are numerous Web servers available on the market; however, there are three that make up the majority of Web servers in use today: the Web server from the Apache Project, Microsoft's Internet Information Server, and Netscape's Enterprise Web Server.

Apache Web Server

Apache remains a major player in the Web server market. One of its key benefits is that it is a freeware application. It has also become known as a Web server with solid reliability, strong performance, and a rich set of features. The keys to Apache's attractiveness and popularity lie in the qualities listed above and its extensibility, its freely distributed source code, and active user support for the server.

Many of the most accessed sites in the world run Apache or Apache derivatives. Public distribution of the source code results in patches for the software being distributed quickly, and allowing public scrutiny helps ensure that security holes in the software are promptly caught and reported. As a result, Apache's large user base has allowed its developers to create a package that is extremely stable and secure and one that is also able to compete more effectively with commercial packages in terms of both raw speed and integrated features.

Microsoft Internet Information Server (IIS)

Microsoft's branding power quickly made its Internet Information Server one of the most widely used Web servers in the Internet marketplace. Although only available for Windows NT, IIS has transformed the NT platform into a viable solution for delivering Web-based applications. It has strong reliability and flexibility. Two of its strongest attractants are (1) it is distributed without a fee, and (2) it is backed by Microsoft.

Like Apache, IIS runs on some of the most accessed sites on the Web. It provides strong capabilities for integrating with application servers. One of the downsides, however, is the lack of support for UNIX platforms. If your business model or technical architecture environment requires running Windows NT, you will likely find yourself electing to use IIS as your Web server.

Netscape Enterprise Web Server (iPlanet)

Netscape's Enterprise Web Server—iPlanet—has earned a spot as a major player among large, high-performing Web sites. It is supported on numerous platforms, including Windows NT. However, it is largely deployed on UNIX-based systems. It also has strong capabilities for integrating with various application servers that provide dynamic Web page capabilities.

The iPlanet Web server is being enhanced with numerous Java capabilities that reflect its partnership with Sun. Under this relationship, it is expected that the iPlanet Web server will excel in its support for Java and other Java-based technologies. This also is the one Web server out of the three discussed here that is not distributed for free.

Application Servers

Application servers are an important component in all aspects of e-commerce, as well as in "modern" application development in general. One of the main roles of the application server is to handle requests between Web browsers and a company's back-end business applications or databases. Since most databases cannot interpret commands written in HTML, the application server works as a translator, allowing, for example, a user with a browser to search an online catalog database for product information (see Figure 7.1). There are several reasons for having an application server handle this connection:

1. To decrease the size and complexity of client programs

2. To allow for caching and control over the data flow, yielding better performance

3. To be able to provide better security for both data and user traffic

The first step in comprehending how application servers work is to understand how a Web server knows to send a request to the application server for processing. The most common way is first to define in the Web server configuration a unique file extension type: for example, files that end with the extension .asp, .cfm, .jhtml, or .jsp. These are all examples of common file extension definitions used on many Web sites. The next step is to tell the Web server what application server to send requests to when it receives an HTTP request for a particular page with a unique file extension. The communication between the Web server and the application server takes place through the Web server's Application Programming Interface (API). Because application servers often implement their own languages (e.g., Cold Fusion, Active Server Pages, Java Server Pages, etc.) for processing their commands, it is likely you would never send requests for pages with different file extensions to the same application server. This will probably change in the future as application servers become more universal. In other words, an application server will be able to process commands from a variety of support interface languages.

So what makes an .asp file and a .cfm file different from a regular HTML file? Upon inspection you would find that there are a large number of similarities between them. In fact, HTML formatting and tags are often contained within application server files. The differences lie in the extra tags, commands, and scripting you

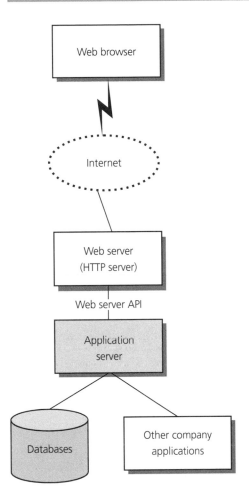

Figure 7.1 Simple application server architecture.

will see in those files. This is what allows the application server to query a database or interface with other applications. Web servers and regular HTML files do not have the capability to perform these functions.

Application servers also provide another important feature that allows for tracking of users between HTTP requests. As noted earlier in this chapter, HTTP requests are stateless; that is, Web servers cannot inherently track which requests are coming from the same user. However, application servers *can* track users among multiple HTTP requests by performing what is called "session tracking."

Session tracking is used in a variety of ways. It allows for the tracking of anonymous users—usually people surfing an Internet Web site—and users that actually log onto your Web site via some type of user ID (and usually a password).

To track sessions, the application server usually creates storage in memory or a database to log information related to the period you are on the Web site. For anonymous users, the information tracked may include advertisements viewed, articles read, and so on. For users that log onto your site, you may want to track profile information and the time that they logged on. It is very common to track time logged on so the application server can automatically log the user off after a period of inactivity. Note that all of this session-tracking information has a high degree of applicability to e-commerce business intelligence, and therefore would almost always be present in an e-commerce data warehousing environment.

So how does the application server know from whom the HTTP request is coming? Pieces of the answer include

- Source IP Address - The IP address of the system making the HTTP request, for example, the PC that your Web browser is running on. This is often not reliable since many ISPs use proxy servers (discussed later in this chapter), resulting in requests coming from the same user using multiple IP addresses.

- Cookies - Tracking session in a cookie (discussed earlier) is a very common practice. This is done by placing a session ID and other related information in the cookie file that resides on the system running the browser. Every HTTP request then sends the information contained in the cookie to the Web server and application server. This way, the application server can compare the session information contained in the cookie with the information it is tracking. Many sites use this capability to such a degree that if you try to disable the use of cookies on your browser, you in fact are unable to even browse a particular company's Web site.

- Attaching Session ID to URL - Session IDs can be sent as part of the URL. For example, this may look like *http://www.mycompany.com/myaccount.jsp?id=SGNB368133GH8765*, where SGNB368133GH8765 represents the session ID. This is probably the safest means for tracking sessions because it would account for the users that disable the use of cookies on their browser. However, it can require a lot of software development on the part of the Web designer to make sure that the session information is part of every link on every Web page.

The use of application servers is almost part of every e-commerce solution today, B2C and B2B alike. This is in part due to their relative ease of implementation and supported functionality. Before application servers, many sites used CGI scripts to provide dynamic capabilities (CGI is discussed later in this chapter). However, when the requirements for a Web site are driven by the scalability and performance requirements of e-commerce rather than billboardware or other noncommerce, lower-volume content, application servers usually win out over the use of CGI scripts.

ASPs

Application Service Providers (ASPs) are third-party companies that manage and distribute software-based services and solutions to customers across a wide area network from a central data center. Basically, ASPs are a way for businesses to outsource some or almost all aspects of their information technology needs. Using ASPs has become a very viable option for companies since software applications and the resources required to support them have become more complex and expensive in recent years.

According to ASPnews.com, ASPs can be broken down into five subcategories:

- Enterprise ASPs - Deliver high-end business applications. Applications that you might expect from an enterprise ASP are SAP, Seibel, Broadvision, and so on.

- Local/regional ASPs - Supply a wide variety of application services for smaller businesses in a local area.

- Specialist ASPs - Provide applications for a specific need, such as Web site services or human resources.

- Vertical market ASPs - Provide support to a specific industry, such as health care, telecommunications, and so on.

- Volume business ASPs - Supply general small/medium-sized businesses with pre-packaged application services in volume, such as payroll.

One final word about ASPs: Longer-duration IT practitioners may recall the era in the 1960s and 1970s when time-sharing bureaus and other types of computer service bureaus would host client companies' mainframe-based and minicomputer-based applications, rather than those companies building their own data centers and purchasing or leasing their own computers. With the advent of PCs, workstations, and servers in the 1980s, the conventional wisdom was to bring applications in-house for better control over these resources.

Now, with the dawn of the Internet e-commerce era, things have swung almost full circle since in many ways (other than the underlying platforms and technology, of course) ASPs are the next generation of time-sharing and service bureaus that had dominated the IT landscape decades earlier. (Like they sing in the 1960s "I'm Henry the VIII I Am" song: "Second verse, same as the first . . .").

Procedural Logic

Nearly any computer programming language has applicability to e-commerce . . . even COBOL! In this section, we'll briefly discuss three "Internet-specific" ways to specify procedural logic as representative of those with which developers may need to work:

- Java
- JavaScript
- CGI

Java

Java is a high-level programming language developed by Sun Microsystems. It was originally developed for handheld devices and television set-top boxes, but was modified in 1995 to take advantage of the Internet and the Web. Like C++, Java is an object-oriented language, but offers simplified features that help to eliminate common programming errors. Furthermore, Java code is compiled into a format, called *bytecode*, that can then be executed by a Java interpreter. Compiled Java code can run on most computers since Java interpreters and run-time environments, known as Java Virtual Machines (VMs), exist for most operating systems.

Java is a general-purpose programming language with a number of features that make the language well suited for use on the Web. Small Java applications, called Java *applets,* can be downloaded from a Web server and run on your computer through the use of a Java-compatible Web browser, including Microsoft Internet Explorer and Netscape Navigator.

The popularity and viability of Java has been increasing exponentially for several reasons. First, it has eliminated some of the complexities of programming that are coupled with C++. Next, its performance has improved greatly through the use of optimized Java Virtual Machines, or interpreters. Lastly, it has demonstrated itself as a good solution for server-side applications that are portable among different operating systems.

JavaScript

JavaScript is a scripting language developed by Netscape to give Web designers the ability to design interactive Web sites. It shares many of the features and structures of the full Java language, but actually is different from Java. (In fact, it was developed independently from Java.) JavaScript can interact with HTML, enabling Web authors to "spice up" their sites with dynamic content. JavaScript is an open language that anyone can use without purchasing. It is supported by Web browsers from Netscape and Microsoft, although Internet Explorer supports only a subset, which Microsoft calls JScript.

CGI

The Common Gateway Interface (CGI) is a specification for transferring information between a Web server (discussed earlier in this chapter) and a CGI program. A CGI program is, as you might expect from the name, any program designed to accept and return data that conforms to the CGI specification. The program could actually be written in any programming language, including C++, Java, or Visual Basic.

CGI programs have traditionally been one of the most common ways for Web servers to interact dynamically with users. Many HTML pages that contain forms, for example, use a CGI program to process the form's data once it's submitted. CGI is considered a server-side solution because the processing occurs on the Web server, not on the system running the Web browser (i.e., the client).

One problem with CGI is that each time a CGI script is executed, a new process is started. For busy Web sites, this can slow down the server noticeably. Thus, the trend toward application servers (discussed earlier in this chapter) began in response to the scalability and performance issue.

e-Commerce Data Warehousing Implications

Until the late 1990s, data warehousing practitioners have typically had a relatively limited "toolbox" (or, if you prefer, "bag of tricks") to use, and decisions to make, when architecting, designing, and constructing a data warehouse. The ETL process *would* be batch oriented; would a tool or custom code be used as the implementation vehicle? What type of database—relational or multidimensional (see the preceding section)—would be appropriate for this environment? Which front-end tool or tools should be used?

Now, however, the "real application" nature of an e-commerce data warehousing environment has not only placed many more tools into these practitioners' toolboxes, but also required many more decisions to be made . . . and for those decisions to be considered in concert with one another. Application integration has come to the data warehousing world as it did to the transactional world in the early and mid-1990s, and all of the discipline required for distributed transactional systems needs to be *formally* applied into the data warehousing arena as well.

Building a comprehensive, detailed e-commerce business model and architecture that clearly indicates

- what data needs to go,

- from where,

- to where,

- under what circumstances, and

- with what constraints

will provide a crystal-clear business blueprint from which these many choices can be made with confidence.

Vendor Web Development Platforms

The volume of material in the previous sections can certainly seem daunting in terms of the number of different pieces to the puzzle that must be considered for e-commerce solutions. One alternative to from-the-ground-up integration is to use a vendor-provided Web development platform. Typically, the environment would be used for the transactional side of an e-commerce environment, with links as appropriate (i.e., Web server, protocols, etc.) to the data warehousing portion. In this section, we'll look at three different Web development environments from IBM, Microsoft, and Allaire.

IBM

The centerpiece of IBM's Internet strategy is the WebSphere software platform.[3] WebSphere is intended to help companies at each stage of e-business[4] development, including supply chain management and the high-volume Web transactions typical of (B2B) e-marketplaces. According to the Giga Information Group, the market opportunity in this area was $585 million in 1999, $1.6 billion in 2000, and will be $9 billion by 2003. Giga also estimated that by the end of 2000, IBM will have 24% market share—up 50% over 1999, making them a dominant player in this space.

IBM's focus on e-business includes product development and marketing campaigns to help companies use middleware as part of e-business operations. (Recall that earlier in this chapter we briefly discussed IBM's MQSeries middleware.) The WebSphere software platform has evolved from a family of Web application servers to a complete family of end-to-end e-business software. It builds on the existing

WebSphere brand with new e-business capabilities to provide a broad and well-integrated middleware package. It combines Web application serving and application integration, along with an array of e-commerce, Web development, and management services under the WebSphere brand.

The WebSphere software platform is based on IBM's Application Framework for e-business and consists of three layers: the Foundation, Foundation Extensions, and Application Accelerators.

WebSphere Foundation

The WebSphere Foundation provides the essential e-business functions of handling transactions and extending back-end business data and applications to the Web, and includes the WebSphere Application Server. The WebSphere Application Server deploys, integrates, and manages Java-based applications and JavaBeans components for the enterprise, and offers a complete set of application services for transaction management, security, clustering, performance, and availability. The WebSphere Application Server for OS/390 is available for enterprise e-business applications.

The Standard Edition lets you use Java servlets, JavaServer Pages, and XML to quickly transform a static Web site into a vital high-performance Enterprise JavaBeans (EJB) server for implementing EJB components that incorporate business logic. The Enterprise Edition integrates EJB and CORBA components to build high-transaction, high-volume e-business applications.

WebSphere Standard Version 3.5 includes many of the topics we discussed earlier in this chapter—a Java development kit, XML, and an HTTP server based on the Apache server, for example—plus support for a variety of operating systems (Windows NT, Windows 2000, Solaris, AIX, AS/400). There is also database access using JDBC for DB2 Universal Database and Oracle.

An advanced version of the WebSphere Application Server, appropriately titled WebSphere Version 3.5 The Advanced Edition, adds the following:

- Improved integration with Lotus Domino, IBM Visual Age for Java, and IBM WebSphere Commerce Suite

- Full support for the EJB 1.0 specification, including both SessionBeans and EntityBeans (container-managed and bean-managed persistence)

- Deployment support for EJBs, Java servlets, and JSPs with performance and scale improvements, including IBM LDAP Directory, which can be optionally installed; a DB2 server that is automatically installed as part of the runtime environment; support for distributed transactions and transaction processing; and management and security controls (including user- and group-level setup and method-level policy and control)

Finally, an Enterprise Edition adds the following to the Advanced Edition:

- Full distributed object and business process integration capabilities
- A transactional application environment integration (from TXSeries)
- Complete object distribution and persistence (from Component Broker)
- Support for MQSeries
- Complete component backup and restore support
- XML-based team development functions
- Integrated Encina application development kit

WebSphere Foundation Extensions

WebSphere Foundation Extensions are integrated services that provide rapid application development, improve the presentation of information and applications, and help meet performance and manageability needs through advanced deployment services. The environment includes WebSphere Personalization and WebSphere Portal Server, which is integrated with WebSphere Transcoding Publisher, the IBM Enterprise Information Portal, and WebSphere Everyplace Suite to provide a foundation for advanced e-business applications.

WebSphere Portal Server, Version 1, delivers a customizable portal and a common set of services on which the user can build a wide variety of applications. Jointly developed with Lotus, the WebSphere portal and services are common to IBM's eCommerce, Collaboration, and Knowledge Management products. By combining WebSphere Portal Server with other IBM products, such as Domino, IBM Enterprise Information Portal, WebSphere Personalization, WebSphere Everyplace Suite, and WebSphere Commerce Suite, it is easier for developers to create enterprise, commerce, pervasive, and vertical portal solutions—useful in both B2C and B2B settings.

WebSphere Personalization, Version 1, provides a choice of both business rules and collaborative filtering technology, allowing customers to optimize personalization of their e-businesses. This advanced technology allows site owners to define and manage the users and content, provides a graphical tool for creating groupings of profiles, and is integrated with WebSphere Studio, making personalized application development easy.

WebSphere Edge Server, Version 1, is designed for creating high-performance Web sites and provides caching, load balancing, and content-based routing support to enhance Web site availability, scalability, and performance. Functionality includes improvements in proxy cache performance, end-to-end SSL support, support for Real Networks streaming media, DiffServ-based traffic routing, and enhanced session affinity for complex transaction support. Edge Server provides a base upon which IBM will introduce services to improve the performance of dynamic applications.

WebSphere Site Analyzer, Version 3.5, is a site analysis tool that provides Web site traffic measurement and reporting functions, providing customers with information they need to improve Web content, performance, and visitor experience. Support has also been added to provide e-commerce shopping cart analysis for WebSphere Commerce Suite V4.1 customers. It also supports Web analytics of WebSphere Distributed Edge Server.

WebSphere Studio, Version 3.5, is a toolkit for creating dynamic Web applications. This software enables developers to create and manage applications for browsers and pervasive devices using a single toolkit and skill set.

VisualAge for Java, Version 3.5, provides a new servlet wizard to generate servlets, JSP pages, and HTML prototypes, allowing developers to quickly test their business logic inside the Integrated Development Environment (IDE) before deploying to a production server.

VisualAge Generator, Version 4.5, provides a powerful, high-end, rapid application development environment for building and deploying multitier, server-centric e-business applications. Its WebSphere RAD (rapid application development) capability means developers can access components directly from programs and can generate Enterprise JavaBeans (session beans), easing the transition to component-based development.

WebSphere Host Publisher, Version 2.2, extends host applications to the Web by consolidating multiple sources of host data into a single Web page with no additional programming. In addition to including WebSphere Application Server Standard Edition, the new version now includes WebSphere Studio to help companies easily develop and deploy advanced e-business solutions. Extensions include the WebSphere Everyplace Suite and WebSphere Transcoding Publisher, which extend the capabilities of WebSphere to mobile computing devices.

The WebSphere Voice Server with ViaVoice Technology enables developers to build voice-enabled Web sites and call centers on the WebSphere platform. It provides a general-purpose Web development tool for building voice applications using VoiceXML. Additionally, the WebSphere Host Integration Solution, which previously included Host On-Demand, Host Publisher, and Communications Server, will include a new version of WebSphere Host Publisher, WebSphere Studio, and WebSphere Application Server Advanced Edition. The WebSphere Host Integration Solution provides a comprehensive and flexible set of Web-to-host solutions for a single price per user, and works with WebSphere Transcoding Publisher to deliver host data to any pervasive device.

Application Accelerators and B2B Integrator

The final piece of the WebSphere picture—the Application Accelerators—are modular and extensible packages such as Lotus Domino, WebSphere Commerce Suite, and, of particular interest to this book's subject, the WebSphere B2B Integrator.

B2B Integrator's features include

- built-in capabilities for communications, security, configuration, and process traceability, which allow for intelligent data transformation, content-based routing, and event-driven business process execution

- promotion of Web-based interaction and collaboration by providing for easy integration with a range of partners, using a variety of industry standard open data exchange protocols, such as RosettaNet, OBI, and Cxml

- support for both message-oriented and object-oriented component interaction

Microsoft

Microsoft communicates a "one-stop shop" message to the marketplace, advocating that their technology can be used to develop and implement systems from the smallest "mom and pop" Web sites to the largest, most complex mission-critical Web sites.[5] Microsoft technology is also being used to host many of the Internet-based technologies used to enable successful Web applications and services. NT servers, for example, are a very common platform today for hosting firewall applications. This section describes some of the Microsoft products used to enable e-commerce solutions.

Site Server 3.0 provides a comprehensive offering that enables businesses to build powerful and cost-effective Web solutions for publishing and delivering relevant and timely information to their employees. Whether the plan is to build a new Web application, migrate an old one to the Web, or add new capabilities to an existing Web site, Site Server can help streamline the information-sharing process.

Microsoft Site Server 3.0 allows users and administrators to publish information easily by providing authors with a structured content submission, posting, and approval process. Users can easily search and find information stored in a variety of sources including Web sites, file servers, Microsoft SQL Server and ODBC databases, and Microsoft Exchange folders throughout their organization. Site Server 3.0 can then deliver information that is relevant to users through personalized Web pages, Active Channels, and e-mail, and enable administrators to analyze usage of the site.

bCentral is Microsoft's "one-stop shop" focusing on small businesses. Small businesses will be able to use bCentral to set up a Web site and bring their business online. Microsoft's message is that small businesses that use bCentral will have "comprehensive reporting on the effectiveness of their online marketing programs, so they can make informed decisions about marketing investments."

Microsoft Visual InterDev 6.0 is the integrated Web application development system for professional programmers. Visual InterDev 6.0 enables Web teams to design, build, debug, and deploy cross-platform Web applications. This environment features a new integrated WYSIWYG (what you see is what you get) editor for ASP and dynamic HTML pages, enhanced database programming tools, and end-to-end debugging facilities for multitier applications built with HTML and Script.

Microsoft's Visual Studio 6.0 is marketed as the complete enterprise development tool suite. Visual Studio allows developers to build scalable applications for Windows and the Web that also integrate with existing systems. The Visual Studio 6.0 development suite enhances developer productivity and provides comprehensive design support with integrated features across all the popular languages. Visual Studio 6.0 Enterprise Edition includes the complete set of development tools for building reusable applications in Microsoft Visual Basic 6.0, Visual C++ 6.0, Visual J++ 6.0, or Visual FoxPro 6.0. In addition, Visual Studio Enterprise Edition adds extensive support for large systems and distributed applications. It offers additional features, including enterprise database development and design tools, team development support, development life cycle support, and development and test versions of the Microsoft BackOffice family of application servers. To take advantage of the latest capabilities for developing Windows 2000 and mobile computing applications, Visual Studio 6.0 includes the Windows 2000 Developer's Readiness Kit and the freely redistributable, SQL Server 7.0–compatible Microsoft Data Engine (MSDE) for mobile applications.

Allaire (Cold Fusion)

Allaire Corporation, founded in 1995, is a provider of e-commerce software products and solutions.[6] They introduced the first Web application server for Windows NT (Cold Fusion) and continue to innovate in areas such as server-side Java development, personalization, and B2B integration. Their strategy has taken them from being a small application server vendor to a company that is a substantial player in the e-business solutions space.

Allaire breaks down their products into three core elements of an e-commerce infrastructure: application servers, packaged applications, and visual tools.

Application Servers

Allaire provides two application servers, Cold Fusion and JRun. Cold Fusion is a robust application server that interprets Cold Fusion Markup Language (CFML), a tag-based server scripting language. (Refer to our discussion of tags with regard to HTML and XML earlier in this chapter.) It supports the following core services:

- Administration - Applications can be managed using a Web browser. These administrative services allow for easy management and configuration across servers and applications.

- Clustering - Cluster services, such as failure and load balancing, allow for increased scalability and reliability.

- Logging - This provides the capability to monitor and track server actions, errors, application behavior, and user behavior.

- Security - Security capabilities include authenticating users, controlling access, securing components, and the ability to integrate with existing security systems.

- State management - Since the Web is by nature "stateless" (as discussed earlier in this chapter with regard to HTTP), Cold Fusion provides a mechanism for tracking users across pages.

- Text indexing and searching - Web applications usually incorporate a significant amount of text-based content. Text indexing and searching services let you query the unstructured textual data in your applications quickly and easily. Cold Fusion uses an embedded version of Verity to accomplish this.

In addition to the core services, Cold Fusion provides the means with which to interface with other systems:

- Databases - Support for ODBC, JDBC, and native database drivers.

- Directories - Connectivity to standard directory services through the Lightweight Directory Access Protocol (LDAP).

- File servers - Access to files servers using the File Transfer Protocol (FTP).

- HTTP servers - Access to other HTTP servers from the application server directly.

- Mail servers - Access to mail servers using the Simple Mail Transfer Protocol (SMTP) and the Post Office Protocol (POP).

- Other connectivity - Interface capabilities to Common Object Request Broker Architecture (CORBA), Component Object Model (COM), and Enterprise JavaBeans (EJB).

Allaire's other application server, JRun, interprets Java Server Pages (JSP), a tag-based server scripting language. It largely supports the same core services that Cold Fusion does with the following additional Java services:

- Distributed objects - Enterprise JavaBeans

- Messaging - Java Messaging Services

- Transactions - Java Transaction API

In addition to the core services, JRun interfaces with other systems, including the following:

- Databases - Support of Java Database Connectivity (JDBC) and native database drivers

- Directories - Connectivity to Java Naming and Directory (JNDI).

- Mail servers - Java Mail API

Cold Fusion and JRun can also be used together. For example, an e-commerce environment might have Cold Fusion providing the dynamic Web page capabilities while JRun provides business logic functionality through Enterprise JavaBeans. Cold Fusion is able to talk to JRun through their native support for EJB connectivity.

Packaged Applications

Allaire currently (2000–2001) has one packaged application, called Allaire Spectra. Allaire Spectra is an application specifically designed for e-commerce. It can be used to address content management, customer relationship management, and online commerce needs. The underlying engine for Allaire Spectra is the Cold Fusion Application Server. Allaire Spectra provides six key services:

- Content management - Provides powerful tools for managing Web site content and allows for in-browser editing

- Workflow and process automation - Ability to create custom workflow and process automation solutions

- Role-based security - Provides the ability to manage users and groups and control access across an e-commerce environment

- Personalization services - Provides ability to profile users, dynamic targeting based upon rules, and the integration of third-party personalization tools

- Business intelligence - Services for logging, measuring, and reporting user activities

- Syndication - Ability to extend an e-commerce solution to partners or affiliates by exposing content and features through a structured interface

Visual Tools

Allaire provides visual tools designed for several different user classes:

- Administrators - The tools give the ability to configure servers, manage distributed applications, deploy applications, monitor performance, and gather operational data. Tools primarily used by administrators include Cold Fusion Administrator (a browser-based server administration tool for Cold Fusion) and Allaire Spectra WebTop (a browser-based tool used for administering the Allaire Spectra application).

- Developers - System programmers, application developers, and designers need to leverage an integrated development environment (IDE). The IDE supports development of HTML, CFML, and JSP as well as support for scripting, database tools, and debugging. Tools primarily used by developers include Homesite (for HTML designers that assist in developing Web sites that support a full range of Web browsers and browser interfaces), Cold Fusion Studio (builds upon Homesite and provides support for CFML, database development, debugging, etc.), JRun Studio (designed specifically for the JSP developer, providing an environment to develop Web applications with Java technologies), and Allaire Spectra WebTop (mentioned previously).

- Business users - Allaire provides Cold Fusion Studio and Allaire Spectra WebTop to business users, the intention being to support as much user-side development as possible.

Networking, Communications, and Protocols

With the Internet foundation and inherent distributed systems of e-commerce data warehousing, an understanding of networking and communications becomes a necessity for practitioners, if only cursorily. A working familiarity with terminology, networking devices and their capabilities, and protocols is essential to prevent situations where a conceptual data warehousing architecture is so totally detached from the underlying implementation environment that the architecture is, essentially, unimplementable.

LANs (Ethernet)

Local area networks (LANs) today predominantly leverage Ethernet technology. Ethernet was originally developed in the 1970s by Xerox Corporation in conjunction with Intel and Digital Equipment Corporation,[7] and is now the primary network method for connecting distributed systems together. Other networking approaches such as Token Ring are still in existence; however, Ethernet switches, network cards, cabling, and other devices have become so cost-effective in comparison, that it is becoming rare to see other architectures.

General Discussion

Ethernet is based upon a bus-based configuration as shown in Figure 7.2. All devices that are connected to the Ethernet bus have a unique address and have the ability to listen for and transmit data at the same time. Throughput on Ethernet networks was

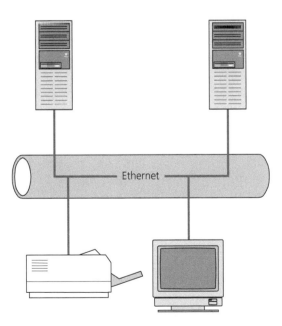

Figure 7.2 Typical Ethernet LAN configuration.

10 megabits per second (Mbps) for many years, but now you can achieve speeds that are in the range of gigabits per second. These are more than 100 times faster than the 10 Mbps speeds. Today, the most common speed is 100 Mbps.

e-Commerce Data Warehousing Implications

Even though much of an Internet-based environment for e-commerce will occur in the wide area network (WAN, discussed later in this section) space, LAN technology and architecture will continue to be a critical piece of all aspects of e-commerce data warehousing: connections of users to local Web servers and application servers, connections of local servers to other servers, and so on. When architecting data transfer flows from one platform to another, or calculating estimated query and report response time, it's important to map any conceptual data flow models into the underlying LAN architecture to assess throughput in various scenarios: "typical" use volumes, peak use volumes (i.e., end-of-month processing), and other scenarios as appropriate.

Interface Devices

Also of importance when architecting a distributed environment are bridges, switches, gateways, and routers.

General Discussion

A *bridge* connects two or more LAN segments and transmits data from one segment to a destination on other segments. If the bridge knows that the destination of a data packet is on the same segment as the source of the data packet, it drops the data packet because there is no need to transmit it. If the bridge knows that the destination is on another segment, it transmits the data packet on that segment only. If the bridge does not know the destination segment, the bridge transmits the data packet on all segments except the source segment (a technique known as *flooding*).

The primary benefit of bridging is that it limits traffic to certain network segments. Figure 7.3 shows a bridge connecting two separate Ethernet segments. This allows devices on segment A to communicate to devices on segment B.

Like a bridge, a *switch* connects LAN segments or even individual devices on the network. A switch maintains a table of addresses to determine the segment on which a data packet needs to be transmitted. It then sets up a dedicated path to that device to send information on. The overall effect is that it reduces traffic on the network by allowing devices to communicate with each other at the same time. Switches operate at much higher speeds than bridges and can support newer functionality.

A common analogy for switches is to think of them as being similar to the telephone network. For example, if you were to make a phone call to a friend, you would

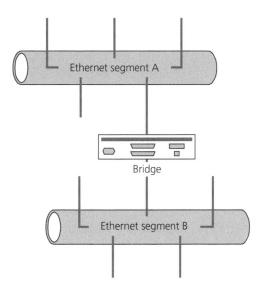

Figure 7.3 Typical bridge configuration.

dial their telephone number—their address on the telephone network. Once your friend answers the phone a virtual connection is established that is dedicated to you and your friend. At the same time, the telephone network is maintaining other virtual connections for other telephone conversations without interrupting your conversation. This is precisely how a network switch works, except that the addresses are network addresses and the communications link is via Ethernet or another network technology.

Gateways are usually a combination of hardware and software that work together to link two different types of networks or systems. The use of gateways used to be very common since many systems did not support a common set of protocols and thus required something to translate between them.

One way to think of a gateway is that it is the network equivalent of the "T" (transformation) portion of a data warehousing ETL set of processes. One or more encoding formats are processed against some standard conversion rules, and the outcome is a new format for the outbound content on the way to its destination.

A *router* can be thought of as a more intelligent device for managing network traffic. Routing involves two basic activities: (1) determination of optimal routing paths and (2) the transport of packets through an internetwork. Transporting packets is relatively straightforward. Path determination, on the other hand, involves performing algorithms to determine the most optimal route to the destination address. To do this, routers have to communicate with each other and maintain routing address tables. Essentially, a router has to have a level of awareness of the network that it is connected to in order to effectively route data packets to their destinations.

An analogy to a router in the data warehousing world is how the DBMS's query planner and other related DBMS subsystems determine (or at least try to determine) the optimal way in which a database query would be handled, based on its rules and awareness of its environment. A single-table query would be handled differently than a particular two-table join, which in turn may be handled differently than some other two-table join, and so on.

e-Commerce Data Warehousing Implications

How important is it really for data warehousing practitioners to understand all the details of these various network interface devices? Basically, the same guidance as was given for LAN technology applies. It is important to have at least a cursory understanding of the underlying networking environment and, in particular, how various portions of that environment relate to one another.

A common occurrence in the world of data warehousing is the use of the "cloud" in architectural drawings to represent "the world out there, whatever it is" or "the networking environment, whatever it is." Certainly, at the conceptual level, "cloud-enabled" data warehousing architecture is permissible when trying to focus on the business architecture, but at some point the cloud needs to be mapped into a real-world environment.

Two of the many examples in which this knowledge is important are the following:

1. Collaborative business intelligence - Increasingly, business intelligence functionality is becoming collaborative in nature, not only in a workflow sense (i.e., routing the results of a report or query to someone else, perhaps on a rule-based basis), but even in a real-time sense—using online conferencing facilities such as Webex (*www.webex.com*) over the Internet or an in-house, LAN-based version. When one group of users is located on one portion of the networking environment and another group of users is located on another portion, it's important to understand the throughput through these interconnection devices as large volumes of data, graphics, and other content flow back and forth.

2. Phased architectural planning - Most enterprise-scale e-commerce data warehousing environments will be constructed in an iterative, incremental manner.

At the same time, most organizations are constantly upgrading their networking and communications environments to meet the needs of e-commerce and an Internet presence in general. Knowledge of the current environment—where the "weak spots" (bottlenecks, etc.) are; what routers and switches and other devices are scheduled for upgrade or even rearchitecting; and other networking-related matters—will help data warehousing planners and architects synchronize their own initiatives with those of the underlying network.

Wide Area Networks (WANs)

WAN connectivity is an essential part of the e-commerce environment, simply because of the inherent wide area distribution of the Internet, a company's potential customer base, its B2B trading partners, and other entities.

General Discussion

The main function of a WAN is to connect two or more LANs, for one or more purposes: providing connectivity to the Internet, providing consumers a means by which they can access your Web site, or providing a private network between a company and one of its other offices or even a major supplier.

WANs are conceptually distinguished from LANs largely by geographic distance. The distance may be across town,[8] across the country, or even across the world. Additionally, a carrier, like a Regional Bell Operating Company (RBOC) or a long-distance carrier company, almost always provides companies with their WAN services.

There are actually two different types of telephone communications companies as a result of the 1984 divestiture of AT&T:

- Local exchange carriers (LECs) - This category consists of the RBOCs, independent telephone companies, and other small telephone companies.

- Interexchange carriers (IECs or IXCs) - Interexchange carriers are most often thought of as long-distance carriers. These are the former AT&T Long Lines organization and other carriers such as Sprint and MCI.

Services that are available from RBOCs and IECs/IXCs that are important to e-commerce include the following:

- Voice-grade services - Leased private analog lines.

- Digital data service (DDS) - Leased digital lines used for data only at speeds ranging from 2,400 bps (bits per second) to 64 Kbps (kilobits per second).

- DS0 service - Leased 64 Kbps digital line.

- Fractional T1 service - Digital lines that are a subset of a T1 service. Often this service is made up of multiple DS0 lines.

- T1 services - Lines that can support voice, data, or multimedia at speeds of approximately 1.544 Mbps. T1 service is made up of 24 DS0 lines, sometimes called channels.

- T3 services - Leased-line service similar to T1, just at a higher rate. This service is made up of 28 T1s (DS1s) to arrive at an aggregate speed of 44.736 Mbps.

- International private lines - Services vary and are provided by certain carriers to international locations through gateway cities. The subscriber usually must lease two lines, one to the gateway and one from the gateway to the international location.

- Switched data services - These services are often referred to as virtual private networks (VPNs). They allow a customer to make use of the carrier's long-distance facilities to configure a private network. This configuration is done through software.

- Packet services - Type of service where data is sent out over a network designed to route data packets. The Internet is an example of a packet-switched network.

There are other connectivity services offered by a variety of carriers that are more often associated with local access and are of particular importance to the B2C side of e-commerce with regard to home and office Internet access speeds available to individuals. These services include

- ISDN - Integrated Services Digital Network, with speeds ranging from 64 Kbps to 128 Kbps.

- DSL - Digital Subscriber Line, over regular copper telephone lines, allowing for speeds ranging from 128 Kbps up to speeds in the Mbps range.

- Cable modem - Service that utilizes the coaxial cable used typically for cable TV. This, however, is a shared medium, so as more users are added to the segment of cable, the slower the speed is likely to be. The speeds for cable modems can reach up to 3 Mbps, although as more users share the segment, this speed may drop.

e-Commerce Data Warehousing Implications

The same points made with regard to LAN technology apply to the WAN environments, but with an "accent mark." Particularly in B2C e-commerce, one of the primary influence factors to many consumers is response time. Though many facets of the WAN environment are outside the control of those architecting and building e-commerce capabilities—public accessibility to DSL or cable modem, for example—it is important to take these factors into consideration.

For example, in Chapter 2 we discussed that one way for B2C companies to address the growing backlash over the personal data collection policies of online retailers was to offer selected consumer-oriented business intelligence housed in the company's data warehousing environment to prospects and customers—sort of a quid pro quo in information exchange. Knowing, for example, that a large portion of a farming-oriented Web site lives in rural areas, and that those rural areas typically lag urban areas in DSL and cable modem availability, should lead the designers responsible for that particular outbound data warehousing functionality in certain directions given lower bandwidths available to their target audience: offering a no-graphics option, minimizing the flow of data to the browser, and so on.

Correspondingly, designers of B2B environments who are likewise exposing portions of their data warehousing environment to trading partners can take advantage of, say, T1 connectivity between the companies to safely plan on large data flows, exchange of applicable multimedia (e.g., instructional videos linked to product assembly or maintenance) in addition to traditional structured data, and so on.

Internet-Specific Networking

LANs, WANs, and the devices that provide interconnectivity among various types of networks are all part of the general information systems infrastructure and architecture "toolbox." That is, non-Internet environments have been built using these infrastructure components for many years.

There are, however, some additional networking considerations that are either exclusively or predominantly related to the Internet that also need to be considered:

- Domain Name System (DNS)

- Firewalls

- Proxy servers

- Web server load balancing

- Internet Service Providers (ISPs)

Domain Name System

The Domain Name System (DNS) is a naming scheme for Internet Protocol (IP) addresses. Every device on the Internet has an IP address assigned to it, and every host name refers to an IP address. The primary purpose for host names is so people can identify the computers by something other than a difficult-to-remember IP address (e.g., 216.32.74.50). It is much easier to remember this address as *www .yahoo.com*.

In fact, it is likely that IP addresses will change. Because of the Domain Name System's higher level of abstraction, it's a more reliable way to name a device or service. When an IP address changes, a domain name server can be updated, so that the old name can be resolved into the new address. DNS helps make the Internet easier and more stable.

Firewalls

The firewall is a system intended to prevent unauthorized access to a private network from a public network (the Internet, in most cases). Firewalls can consist of hardware, software, or a combination of both. Firewalls are commonly placed between a company's intranet and the Internet and only allow communication that meets certain criteria. It does this by examining information contained in the data packets that are sent across the network and comparing it to a set of rules. If this information meets the criteria defined by the rules, the firewall will allow the packet of data to pass through. By design, anything that is not specifically allowed is prohibited by the firewall.

Additionally, a firewall can limit communication from a computer on the Internet to certain computers on your private network. For example, a computer on the Internet may be able to access one of your Web servers on your private network, but not a database server. This is important for B2B transactions since you may want to allow certain companies access to your internal systems and exclude all other users from accessing those systems.

Proxy Servers

Proxy servers usually are found between a user and the server providing the information or services the user is requesting. The proxy server intercepts all requests to the "real server" (the server that houses the content) to see if it can fulfill the request itself. If not, it forwards the request to the real server. Some firewall products also have proxy capabilities, so sometimes the two functions are combined into a single device.

Proxy servers are targeted to address two main objectives: (1) to improve performance, and (2) to filter requests. Proxy servers can dramatically improve performance for some groups of users since they save the results of all requests for a predetermined amount of time. For example, a user loads a company's home page through a proxy server. Later, another user requests the same company's home page. Rather than sending this request to the Web server to fulfill the request, the proxy server simply returns the home page that it already obtained for the first user.

Proxy servers are often on the same network as the user, which results in a much faster operation. Major online services such as America Online utilize many proxy servers.

Proxy servers, like firewalls, can also be used to filter requests. For example, many companies use proxy servers to prevent employees from accessing specific Web sites. In addition, logging and reporting capabilities within the proxy server can give you an audit trail for user activity.

Web Server Load Balancing

Load balancing is the process to distribute requests across multiple Web servers (actually, servers of any type, though for this discussion we're dealing with Web servers), each of which could itself handle a particular request (see Figure 7.4).

This load-balancing "solution" can be made up of hardware, software, or a combination of both. The goal is to distribute processing and communications evenly across a computer network so that no single server or system is overwhelmed. This is especially important for networks where it is difficult to predict the number of

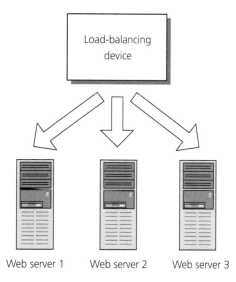

Web server 1   Web server 2   Web server 3

Figure 7.4 Load balancing in an e-commerce environment.

requests that will be directed to a server. Large Web sites typically employ two or more Web servers in a load-balancing scheme. If one server becomes overburdened, requests are forwarded to another server for additional capacity.

Internet Service Providers (ISPs)

Internet service providers are companies that provide access to the Internet. For consumers, ISPs usually provide an access telephone number and a logon ID and password to obtain dial-in capabilities to access the Internet. These same ISPs may also provide higher-speed broadband access into the Internet through the use of cable modems or Digital Subscriber Line (DSL) services. Some examples of ISPs include America Online and MindSpring.

In addition, ISPs also provide services to companies. They can provide a direct connection from a company network to the Internet. Some examples of ISPs providing these services include UUNet and Qwest.

Consequently, ISPs need to be architected into all types of e-commerce solutions, whether consumer oriented or business focused.

e-Commerce Data Warehousing Implications

All of the discussion points made earlier in this section apply with regard to Internet-specific networking capabilities: at least a cursory understanding of these technologies and systems is important to ensure proper architecture for all aspects of the e-commerce environment, business intelligence as well as transactional.

User-Facing Technology

Finally, we briefly discuss two different types of user-facing technologies—Web browsers and personal digital assistants—and their data warehousing implications.

Web Browsers

Not much really needs to be written about basic Web browser functionality, given that the Web browser was *the* "killer ap" of the 1990s and, for all intents and purposes, has enabled the e-commerce era. Earlier in this chapter, we briefly mentioned Netscape's Navigator and Microft's Internet Explorer products, the two marketplace leaders in the browser space.

For purposes of our discussion, though, it's worth reiterating some of the points we made earlier with regard to HTML and XML. First, the interfaces between the browser and the rest of the underlying environment are evolving and will continue to do so. HTML, ubiquitous though it may be, is "old technology" and has its limitations as the Internet continues to move away from static interaction models to dynamic, commerce-based systems. Consequently, it's important to track the trends and advances in browser technology to ensure that the user side of data warehousing is synchronized with available capabilities.

Additionally, we discussed the concept of the "passive information consumer" earlier in the chapter and noted that several different approaches exist to support these users: browser capability embedded into front-end data warehousing reporting and query tools or through the standard browsers (Netscape Navigator or Microsoft Internet Explorer) themselves. User-side data warehousing architecture needs to factor the passive information consumers into the overall picture and, correspondingly, make product determinations based on cost factors as well as technology.

Personal Digital Assistants (PDAs)

In a world where mobile phones and handheld devices like the Palm Pilot are so widespread, the basic concept of the personal digital assistant is fairly well known.

Using a PDA in the world of e-commerce is a natural progression, but it has been a slow journey so far, mostly because of limitations in current (2000–2001) technology. Because of their size, entering data into a PDA requires either a very tiny keyboard or some form of handwriting recognition system. The problem with the very tiny keyboard approach is that they're too small for touch-typing. The problem with handwriting recognition is the difficulty in making it work effectively (though handwriting recognition technology is light-years ahead of where it was only a few years earlier in the mid-1990s).

The solution to the handwriting recognition problem has proven to be the Graffiti handwriting system. This relies on a touch-screen display and a simplified alphabet for data entry. Typically, PDAs with the Graffiti system provide the option to write directly onto the display, which translates the input into text, or to open up a dedicated writing space, which also provides online examples and help.

Manufacturers of PDAs have been challenged to provide that functionality that makes them a "must have" in business in general and specifically in e-commerce. Products that combine the capabilities of mobile phones and PDAs are well positioned to deliver that "must have" aura. The ability to conveniently and inexpensively access the Internet with a single device took a significant step with Palm Computing's launch of their wireless Palm VII in late 1999.

Kiosks and, in the future, ATMs can be other user interfaces. Kiosks, in particular, are increasingly found in physical retail locations. For example, every Target store has a Gift Registry Kiosk. These are (or can easily become) Web-based e-commerce tools.

e-Commerce Data Warehousing Implications

An increasingly mobile workforce in many companies has radical implications on the delivery of business intelligence to out-of-office users. The traditional approach of those individuals periodically synchronizing a store of data (such as Cognos PowerPlay cube) on a laptop with the main data warehouse's content via dial-in lacks the timeliness in many business models.

With wireless capabilities linked to mobile devices through protocols such as WAP (see the discussion earlier in this chapter), users of these devices can be considered part of a company's business intelligence user community even without laptops or other more traditional personal computing devices. Consequently, information delivery to these users via their PDAs—as well as the ways in which users request information from those same PDAs—becomes part of the e-commerce data warehousing puzzle.

Even for deskbound or laptop-based mobile users, advances in browser technology and interfaces need to be considered. Originally, the browser was the "thinnest of clients" in terms of primarily being a display-only piece of software; all logic was handled elsewhere (Web servers, application servers, etc.). Now, with plug-ins, applets, and other browser-based logic, the browser becomes a more active player in Web-based business applications (and even in Web surfing).

Therefore, the overall e-commerce data warehousing architecture needs to consider the company's internal desktop environment (what browser is standard issue and what its capabilities are), as well as those of its intended e-commerce users— consumer oriented and B2B alike—outside of the boundaries of its own enterprise.

Summary

A wealth of information has been covered in this chapter, so consequently none of the many topics has been covered in anywhere near the detail that a practitioner specializing in that area would need to know. However, from a data-warehousing-specific point of view, basic familiarity with terminology, capabilities, and other key aspects of each is usually sufficient to successfully plan and architect any data warehousing environment, whether for e-commerce purposes or otherwise.

Readers who find themselves needing to learn more about any particular topic because of project-specific reasons or even general interest are directed to other texts that focus on that particular topic in detail.

Endnotes
1. D. Amor, *The E-business (R)evolution,* Prentice Hall PTR, Saddle River, NJ, 2000, page 336.

2. More information about relational database technology and the SQL:1999 standard can be found in Jim Melton and Alan Simon, *Basic SQL:1999—Understanding Relational Language Components,* Morgan Kaufmann Publishers, 2001.

3. Information in this section is from discussions with IBM executives and technologists and from IBM's Web site *(www.ibm.com).*

4. IBM officially uses the term "e-business" rather than "e-commerce," so for this section we'll retain IBM's terminology. As we noted in Chapter 1, it's the authors' belief that the two terms can be used interchangeably.

5. Information in this section is from discussions with Microsoft executives and technologists and from Microsoft's Web site *(www.microsoft.com)*.

6. Information in this section is from discussions with Allaire executives and technologists, and from the company's Web site *(www.allaire.com)*.

7. An interesting side note: Of the three original codevelopers of Ethernet, Intel was originally the "little guy." It's very interesting how, as the technology landscape evolves, companies rise dramatically or fall from grace . . . or, in the case of Digital Equipment Corporation, cease to exist at all.

8. The term *metropolitan area network* (MAN) isn't as commonly used as LAN or WAN, but refers to an "across-town" network, usually for a single company. For our purposes, MANs are subsumed into the discussion of WANs.

8

Products for e-Commerce Intelligence

In Chapter 7, we discussed the many different components that comprise an end-to-end solution for e-commerce business intelligence, from the underlying data warehousing environment to the infrastructure to various user-facing options and technologies.

One topic that was not covered in Chapter 6, however, was that of commercially available products that can provide a great deal of the user-side functionality, an alternative to custom-developed solutions. In this chapter, we'll take a brief look at three different vendor approaches to off-the-shelf front-end products:

- Vignette

- Ithena

- Revenio

We selected these three vendors from the hundreds of possibilities (more on that in a moment) as representative of three different paths that vendors are taking toward the area of e-commerce business intelligence and data warehousing. Vignette comes to this discipline by expanding on its initial e-commerce transactional and content management offerings, courtesy of several strategic company acquisitions. Ithena, on the other hand, is a wholly owned subsidiary of Business Objects, a leading data warehousing tool vendor, and was established with the objective of focusing solely on customer intelligence. Finally, Revenio is representative of the no-prior-legacy approach of an entirely new start-up beginning their product development with a clean slate.

Some readers may be wondering about products from their own favorite vendors—MicroStrategy, Informatica, Broadvision, E.piphany, or one of hundreds of others that can be categorized into this space. By no means are we endorsing any one of the three vendors' product offerings that we discuss in this chapter, in comparison with each other or with offerings from any other vendor. Rather, our discussion in this chapter is meant to be instructive and representative of what the reader might expect to find when evaluating commercial products for his or her own environment.

Any individual company's product evaluation and selection must be driven by that company's overall e-commerce strategy and its accompanying business intelligence strategy, as was discussed in Chapter 2. By following that sequence of activities, commercial products can then be evaluated for suitability to that company's particular environment. Too often the opposite happens: a product is selected for some reason, and a company struggles to adapt its desired business processes to the capabilities (or lack thereof) of a product to which it has just committed itself.

So again, consider the discussion in this chapter to be informative and representative, rather than any kind of statement of endorsement.

Vignette

Vignette Corporation is an Austin, Texas–based company founded in 1995. Vignette's original e-commerce focus was in the Internet content management space and then later in B2C personalization, but through a series of acquisitions and internal product development and enhancement it has broadened its focus into other e-commerce areas, including e-business intelligence.

The V/5 e-Business Platform

Figure 8.1 illustrates the overall Vignette V/5 e-business platform. Note that underneath e-business[1] applications—transactional as well as analytical—a variety of platform services exist based on various pieces of the Vignette product line: content management, life cycle personalization, communications, and so on.

With regard to e-business intelligence capabilities, the Relationship Marketing Server component is the focus of our subsequent discussion.

Relationship Marketing Server Overview

Figure 8.2 illustrates the premise behind the Relationship Marketing Server: customer actions from various channels relate to one another during some defined timeline, the idea being to acquire in-depth understanding of customer behavior.

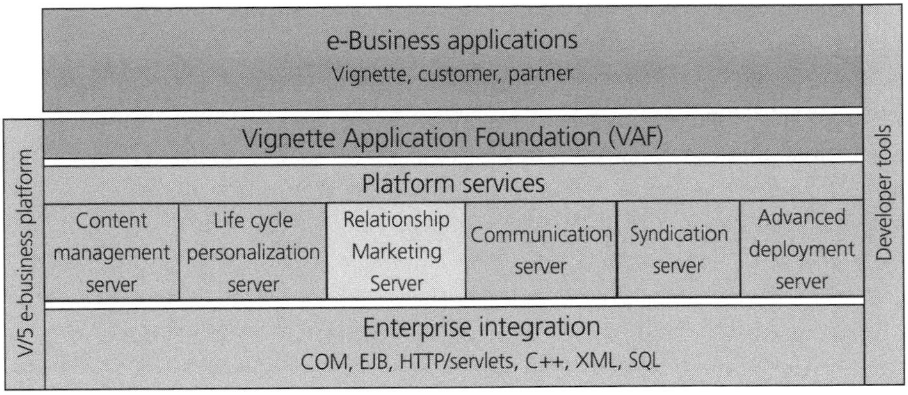

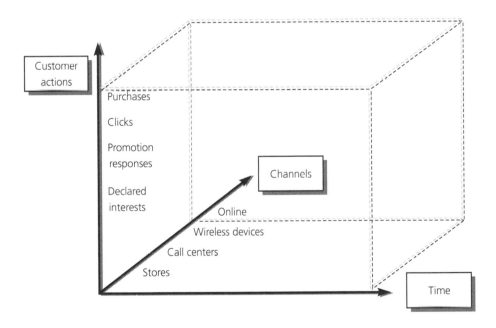

Figure 8.1 The Vignette V/5 e-business platform.

Figure 8.2 Relationship Marketing Server principles.

As shown in Figure 8.3, a "knowledge hub"—essentially a specialized e-business data warehouse—is the recipient of various types of information such as transactions, clickstream data, promotion responses, and demographic data, all of which can be used to measure e-business performance. After synthesizing this information, a variety of analytically focused functions—data mining and analysis, audience profiling and segmentation, and campaign management—can occur to develop insights and drive targeted and focused actions. The objective is to provide a "closed loop" in which transactional activities are synthesized together; business intelligence and analytics occur that drive subsequent transactional activities; those subsequent transactional activities are then synthesized and analyzed; and so on.

The core aspects of data mining (e.g., statistical modeling) are targeted to provide output related to relationship marketing: identifying cross-selling opportunities or early warning of profitable customers showing signs of defecting to a competitor, for example.

Audience segmentation uses two different sets of user-defined criteria as input to its segmentation algorithms. The first is labeled as "basic criteria" and includes

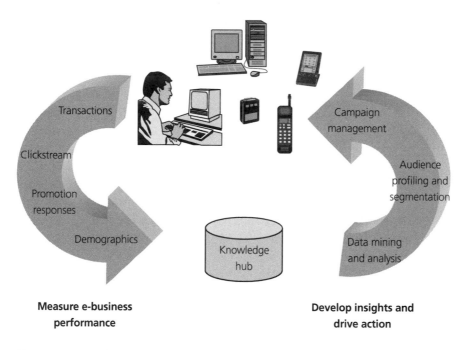

Figure 8.3 Data flows in a Vignette Relationship Marketing Server environment.

rudimentary lists, counts, and dates such as which products have been purchased; what content has been viewed online; what the date of last contact was; the customer's geographic location; and so on. This basic criteria is augmented with "advanced criteria" derived from the data mining capabilities discussed above. Advanced criteria might include lifetime customer value scores, retention forecasts, page views per session, and other scores.

In addition to the two different types of user-defined criteria, the V/5 Relationship Marketing Server also uses clustering techniques for interactive segment discovery. Taken together, these techniques can provide the foundation for subsequent operational action, such as campaign management. People that have attributes in common get put in a group, the premise being that if they act similarly in one area, they might do so in another. Therefore, the system looks for correlations, such as two people who share the same or nearly identical demographics purchasing the same items during one month. Quite possibly, they would both be susceptible to the same type of marketing campaign for a targeted product set. Note that clustering and campaign isn't just for B2C e-commerce, but also for B2B environments.

The Relationship Marketing Server campaign management capabilities include a user interface through which you can define and manage the "rules" of a particular campaign, such as

- "who" - what segments, clusters, or individuals should be the target of the campaign

- "what" - the various content assets that should be presented as part of the campaign (e.g., special promotions, product lists, etc.)

- "when" - whether a campaign should be manually scheduled or use event-based triggers

- "where" - what channels of communication should be part of the campaign (Internet Web site for online shoppers, e-mail, pagers, PDAs, WAP-enabled phones, etc.)[2]

- "how" - the content presentation style

V/5 Relationship Marketing Server Architecture

Figure 8.4 illustrates the technical architecture underlying the V/5 Relationship Marketing Server. Note that a number of databases shown comprise what is essentially a data warehousing environment: the analysis database, the visitor database, and the system database. Various pieces of information flow among these databases

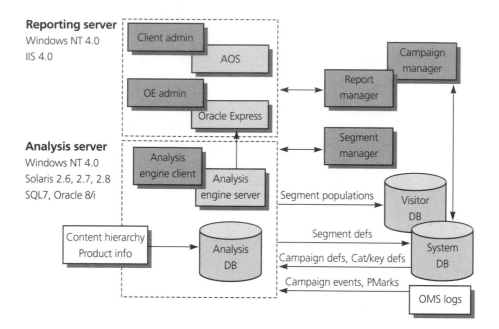

Figure 8.4 The V/5 Relationship Marketing Server architecture.

in a formalized manner, according to the business rules of the V/5 environment and its various engines and managers.

Ithena

Many readers will be familiar with Business Objects, the data warehousing product vendor in the front-end tool space. Its current flagship product, WebIntelligence, is a Web-enabled version of its long-time query and reporting tool that shared the company's name.

Business Objects decided to address the customer intelligence area by not only creating a new, specialized tool, but by also creating an entirely new company. Ithena is a wholly owned subsidiary of Business Objects, and its flagship product, e-CI, provides CRM analytical capabilities.

Ithena e-CI uses many components from its parent's product suite (such as WebIntelligence for reporting and querying), integrated together in a best-of-breed manner and augmented by custom-developed capabilities. The result is an analytical engine that operates on top of an underlying data warehouse, but specifically focused on customer intelligence rather than general-purpose business intelligence.

Ithena e-CI Premise

In Chapter 2, we discussed the premise of B2C customer intelligence and the various levels from basic services to various forms of extended intelligence services that are operational in nature, in addition to the after-the-fact reporting aspect. Using content from an e-commerce data warehousing environment, Ithena e-CI identifies, analyzes, and predicts changes in customer behavior, enabling businesses to "treat different customers differently" according to buying habits, loyalty, and other attributes that are discovered, analyzed, and presented to business users. The objective of Ithena e-CI is to enable its users to maximize its overall customer value by proactively and intelligently managing *individual* customer relationships. In essence, Ithena e-CI is valuable for companies undergoing a fundamental internal paradigm shift from being product-centric or campaign-centric in their operations to becoming truly customer focused in a one-to-one sense.

Ithena draws a distinction between a campaign-centric organization as compared to a customer-centric one as follows. A campaign-centric organization uses data mining or other discovery-oriented (i.e., "tell me something interesting") processes against large volumes of data. Based on the results of the analysis, specific campaigns will be created that target customers and/or prospects who are likely to be attracted by a specific offer.

The behind-the-scenes activities necessary for campaign-centric customer interaction are often hindered by the granularity established in the statistical models underlying a specific campaign strategy. Very often, changes in individual customers' behavior aren't detected in a timely enough manner for a company to proactively approach those customers in a very focused manner; the reason for the lack of detection is because of the granularity of the segmentation algorithms and the lack of capturing detailed enough data about *individual* customers in the data warehouse.

So whereas campaign management can be an effective tool in some companies' overall CRM analytics strategy and for subsequent customer-facing operational activities (e.g., marketing and selling), other companies may wish to take a more fine-grained approach. Ithena's intention is to provide those capabilities in its e-CI product.

Key Concepts in Ithena e-CI

Ithena builds its e-CI product around four key concepts:

- Best practice analytics
- Probes

- Joiners and Leavers

- ChangeAgents

Best Practice Analytics

e-CI includes over 20 hardwired analytical capabilities within the product, based on best practices within the CRM analytics space. These include the following:

- Seasonality analysis

- "Raw versus smooth" analysis

- Loyalty and turnover metrics

- Customer vintages

- Cross-segment comparison

- Segment migration analysis

Using these capabilities, knowledgeable and experienced users can, with relative ease, receive informative reports about individual customers and aggregated groups from information resident in the data warehouse. A key aspect of e-CI, like many other CRM analytics tools, is the creation and management of segments (indicated above by the areas of cross-segment comparison and segment migration analysis). As we noted in Chapter 2, it's up to the individual organization to define the segmentation model or models it wishes to use, and these models can vary widely in complexity. For some organizations, a relatively simple segmentation model may be sufficient, containing only a few broad categories such as "loyal customers," "browsers-not-buyers," or "reacquired customers." In other situations, deep behavioral analysis such as those found in the Yankelovich ID categories[3]—"Go-getters," "young and restless," and "band leaders," for example—can provide the foundation for an organization's segmentation model.

Regardless of the particular segmentation model an organization elects to use, a key aspect to e-commerce customer intelligence is not only determining which customers and prospects belong in which segment but also tracking movement of customers across those segments over time. And, ideally, movement should be tracked *and acted upon* as quickly as possible in time for an organization to possibly influence customer behavior back into more positive segments (e.g., "loyal customers" rather than "on their way out"). Doing so is where the other three key Ithena e-CI capabilities come into the picture.

Probes

In e-CI terminology, a probe is an aggregate measurement attached to a particular customer segment. A probe can be as simple as the count of membership within that segment or the frequency of making a purchase, or as complex as the calculated life-time value of that segment. In effect, a probe operates like a thermometer for that customer segment, indicating to e-CI users what the "temperature" is at any given time.

It's important to note that there is a distinction between an e-CI probe and the result of a simple query against rows of data for customers in a segment. e-CI probes are designed and coded to be automatically refreshed at user-specified intervals, in effect providing automatic "push" capabilities against the underlying data. Further, the resulting value of a probe is data in a result set that can be further analyzed.

Joiners and Leavers

Joiners and Leavers are groups of customers who have moved between segments as a result of changing some aspect of their behavior. Each customer joins or leaves a segment at an individual level, and as a result is grouped together with similar customers who have also moved between segments; the group is known as a *Joiners and Leavers segment* (i.e., a segment in addition to the core customer segmentation model the organization has established, which contains customer information relevant to joining and leaving).

Tracking Joiners and Leavers enables organizations to quickly identify opportunities and threats at the individual customer level, rather than having to do so at the group level and then relying on campaign management and the accompanying time lag before being able to reach targeted individual customers. For example, a customer can be tagged as a joiner of a "likely to churn" segment based on the results of an e-CI model that notes a reduced outstanding account balance coupled with increased time between purchases as compared to prior purchasing history. The business model may then call for increased outbound activity (e.g., e-mail solicitations) or specialized responses for inbound activities such as shopping at the company's Web site or calling into the call center. Campaign management can come into play at that point, should the company be conducting a specialized customer retention campaign.

ChangeAgents

An e-CI ChangeAgent is a rules-based capability in which business rules are attached to either Joiners and Leavers or probes, the objective being to enable "closed-loop processing" for purposes such as targeted exception-based marketing. Figure 8.5 illustrates the high-level relationship between ChangeAgents and the overall e-CI environment, including "alert channels" (e.g., Internet, e-mail, PDAs, etc.) as well as specific actions (e.g., campaign management, call center contact, etc.).

ChangeAgents act as triggers that can, upon realization of a particular business rule, automatically "fire" actions by other integrated system components (e.g., CRM

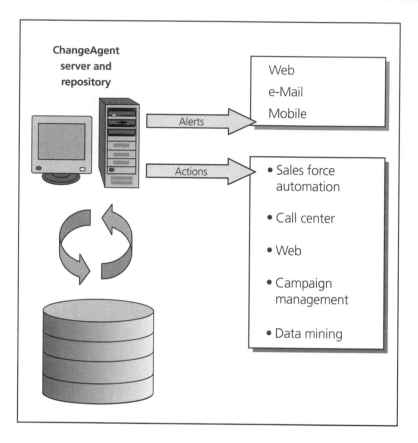

Figure 8.5 Relationship of ChangeAgents to other e-commerce entities.

core applications, or as discussed next with regard to Revenio Dialog, a dialog marketing engine). Essentially, an e-CI ChangeAgent is the Ithena analog of a database trigger and its relationship to a database stored procedure: a codified business rule deeply embedded within the application infrastructure.

Ithena e-CI Architecture

Figure 8.6 illustrates the conceptual high-level architecture of an Ithena e-CI environment. Note the various sources of data—CRM core applications (e.g., call center and sales force automation), clickstream data, and other (e.g., "external") applications—that feed into the underlying data warehouse. As was discussed in Chapters 1 and 2, an effective e-commerce data warehousing environment needs to include not only traditional forms of data (e.g., information about customers, products, channels, etc.) but also data related to e-commerce such as clickstream activity.

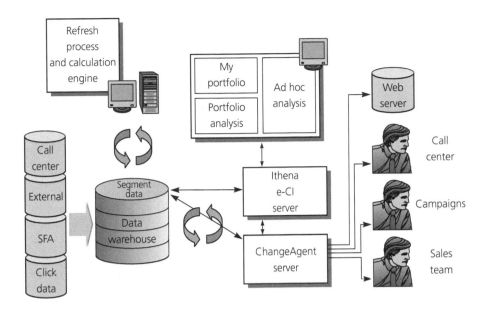

Figure 8.6 Ithena e-CI conceptual architecture.

Ithena e-CI in Other e-Commerce Business Models

Though it's common to think of customer intelligence services primarily in a B2C setting, a product such as e-CI also has applicability to other e-commerce business models such as B2B or, as discussed in Chapter 5, G2C (government-to-citizen). The basic concepts of segmentation and Ithena's segmentation-related capabilities—probes, Joiners and Leavers, and ChangeAgents—can be applied just as readily to analyze, for example, the behavior of B2B trading partners and their purchasing agents, or activity among residents of a state with regard to their usage (or lack thereof) of online e-government services such as vehicle registration.

Revenio Dialog

Revenio, founded in 1999, is a company based in Burlington, Massachusetts. The fundamental premise of the company's flagship product, Revenio Dialog, is to enable companies to move their e-commerce marketing activities beyond batch-oriented, time-lagged business processes such as campaign management to an environment featuring a high degree of interactivity: two-way, continuous, and long-running communications.

Dialog Marketing Premise

The key enabler to the discipline of *dialog marketing* is the Internet, although dialog marketing uses multiple channels to communicate effectively with each customer. Rather than use e-mail and other asynchronous online capabilities to, essentially, mimic pre-Internet marketing models (using direct mail, for example), the concept of dialog marketing attempts to engage the customer and, as quickly *and intelligently* as possible, steer the customer's decision processes through an ongoing exchange of information between a company and its customer that leads toward a decision to purchase and builds an ongoing relationship that fosters customer lifetime value through repeat purchases (Figure 8.7).

A Simple Example of Dialog Marketing

Figure 8.8 shows a simple example of dialog marketing. The cycle begins at the time a customer makes a purchase, by engaging the customer in a "cross-sell dialog" with the intention of obtaining the customer's permission to contact him or her at some future time or (in the case of this example) when some future event occurs, such as the availability of a new product.

After receiving the customer's permission, and upon the occurrence of the event that triggers the next phase of the dialog, the customer is contacted (via e-

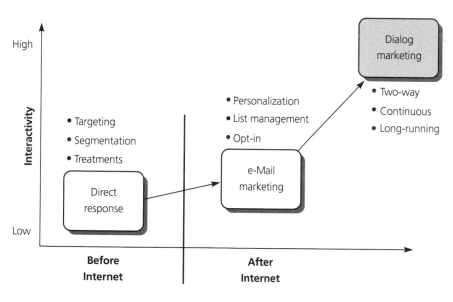

Figure 8.7 The evolution toward dialog marketing.

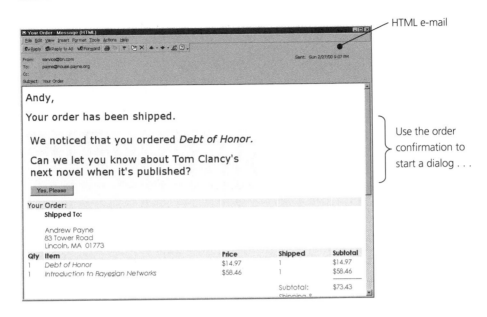

HTML e-mail

Use the order confirmation to start a dialog . . .

Figure 8.8 Beginning the dialog marketing cycle through cross-selling.

mail in this case) to notify him or her of the new product being available (Figure 8.9). As illustrated in Figure 8.9, the customer is given several options, from an immediate purchase to the option to receive additional information or even to decline the purchase in favor of a complementary product (the paperback version of a book, in this example). All the while, the dialog between business and consumer continues.

As illustrated in Figure 8.10, the dialog flow can be constructed so that the customer is contacted at appropriate intervals, governed by the business rules in combination with the events that have occurred along the way. For example, Figure 8.10 illustrates that should the customer have asked to wait to see book reviews that are now available, upon reestablishing contact with the customer he or she is also given the option to basically say "leave me alone"—the "I Already Bought It" link—rather than to commit to a purchase right now or to wait for the paperback version.

All the while, the dialog marketing environment can be collecting data about the interaction and storing that in the underlying data warehouse (discussed later). For example, customers who ask for reviews, but then upon receiving those reviews indicate that in the meantime they have already purchased the book, can be appropriately categorized (e.g., "opportunistic purchaser" or some other category indicating that e-tailer loyalty might not be a characteristic of that customer).

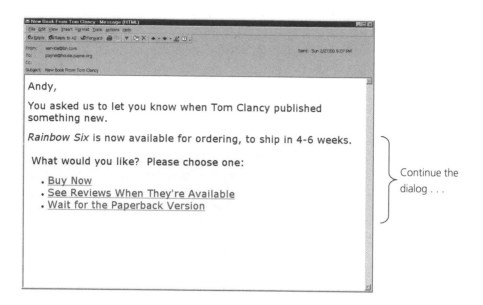

Figure 8.9 Reestablishing contact with the customer.

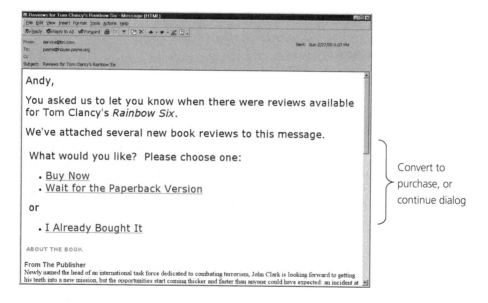

Figure 8.10 Continuing the dialog.

Underlying Data Warehousing Environment

So where does data warehousing fit into a dialog marketing environment? Ideally, Revenio Dialog would sit on top of an underlying data warehouse that at a minimum would contain the following information:

- Customer information (name, address, contact information, etc.)

- Product information, including relationships between products: which ones are complementary to each other for cross-selling, which ones are "upsells" or "downsells" of others, etc.

- Customer purchase history, categorized by channel (online, in-store, telephone, etc.)

- Customer "dumped shopping cart" history

- Customer browsing/clickstream activity

- Customer responses to dialogs

- Summarized statistics (i.e., product sales by channel for previous week, previous month, comparisons to prior year, etc.)

- Customer segmentation or other CRM analytics (e.g., categorizing customers based on their behavior in relation to their responses to dialogs)

Even though the most "visible" capabilities of Revenio Dialog are those that are Internet based for customer interaction, the environment as a whole is architected to operate in a click-and-mortar e-commerce model. Figure 8.11 illustrates the high-level architecture and underlying technology of the environment. Note that in addition to e-mail and Web-based dialogs with users, other channels can be designated as part of the overall customer contact strategy, such as telephone, mail, and fax.

It's also interesting to note that while conducting dialog-based business with customers, data quality and integrity can be "operationalized," as discussed in Chapter 9. For example, Figure 8.12 illustrates how multiple customer contact channels can be used not only to reestablish contact with a customer when, for example, an e-mail address change isn't known to the company, but also to provide a conduit for customers themselves to "self-correct" invalid (e.g., out-of-date) information. Those corrections (the new e-mail address, in this case) are then propagated into the company's e-commerce environment, including the data warehouse. Alternatively, the lack of an alternative-channel response from a customer can also be used as part of the CRM analytics, perhaps segmenting the customer as "lost, doesn't want to be found" or "lost, couldn't contact through alternative channel."

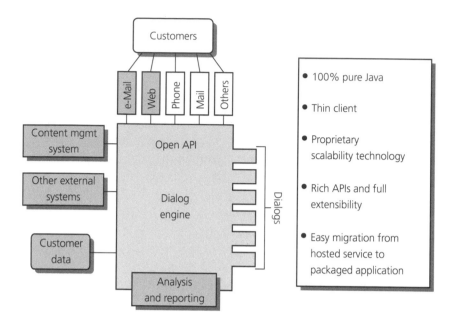

Figure 8.11 Revenio Dialog architecture.

Figure 8.12 Alternative channels and data quality.

Designing and Building the Dialog Marketing Environment

Revenio Dialog supports building a dialog marketing environment through two primary tools, plus information and technology related to multiple communications channels (see Figure 8.13).

IT developers and end users (e.g., marketing professionals) use a palette of "shapes" to create scripts and logic flows that contain various customer contact points, requests to obtain permissions, queuing subsequent conversations, and decision points (see Figure 8.14). Users can also create their own shapes to address their specific dialog marketing application needs.

Key to this book's topic is that the logical flow of individual activities—both customer-facing (e.g., dialogs) and behind-the-scenes—should be deeply embedded with business intelligence obtained from the e-commerce data warehousing environment. For example, the alternatives available at key decision points and the guidance for subsequent dialogs on each path might be driven not only by the customer's response to a dialog at that very moment, but also by the customer's purchase history, segmentation and classification information, product availability, or other information obtained from the underlying data warehouse and external "events" such as Tom Clancy publishing his next book.

For example, suppose a customer makes several online requests for product information. The underlying logic of the dialog may call for looking up the customer's profile in the data warehouse, where it is noted that this person is tagged as

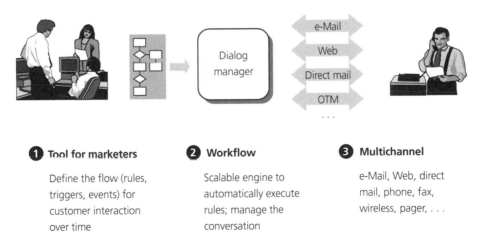

1 **Tool for marketers**

Define the flow (rules, triggers, events) for customer interaction over time

2 **Workflow**

Scalable engine to automatically execute rules; manage the conversation

3 **Multichannel**

e-Mail, Web, direct mail, phone, fax, wireless, pager, . . .

Figure 8.13 Revenio Dialog development environment.

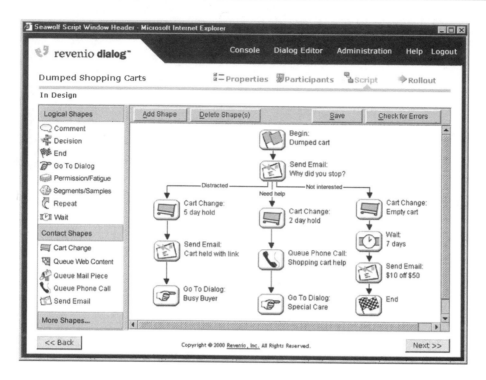

Figure 8.14 Revenio Dialog development palette.

"troublemaker—watch out!"—not because of what is occurring during the course of the current dialog, nor perhaps even from the customer's prior interactions with the company. Maybe the person is included in a list of "B2C deadbeats" obtained from a provider of syndicated data, indicating past problems such as failing to pay for goods purchased through an online auction site.

The possibilities for using data-warehouse-resident content in the course of dialog marketing are nearly endless. The fundamental premise is to ensure that the transactional business logic, as implemented through (in this case) the palette shapes and workflow, aren't solely transactional in nature but rather have the appropriate interweaving of business intelligence content into the customer-facing processes.

Supported e-Commerce Business Models

Finally, it's important to note that even though the examples in this section (provided courtesy of Revenio) are oriented toward B2C e-commerce, the concept of dialog marketing—and how Revenio Dialog might be used—also applies to B2B, as well as e-commerce models for government commerce and employee relations discussed in Chapters 5 and 6.

In a B2B setting, for example, dialogs can be scripted for relating to a trading partner's purchasing manager, helping not only to steer that person toward a decision to purchase but also to establish a degree of "intimacy" in the human element of the B2B trading between those two particular companies. Or, perhaps, a dialog can be created such as the following:

- Upon completion of the dialog for your company's products, ask the purchasing manager what other products he or she needs to find that your company may not produce or resell.

- Receiving the list, you can request permission to establish contact between that person's company and another B2B partner of your company that does deal in the desired product(s), thus establishing a "value chain" involving multiple companies.

The key point to remember is that complex dialogs have traditionally been difficult to build programmatically, particularly in e-commerce environments. Using a tool such as Revenio Dialog in which these dialogs can be created graphically—and appropriately linked into content from the underlying data warehousing environment—can help build the desired level of business-intelligence-enabled e-commerce capabilities.

Summary

As we noted at the beginning of this chapter, the three vendor products discussed in this chapter are representative of various types of business intelligence tools that e-commerce practitioners will typically find themselves using. Two key points to note:

- Classical data warehousing business intelligence in the form of after-the-fact, general-purpose reporting and querying is typically not sufficient for an organization to achieve the desired degree of integration between the transactional and analytical sides of e-commerce.

- While CRM analytics such as segmentation and accompanying analysis have been available in tools for a while, adding e-commerce into the picture—particularly for click-and-mortar companies or in nonconsumer settings (e.g., B2B e-commerce)—sufficiently complicates the underlying data warehousing environment with regard to the data that needs to be stored and synthesized, the number of sources from which the transactional data will be acquired, and other data warehousing facets. Consequently, the traditional demarcation between CRM and data warehousing that we noted in Chapter 1 must be overcome for tools such as those discussed in this chapter to function to their fullest potential.

Endnotes

1. In this section we will use the term "e-business" rather than e-commerce given that Vignette uses that term for its product line and environment.

2. PDAs and WAP were discussed in Chapter 7.

3. Cited in *USA Today,* August 1, 2000, Pages B1 and B2—a Yankelovich ID research study in which consumers were divided into 8 categories that are further comprised of 32 subgroups.

9

Data Quality and Integrity Issues

The areas of quality and data warehousing have had an uneasy relationship since the modern data warehousing era began in the early 1990s. Hardly anyone would argue with the need for high-quality, correct data as a key underpinning of business intelligence and decision support. And nearly every data warehousing architecture diagram that has ever been produced illustrates how the extraction/transformation/ loading (ETL) process is infused with quality assurance processes, often labeled as "data cleansing" functions.

Yet when actually deployed, many—arguably most—data warehousing environments are burdened with quality problems of one form or another. Decisions made on the basis of data warehousing content are questioned; two or three data marts with overlapping data content provide different results to the exact same query; and so on.

And now, in the context of e-commerce, the data quality problem worsens. Why? As we'll discuss in this chapter, there are several reasons, including an increase in cross-enterprise data sharing for B2B scenarios and the need to incorporate consumer-provided data into B2C data warehouses. We'll explore the problems and present tactics to deal with the issues and to help ensure that e-commerce data warehouses contain accurate, correct data for business intelligence purposes.

A Brief Overview of Data Quality and Data Warehousing

Since the mid-1970s, students studying computer science or business information systems have had the importance of data quality impressed upon them. "Garbage in, garbage out"—abbreviated as "GIGO"—has long been a watchword. In the realm of transactional applications, initially enforcing data quality (or at least attempting to do so) typically takes the form of edit checking during data input processes: making sure that all mandatory fields are included by the person inputting the data, ensuring that data values fall within permissible ranges or lists of values, and so on. Then, following data storage, the second realm of data quality takes place when existing data is accessed, modified, and then the new values are stored in the file system or database.

When properly and comprehensively accomplished, the quality of an application's underlying data should be as close to 100% correct as possible. But in the real world, however, errors and other quality problems begin creeping into the data from the very outset through inadequate or missing edit checking, often occurring as modifications are made to an application following its initial deployment (i.e., edit checking is often overlooked in the rush to get subsequent versions of an application deployed). Additionally, as an application evolves from one version to another, its internal logic typically becomes confusing and difficult to understand, leading to down-the-road quality problems as data is used and modified at some point after its initial entry and storage.

Which brings us to the data warehousing side of the problem. "Standard" data warehousing processes assume that there will be some degree of quality problems in the source data that is being extracted, manipulated (e.g., undergoing transformation and perhaps being synthesized with similar data from another application), and loaded into the data warehouse. This is why, of course, the typical data warehousing architecture includes processes to "cleanse" data prior to the loading processes.

Ideally, the flow of data-quality-related processes within a data warehousing environment should look something like Figure 9.1. In addition to "fixing" data before permitting its movement into subsequent data-warehousing-related processes, the data warehousing environment *should* communicate its quality-related findings back to the source application(s) in one form or another. At the very least, a log file of discovered problems should be sent back to the "owners" of each source application so the application maintenance developers can study the problems and attempt to identify the cause . . . and then perform any necessary database updates and/or application code changes to clear the problems and prevent them from recurring, as illustrated in Figure 9.1(a).

The more highly automated alternative shown in Figure 9.1(b) has a "quality control engine" attached to a source application. This engine fields the log file of problems discovered by the data warehousing environment, attempts to correct as much of the problematic data within the source file system or database as possible, and then attempts to identify the cause(s) of each problem, that is, which edit-

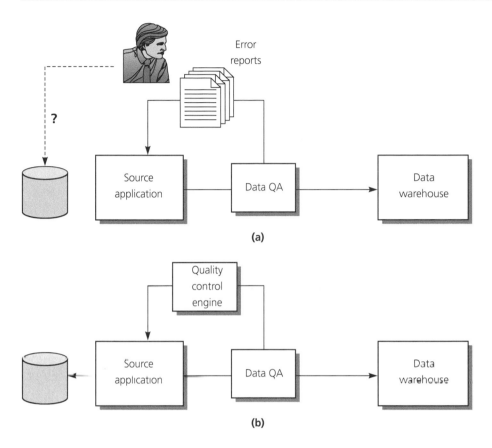

Figure 9.1 Data quality as an end-to-end set of processes involving the source applications: (a) manual and (b) automatic application of QA results to source application data.

checking functions may be incorrect or which application modules may have inadvertently introduced the error.

However, as nearly every data warehousing practitioner knows, neither of the two solutions shown in Figure 9.1 is likely to be employed in any real-world environment. The unpleasant truth is that even though data quality *should* be an end-to-end proposition within an enterprise, the reality is that the owners of source applications typically have little or no interest in propagating quality-related changes back to their application environments unless absolutely necessary. Most transactional applications have little need for accurate historical information within the realm of their responsibilities; they simply "lock data away" once it's no longer of use, and to the keepers of those applications, if someone else (i.e., the data warehousing

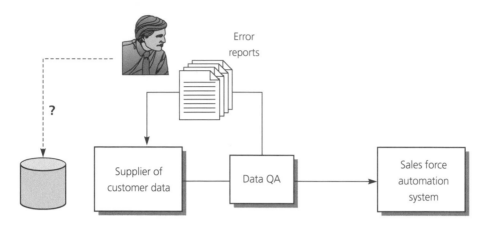

Figure 9.2 CRM applications affected by ongoing data quality problems.

architects and developers) want to extract data for analytical and reporting purposes, that's fine, as long as no additional work comes trickling back to those responsible for the source applications.

This lack of interest in and cooperation with regard to data quality isn't solely a data-warehousing-related problem, either. IT practitioners who specialize in CRM applications such as sales force automation (SFA) or call centers typically face the same issues, as shown in Figure 9.2.

While few within an organization will argue with the need for SFA or call center applications, the owners of (as an example) a legacy application that contains customer data that must be initially loaded into SFA and call center environments and subsequently refreshed on a regular basis typically take the same view of data quality as discussed above: "Don't expect us to do anything about data quality unless it directly affects our own application."

Before moving on, we want to more formally define the phrase that we've used a number of times so far in this chapter—"data quality"—as well as a closely related term, "data integrity." Without degenerating into an argument about semantics, we define "data quality" as referring not only to whether or not an actual error is present in some piece of data (e.g., an incorrect spelling of a person's last name, or an individual's previous address but not his or her current address), but also to the "usefulness" of the data. For example, a customer information database that's part of a B2C environment may be structured in its schema to contain columns for

- "core" customer information (e.g., name, address, telephone number, credit card number, etc.)

- "extended" customer attributes, such as which of the company's channels (e.g., physical store location, Web site, telephone ordering, public kiosk, etc.) that customer has used, and historical activity through each channel

- customer preferences and similar information, such as hobbies, profession, business and personal travel patterns, and so on

Suppose that the company wants to build a comprehensive data warehousing environment containing the ever-illusive "whole-customer view" from which customer segmentation, campaign management, dialog marketing, and the other B2C analytically driven processes discussed in Chapter 2 will occur. Consider, though, that the company's "mortar-side" applications (e.g., the physical location side of a click-and-mortar B2C company) have typically not collected much, if any, of the extended customer information or the customer preferences. Will a data warehouse that is heavily dominated by data from the "click side" (e.g., the company's Internet e-commerce applications) be useful in designing marketing campaigns that span the company's physical locations and online presence? Perhaps . . . or perhaps not. In this context, "data quality" can refer to not having adequate amounts of data from one or more sides of the business to make information-based decisions with a high degree of confidence. It's not that the data is error-prone; rather, when viewed in an aggregate sense, the data is not of a high-enough quality to effectively support information-driven business processes.

We will also occasionally use the term "data integrity" as we did in this chapter's title. Though in a general sense, the phrases "data quality" and "data integrity" are often used interchangeably, we will use "data integrity" to refer to situations where there must be some type of correlation of data items in different locations with one another. This correlation might occur within the enterprise (e.g., ensuring that the count of active online customers in the data warehouse matches the count of active online customers if obtained from the company's e-commerce application) or across enterprises (e.g., that changes in one company's database to add a new purchasing agent are reflected in the databases of its B2B supply chain trading partners).

B2C Considerations and Complications

Think of some of your own interactions with a Web site in the past few years when you were filling out a "personal information form" to register for a free newsletter, a free e-mail account, or some other Web-provided service. Which telephone number did you enter: business or home? Did you even enter a truthful telephone number, or did you think to yourself "That's none of their business" and enter your area code followed by random digits instead of one of your actual telephone numbers?

When asked about topics in which you are interested, did you carefully study the list or did you just check off one or two items to get past that item and finish up the questionnaire as quickly as possible? When presented with a list of 10 different items and asked which one from that list is the means by which you first heard of the Web site, did you answer truthfully or just check off one of the items simply to move on?

All of the questions above are indicative of a data quality complication—and a serious one, at that—when data warehousing and business intelligence are applied to B2C environments. Simply put, there is a low degree of confidence in the quality of data provided as a result of self-entry processes on the part of consumers.

To be fair, this problem isn't unique to B2C e-commerce environments. Think about paper warranty cards: what percentage of respondents checks the box that *accurately* represents their household income, or takes the time to thoroughly scan a list of the company's other products to answer which ones the consumer has purchased within the past 12 months and which ones are likely to be purchased within the next year?

B2B Considerations and Complications

B2B environments have their own unique data quality complications that must be taken into consideration. As we discussed in Chapter 4, the two major forms of B2B—supply-chain-oriented and marketplace-centric—both share the common characteristic of crossing enterprise boundaries with regard to conducting e-commerce and in exchanging relevant data.

Consider first marketplace-centric B2B e-commerce. Many of the same data quality issues inherent in B2C environments are likely to surface, simply due to the fact that many sellers and buyers are interested only in (or primarily in) maximizing their financial benefit through using a vertical market exchange. In registering with an exchange, a purchasing agent (from the buyer side) or the person on the seller side responsible for listing goods is just as likely to provide inaccurate information as a consumer registering with a C2C auction site (remember that C2C can be considered a subset of B2C e-commerce, as we discussed in Chapter 3). There is nothing "wrong" in doing so, at least with "wrong" equating to dishonesty or unethical practices. Simply stated, the prevalent view among those responsible for representing their companies in a B2B exchange is likely to be "Someone else's data collection and analysis—whether being done by the exchange itself or other companies who gain access to information I provide—is of little concern to me, so what's in it for me to list how many employees we have in our company, what other channels we use to purchase raw materials or supplies, and so on?"

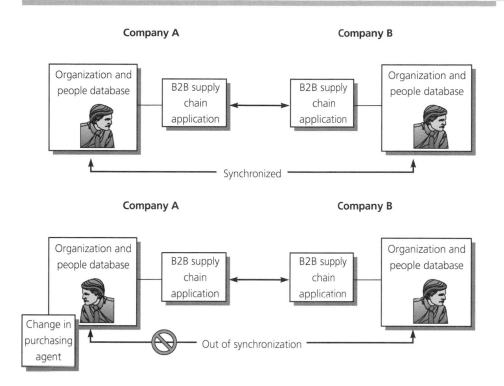

Figure 9.3 Data integrity issues in an automated supply chain environment.

Even in supply-chain-oriented B2B e-commerce, in which companies explicitly designate each other as trading partners and build Web-based environments for their unique supply chain needs, data integrity is likely to be problematic. Consider a typical situation as illustrated in Figure 9.3. Key pieces of information may be updated within the applications of one trading partner, but because the supply chain system crosses enterprise boundaries, those changes are typically not propagated to other companies' systems in a timely manner, often leading to down-the-road coordination problems.

Finally, it should be noted that even in "non-e-commerce" B2B situations there are data quality issues that need to be dealt with. For example, Alan Simon was conducting a data warehousing requirements workshop in early 2000 in which a participant noted that the company had recently rolled out an SFA environment . . . but it had been documented that many of the salespeople were just entering "anything" for key pieces of data such as the details of client contacts and number of product samples distributed to prospective client businesses. Why? The view held by many members of that company's sales force was that their job was solely to take orders and sell products and then move on; everything else, including providing accurate data about other steps within the overall sales life cycle, was irrelevant and a nuisance. Clearly, attempts by this company to bring this SFA data into a data warehouse for analytical and decision-making purposes would be problematic, in a way that no "traditional" data cleansing processes would be able to resolve.

Solving the Data Quality Problem, Part 1: Source Data Analysis

Now that we've identified the major data quality and integrity issues likely to be encountered in e-commerce environments, let's focus on solutions to ensure that the time and effort devoted to building supporting data warehousing environments doesn't result in an environment that is architecturally sound, yet delivers little or no business value because of data quality and integrity issues.

The first line of defense in an e-commerce data warehousing environment—B2C or B2B—is the same as in nearly any data warehousing environment, regardless of its purpose: conducting an extremely thorough, *hands-on* source data analysis. The phenomenon of data warehousing—that in almost all situations, a data warehouse's contents is exclusively drawn from other applications rather than being created as a part of the data warehouse's own processes (as would be done in, say, an order-entry application)—means that a large part of the data quality challenge is *out of the hands* of those responsible for building and maintaining the data warehouse.

A key component of any data warehouse project is to map the warehouse's data structures back to those from one or more sources, the result being the set of data transformation processes that must occur to create the data warehouse's contents (see Figure 9.4).

A common mistake made by many data warehousing practitioners is to rely solely on the data structure definitions from the various sources (e.g., database schemas, field definitions within a flat file, etc.) as they design and develop transformation processes. As these practitioners learn, the contents of any given data source often don't match the structure. Sometimes, the mismatch is quickly found once the first transformation process fails during development, such as the file definition in the application's documentation stating that the customer identifying number is 11 alphanumeric characters with no duplicates, when in reality the customer identifying number is now 12 alphanumeric characters and duplicates do exist (they're just flagged in the file as being "logically deleted" so the application ignores those records).

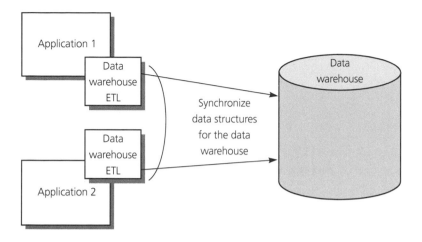

Figure 9.4 A typical data warehousing transformation process.

But in other cases, the mismatches are much less obvious, such as the database column titled CUSTOMER_INFO_CHANGE_DATE that still contains a date value in each row in that table . . . but more than a year ago, the application was changed to use that column for the date the customer last contacted the call center as part of a frantic company effort to roll out a new customer quality initiative in the face of rising customer dissatisfaction ratings. Rather than add a new column to that database table, some application developer or analyst or business manager determined that storing the date the customer's information (e.g., address, phone number, etc.) was last changed was no longer important and the field could be reused going forward for the quality initiative to save disk space.

The key to identifying and resolving situations such as those discussed above, and tens of thousands of other similar situations, is to use the source data structures as a starting point rather than *the* authoritative guide . . . and to ensure that enough project time is allotted for a thorough hands-on source data analysis effort.

By "hands-on source data analysis" we don't mean purchasing a high-priced data quality tool, something that IT project budget holders often balk at doing. Rather, source data analysis can be best accomplished—and in a very cost-effective manner—by "turning the analysts loose" with SQL or a simple reporting and analysis tool such as SAS (a commonly used statistical package from the SAS Institute) or Focus (a tool from Information Builders, Inc.—IBI—that is commonly found in mainframe environments as well as in its desktop version). The directions to the analysts conducting the source data analysis should be stated very simply as "go forth and find things" by digging through the data.

Two quick stories, experiences of Alan Simon on past data warehousing projects, illustrate the value of source data analysis and how it can best be accomplished. In the first situation, a contract management data mart built in the mid-1990s for a pharmaceutical company, the data mart project was occurring in parallel with a legacy system migration effort. As part of the legacy system migration, converted data was available every 2–3 weeks in the form of an AS/400 relational database, and this database was copied to the data mart's hardware platform (another AS/400) for use by the data mart project team.

The author was conducting the source data analysis and came across a set of master customer database tables, one of which contained information about supermarket chains, drugstore chains, hospital companies, and other customers of that pharmaceutical company. Another table contained a comprehensive list of physical locations (individual hospitals, supermarkets, drugstores, etc.), all of which were linked back to the "master record" in the first database table. Recalling a college summer job as a janitor in a supermarket in the Phoenix area, the author did an SQL "join" operation to display a complete list of that company's locations in the Phoenix area to see if the store in which he had worked was still there. The results set did show that particular store, plus other nearby stores in which he had shopped or knew people who had worked there . . . plus a supermarket location from a different chain and several drugstore locations from a well-known national drugstore chain. Curious, a number of other SQL join operations commenced, with many of the other results sets showing similar confusing intermixing of physical locations. The reason: errors in the data conversion process of the legacy system migration project that hadn't been caught. Having caught these errors as part of the data mart project's source data analysis, not only was the team able to avoid loading incorrect data into the data mart's database, but the new source application's own data was corrected prior to the system being rolled out to the users.

The second situation occurred several years later as part of a data warehouse project at one of the world's leading consumer product companies. As part of this project, external market share data was being purchased from a leading provider of consumer-oriented marketing information, to be loaded into the data warehouse. Drawing on past experiences such as the pharmaceutical data mart project discussed above, the author outlined work processes for team members to proceed with hands-on data analysis for each of the seven or eight sources that would be providing content to the data warehouse. Some grumbling occurred among some of the team members from the client company (the project was being conducted by a mixed consulting-client team), claiming that their company paid the external data supplier extra for absolutely top-notch data cleansing services, and that the incoming data was "flawless." Finally agreeing to perform some representative hands-on source data analysis, they quickly discovered a handful of dates in the source data in the 12th century (1100s). Now, convinced as to the utility of source data analysis, they proceeded to do so for the other data sources as well.

Whether the sources for an e-commerce-related data warehouse are the traditional ones that have been supplying data warehouses for a number of years, or you're dealing with newer Internet-specific application environments, your activities should be the same: get your hands on the data, dig through, and see what's there—not only potential quality and integrity issues but also hidden business rules, such as undocumented relationships among various pieces of data. After doing so, the data quality and integrity when your data warehouse is initially deployed is certain to be better than if you relied solely on documentation about the source data structures.

Solving the Data Quality Problem, Part 2: Operationalizing Data Quality and Integrity

Quickly refer back to the last sentence of the preceding section, and note that we explicitly mentioned that hands-on source data analysis will improve data quality when your data warehouse is *initially deployed*. As we noted earlier in the chapter, however, as time moves forward it is very common for data quality and integrity to degrade as changes occur within the overall end-to-end environment.

The primary reason for degraded data quality has nothing to do with technology, but rather falls within the realms of organizational-related issues as well as methodologies and processes. Simply stated, data quality management is almost universally viewed as belonging to the IT organization rather than being part of the overall business processes of the company. Consider all of the topics we've discussed in this chapter, both on the problem side and (so far) on the solutions side. All are technology focused.

In traditional data warehousing environments, the "left-to-right" one-way flow of data from source applications to the data warehouse occurs mostly in a behind-the-scenes manner. Even consumers of data-warehouse-provided business intelligence, from rudimentary reports to online analysis to key business and performance indicators, care very little about the processes that must occur to build and maintain the data warehouse. To their way of thinking, "It's all overhead," and the more that can be streamlined in terms of time and money, the better.

Now consider the B2C complications we discussed earlier in this chapter in the form of relying on data self-entry on the part of consumers. When their fax number changes, or they get a new e-mail address, how many consumers think to update that contact information with companies with which they conduct business? With some companies, such as the bank in which a person has his or her checking account or a stock brokerage, they will go to the effort to update their contact information. But a click-and-mortar retailer? Even one from which that person has made more than a few purchases in the past? Probably not.

Consequently, one key portion of a B2C company's data warehousing environment—*as well as their operational environment*—will likely see decreasing data quality over time as changes occur to contact information in their customer base, but the company has little or no visibility—at least in a timely manner—to those changes. Simply providing a hyperlink on their Web site for consumers to click on, and then go to a "change contact information" page, is insufficient.

Other information grows out of date as well, or perhaps becomes detached from a customer's main information as a result of, say, using a different credit card than that previously recorded for the customer: product preferences (e.g., what types of books or music the consumer buys), hobbies, and so on.

A solution is to "operationalize" the data quality processes by closely coupling them with other customer-facing business processes. For example, suppose a B2C click-and-mortar retailer builds a data warehouse in which customer information is gathered, consolidated, analyzed, and then fed into targeted marketing functions. Part of the targeted marketing might be to contact selected customers in some way, typically by e-mail, to let them know of new product availability, upcoming sales, and so on through the Web site.

Some portion of e-mail contacts will invariably bounce back as undeliverable. For example, people change employers, and perhaps a consumer used his or her business e-mail as the primary online contact vehicle rather than a personal e-mail account; after changing jobs, that contact point is lost.

An overly simplified campaign management or targeted marketing process might build a list of bounced e-mail addresses and simply flag those customers in an operational database as "cannot reach right now." Not only does the company "give up" (for at least a while) in attempting to sustain contact with these customers, it is likely that this "cannot reach right now" designation may not necessarily propagate its way into the data warehouse, and subsequent reporting and analysis may be incorrectly skewed by failing to take this loss of contact into consideration.

An alternative is to introduce a more complex set of processes, based on a "whole-customer view" that can be built within the data warehouse through information from multiple sources (see Figure 9.5). Whereas the online fill-in-the-blank customer registration form collected only data essential for successful B2C transactions (the goal being to keep a new customer from getting frustrated at the data collection process and simply leaving the Web site), the catalog system collects not

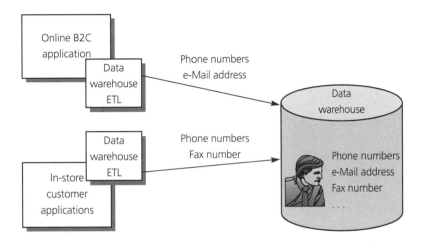

Figure 9.5 A "whole-customer view" portion of a B2C data warehouse.

only home and business phone numbers (as does the Web site) but also a fax number, if available.

The operationalized data quality processes might go something like the following:

1. Build the list for the targeted marketing effort, and send e-mail messages.

2. Build a list of bounced e-mail addresses.

3. Process the bounced e-mail address list against the whole-customer view within the data warehouse, and where alternative contact information (phone numbers, fax numbers, etc.) exists, build a "Stage 2" targeted marketing effort that consists of

   • the same offer as was originally offered by e-mail

   • a notice along the lines of "We apparently don't have your current e-mail address"

   • some inducement (e.g., an additional discount off the order) for the customer to go to the Web site, log on using his or her ID and password, and update the e-mail contact information

Perhaps the Stage 2 effort would be a fax-based one, or alternatively the company's call center could take charge of the outbound sales calls and attempt contact via either business or home telephone. If the company has performed a house-holding function as part of building the data warehouse (e.g., linking family members who all have individual accounts), contact could be attempted through some other family member.

Should the Stage 2 contact attempt(s) fail (e.g., the person can't be reached in any way), he or she could *then* be flagged as "cannot reach right now." Should contact be successful but within some designated time there is no online update of the e-mail address, the customer might be flagged as "reachable, but unresponsive" or some other appropriate designation. Subsequent shopping patterns, if any, can then be monitored and propagated through to the data warehouse's whole-customer view. For example, if that customer does shop in one of the retailer's physical locations (determined either through an ID card, or perhaps through credit card use) but still does not take advantage of the online sale or update the e-mail address, a classification might be made noting that the customer possibly prefers to shop in physical retail outlets rather than online, and targeted marketing efforts for in-store shopping could then be sure to include that person.

There are any number of variations of the above. For example, if the click-and-mortar retailer has an in-store kiosk at which customers swipe their ID cards to receive customized in-store coupons, a trigger might occur through which the customer is either prompted to enter his or her e-mail address right there at the kiosk (with appropriate inducements, such as an in-store cash-back coupon that can be immediately used that day), or perhaps simply notified via the kiosk's screen that the company has lost e-mail contact, to go to the Web site and update the e-mail address in exchange for an additional discount, and so on.

From a technology standpoint, processes such as the above could be cobbled together using custom code in concert with marketing-oriented CRM packages, or alternatively a dialog marketing package such as Revenio (see Chapter 8) could be used to build the appropriate end-to-end foundation and flows. More important than the technical building blocks, however, is to understand that by coupling processes related to data quality with operational business processes such as marketing and selling goods to customers, most or all of the resistance toward data quality disappears because it is no longer seen as an overhead function that adds little if any real business value. Rather, data quality becomes an inherent part of operational business processes, and to decouple the two comes to be thought of as inconceivable.

Operationalizing data quality also applies to B2B settings. As illustrated in Figure 9.6, a supply-chain-oriented B2B environment might establish a "data quality channel" through which trading partners actively exchange updates about key pieces of data, outside of their regular buying and selling channels. XML (see

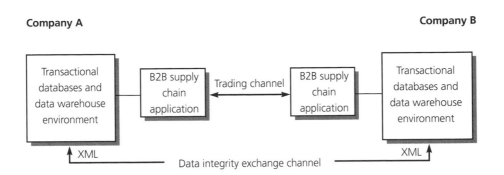

Figure 9.6 A B2B supply chain "data quality channel."

Chapter 7) would be a particularly appropriate mechanism through which this channel could be built and data exchanged.

There is one final item from a technology point of view that must be noted. Near the beginning of this chapter, we mentioned that in most traditional data warehouse environments, there is little incentive on the part of the owners of transactional applications to actively participate in data quality processes, and those responsible for the data warehouse often fight a losing battle to establish *and maintain* data quality and integrity between the source applications and the data warehousing environment. However, as should be very clear from the scenarios presented above, it is impossible to operationalize data quality without adequate "feedback loops" between the data warehousing environment and that of the source applications. The traditional one-way flow of data and control information from the source applications to the data warehouse—with nothing coming back the other way—simply won't suffice in an e-commerce setting.

Summary

Data quality and integrity will continue to be a challenge as long as computers exist. As we've discussed in this chapter, companies that embrace e-commerce, whether in a B2C or B2B setting, find themselves with many new data quality and integrity challenges that they haven't had to face in more traditional computing environments in the past. Yet, at the same time, the capabilities provided through e-commerce, from the openness of the Internet to building blocks and products that are used in e-commerce settings, also provide new weapons to be employed in the ongoing quality battle.

The two key points made in this chapter worth repeating are

1. By operationalizing data quality, much of the traditional resistance will disappear because data quality is now viewed as an inherent and essential part of ongoing business processes.

2. It is essential that an organization's data warehousing architecture evolve from the traditional one-way flows of information to embrace end-to-end, ongoing exchange of data between source applications and the data warehouse.

10

Information Privacy and Systems Security Issues for e-Commerce Environments

The overwhelming adoption of the Internet as a tool for conducting commerce has resulted in two competing forces that are constantly at odds with one another in a very public forum. Specifically, *ease of access* needs to be counterbalanced against *security and privacy needs*.

Actually, for quite some time this fundamental paradox has existed between security and privacy and information access. However, the "battleground" for these competing forces has typically been within the technology and systems realm, occurring mostly behind the scenes and away from the forefront of businesses' mainstream operations.

The Internet, however, has brought this issue to the forefront. In addition, one of the key components of e-commerce and doing business over the Web in general is to capture information on consumers and partners so that the electronic presentation of information can be massaged to more effectively market, sell, or serve customers. The collection, organization, categorization, and distribution of information about individuals, and the groups they belong to, causes many concerns about "how much" information is enough and what information should be kept private and what information should be open to the public.

The security and privacy picture is further complicated by the very nature of data warehousing: building a consolidated store of information to enable one-stop shopping for business intelligence purposes. Since the early 1990s and the birth of the modern data warehousing era, security has been somewhat of a sore subject in this realm. Architects and planners almost always include requirements stating their intentions that the resultant data warehouse will be a secure environment and follow all applicable privacy guidelines governing its content (e.g., keeping individuals' credit scores private, or maintaining the confidentiality of other types of consumer financial information), yet as projects proceed and the inevitable challenges surface, security is often recategorized as a "post–Phase I" feature that rarely surfaces. Typically, the only security applicable to the data warehousing environment is user authorization via login IDs and passwords, and rudimentary database security (e.g., which users have permission to view specific data). Advanced security of the type we'll discuss in this chapter often never surfaces again during that environment's life span.

And now, we couple the traditional challenges of data warehousing security with those inherent in the Internet in general and e-commerce in particular, and the result is a potential nightmare for any organization that doesn't give adequate attention to security and privacy issues from the very beginning of a project through development and deployment, and into ongoing operations.

This chapter takes a look at the fundamental paradox that exists between protecting our privacy and the need to access and distribute information. The chapter also discusses common security threats, risks, and options for countermeasures to protect and enhance the security of an e-commerce environment.

Much of this chapter's material transcends needs specific to data warehousing environments, for one very simple reason: security and the protection of privacy requires a comprehensive, end-to-end, all-encompassing effort. It is *impossible* for planners and architects to build a secure e-commerce data warehousing environment without factoring in the security environments and issues of the organization's

- legacy systems

- networking and communications infrastructure

- cross-enterprise communications and information exchange with other companies

- Internet environment (both company-specific and the Internet in general)

As was noted in the introduction to Part II, readers not directly involved in the security aspects of e-commerce data warehousing may wish to skim this chapter rather than read it in detail, at least at present. We strongly suggest, however, that every reader at least skim the material that follows to gain a working familiarity with security and privacy issues as they relate to the Internet and e-commerce.

These fundamental issues *will* percolate into the data warehousing realm, so it's essential to understand privacy and security issues of the topics we'll discuss, such as cookie data and aggregated publicly purchased behavioral and profiling information.

Failing to consider these issues often results in architecting and designing an e-commerce data warehousing environment that lacks adequate security, or perhaps can't even be used as envisioned because of privacy issues and related legislation.

e-Commerce Foundations That Underlie Privacy and Security Needs

In today's marketplace, a key aspect of business-to-consumer (B2C) e-commerce is the belief that the consumer experience should be customized to reflect the individual's preferences, wants, lifestyle, and interests. This approach requires that information about the individual be captured, organized, and subsequently used the next time the individual logs onto the Web site, and is commonly referred to as *personalization* (see Chapter 7).

Acting on Personalization Information

Personalization leads to the desire to capture, organize, and use various types of information to reflect buying patterns of individuals and groups . . . and to act upon that collected data in an informed manner. Information can be collected based on *what* people buy, *how* they buy, and *why* they buy. The collected information can be captured and organized using a data warehousing environment before flowing to a company's other organizations (e.g., customer service, sales, marketing, etc.). The specific technical implementation is dependent upon the desired level of integration, business model, and relative importance of the information to the direction of the business. Independent of the technical implementation, the name of the game in B2C is to collect, organize, trend, and target selling and marketing activities at specific consumers and groups of consumers.

Buying and Selling Collections of Information

The Internet has also spawned a new era in businesses that simply collect and sell information about individuals, their demographics, and their buying patterns. In the past, "offline" versions of these businesses typically relied on data samples and statistical grouping and sold aggregated information about customer behavior. Now, with online tracking of individual transactions, shopping habits, and Web usage patterns in general—and attempts to match that highly detailed online tracking information with the actual individuals to whom the data belongs—not only do new data aggregation businesses exist, but the result is an entirely new class of security and privacy issues.

This type of information is naturally considered in today's digital commerce economy to be very valuable. Such information could be analogous to having a retail store in just the right location, with just the right products, and having just the right customer service. The digital economy allows this customization to occur in seconds rather than the months and years in the old economy of brick and mortar.

Information Accessibility via the Internet

The most profound difference in information access today, compared with that of the 1980s into the early 1990s, is convenience. Many types of information have always been available through the Freedom of Information Act (for example), but the time involved in filling out the forms, getting the forms to the right government agency, and then waiting 4–12 weeks to receive a large bulky document was very inconvenient and time-consuming. Today, that same process may take less than a few minutes to locate, select, and download the same information. The Internet provides broad and comprehensive access to information, but more important than that, the access is now convenient and expedient.

The amount and types of information that can be accessed via the Internet is absolutely amazing. The number of Web sites available to the average Internet user changes daily, with thousands of new Web sites added each week. Personal information, such as buying habits, birth date, death records, home address, telephone numbers, political association, church association, employer, schools attended, credit history, marriage history, and so on, can be organized, compiled, and manipulated so that valuable information emerges.

Organizations exist today that do nothing but buy, collect, and organize such information. Once sufficient information is collected and organized, these organizations sell this information to other organizations that are in business to sell products and services. The information is used to target specific demographic groups believing that the information will serve to dramatically increase the likelihood of a purchase when the product or service is presented to the preselected demographic group. Chat groups and listservs also provide a means for capturing thoughts, ideas, passions, and opinions on specific subjects. Many individuals also set up personal Web sites. These sites often include information about their personal lives such as photos, likes and dislikes, profession, single or married, children or not, and so on. Much of this information, just a couple of years ago, would have been considered too private to put on the Web.

Some examples of the information available on the Web today include

- Individual information - name, address, phone, e-mail, photographs, political affiliation, bank records, credit history and reports, news articles, criminal justice records, business credit and company financial records, family information, mailing lists, professional associations, tax records, insurance records, adoption records, genealogical records

- Public information - licenses, motor vehicle records, consumer credit reports, earnings history, education history, worker's compensation history, medical records, resumé

- Legal information - previous lawsuits, business partnerships, extended credit, pending lawsuits

Search technologies via search engines are making the identification of information easier and easier. Finding personal information about a particular individual can be accomplished in a matter of hours today with the advanced search technologies that are available. Table 10.1 provides a list of popular Web search engines.

Along with generalized search engines, there are also quick ways to find people and information about people. Some of the popular "people" information Web sites are shown in Table 10.2.

Information Privacy—Are There Any Protections?

As discussed previously, access to information on our personal lives, our jobs, and our buying habits is already available, and becoming more available every day. Moreover, advanced search technologies are being developed that make rapid access to information easier every day. Believe it or not, there are laws in place to protect the privacy of information. For any information practitioner, it is important that these laws be understood and managed into any e-commerce strategy.

Table 10.1 Popular Web search engines.

Web Search Engine	URL
Alta Vista	*http://www.altavista.digital.com/*
Excite	*http://www.excite.com/*
Infoseek	*http://www.infoseek.com/Home*
Infospace	*http://www.infospace.com/*
Lycos	*http://lycos.cs.cmu.edu/*
Magellan	*http://www.mckinley.com/*
WebCrawler	*http://www.webcrawler.com/*
World Wide Web Yellow Pages	*http://www.mcp.com/newriders/wwwyp/*
Yahoo!	*http://www.yahoo.com*

Table 10.2 Popular Web sites to locate information about people.

Web Site	Description
http://www.switchboard.com	Virtual telephone directory
http://home.netscape.com	Includes a "people icon" that provides search capability for personal information about people
http://www.lycos.com/pplfndr.html,	Designed to help you find people and information about specific individuals
http://www.yahoo.com/search/people,	Designed to help you find people and information about specific individuals
http://www.excite.com/Reference/people.html	Designed to help you find people and information about specific individuals

The Privacy Act of 1974 (Public Law 93-579, 5 U.S. Code 552a) sets restrictions on the collection and transfer of personal data by government agencies and provides for citizens to sue government agencies that violate this act. Federal law restricts access to credit information to those with a need to know. Organizations with a "need to know" may include banks, mortgage companies, and rental agencies. Many state laws protect personal information. Medical records are an example of information that is typically protected by state laws. Nevertheless, access to much of our personal information is simply unregulated.

Access to personal credit information is regulated and controlled by the Fair Credit Reporting Act (Public Law 91-508) and is generally believed to be one of the more private areas of our personal records.

The Current State of Web Site Privacy

The following information is provided from a report produced by Georgetown University.[1] This report was updated as recently as August 2000 and reflects the current state of privacy policy on the Internet.

The Georgetown Internet Privacy Policy Survey is a progress report to the Federal Trade Commission on the extent to which commercial Web sites have posted privacy disclosures based on fair information practices. The study was initiated by the private sector and was funded by small contributions from 17 different companies and organizations.

Media Metrix provided the data for the study. The sample consisted of 361 dot-com Web sites visited by consumers at home drawn from a sampling frame of the top

7,500 URLs ranked by audience during January 1999. The unduplicated reach of the sampling frame is 98.8%. Data was collected by 15 graduate student "surfers" during the week of March 8–12, 1999. The surfers completed a survey form for the URLs in the sampling pool until the target of 300 Web sites had been reached. Because the sampling frames for the 1998 FTC study and the current Georgetown study were drawn from different populations, extreme care must be exercised in making direct comparisons between the results of the two studies.

The study results address three questions:

1. What personal information do Web sites collect from consumers? 92.8% of the sites in the sample collected at least one type of personal identifying information (e.g., name, e-mail address, postal address). 56.8% collected at least one type of demographic information (e.g., gender, preferences, zip code). 56.2% of the sites collected both personal identifying and demographic information. 6.6% of the sites collected neither type of personal information.

2. How many Web sites posted privacy disclosures? 65.9% (238 sites) of the 361 sites in the sample have posted at least one type of privacy disclosure (a privacy policy notice or an information practice statement). 36% (131 sites) posted both types of disclosures. 34.1% (123 sites) did not post either type of privacy disclosure.

3. Do these disclosures reflect fair information practices? The content of all privacy disclosures were analyzed for four elements of fair information (notice, choice, access, and security) and whether or not they posted contact information to ask questions or to complain about privacy. Of the 236 Web sites that collected personal information and posted a privacy disclosure, 89.8% included at least one survey item for notice, 61.9% contained at least one survey item for choice, 40.3% contained at least one survey item for access, 45.8% contained at least one survey item for security, and 48.7% contained at least one survey item for contact information. 13.6% (32 sites) of the same 236 Web sites (or 9.5% of the 337 Web sites that collect at least one type of personal information) contained at least one survey item for all five elements of fair information practices: notice, choice, access, security, and contact information.

How Can Information Be Collected?
A Discussion of Cookies

As was discussed in Chapter 7, a cookie is a tiny piece of information written to the hard drive of an Internet user when he visits a Web site that offers cookies. Cookie files are very small, having no more than 255 characters and 4K of disk space. Cookies can include a variety of information, including the name of the Web site, where on the site the user visited, passwords, and even user names and credit card numbers that have been supplied via forms. Cookies are intended to be retrievable only by the site that issued them, and link the information gathered to a unique ID number assigned to the cookie so that the information is available from one session to another.

The Purpose of Cookies

Even though cookies are often a key part of a business's campaign management, CRM analytics, and other information-based business operations—and consequently cookie-provided data is often a key part of an e-commerce data warehousing environment—it's interesting to note that cookies were originally designed to benefit the end user or consumer. Online organizations that required user IDs and passwords could store this information in the form of a cookie. This way, repeat visitors to a site could avoid having to fill out form information on each visit. Likewise, some online search engines such as Infoseek use cookies to "remember" users and offer them customized news and services based on their prior use. So as originally designed, cookies were intended to be a time-saving device for computer users and consumers. For example, instead of having to send a credit card number over the Internet multiple times, an online vendor could read a user's cookie and match it to a stored profile that would contain that information. Cookies were also initially designed to track Web page usage to help Web site designers understand which pages were most effective. This information could then be used to guide future development and design efforts as well as planned Web page maintenance and update schedules.

Cookies and Consumer Targeting

Since cookies can be matched to the profile of a user's interests and browsing habits, they are a natural tool for "targeting" advertising to individual users. Cookies were soon used to target advertisements such as changing banner ads to users whose profiles match those of likely consumers of the advertised products. Another advantage of using cookies is to ensure that specific consumers were not overwhelmed with the same advertisement over and over again. The ability to track user/consumer habits and match these habits against advertising is a logical and obvious fit for targeting the sale of specific products. For example, if a consumer inquires several times about the subject of fishing, it follows that an advertisement focused on selling fishing equipment would have a greater chance of success.

Cookies—Fundamental Privacy Risks

Proponents of Internet privacy disagree with the use of cookies for a variety of reasons. Chief among them is that cookies are stored on a user's PC without their knowledge. Many Internet users are unfamiliar with cookies and especially are unaware that information about that person's Web surfing habits is being stored on their own computer and is accessible to Web sites being visited. Before the upgrades of popular browsers like Netscape and Microsoft Internet Explorer, cookies were placed anonymously and without alerting the user. In fact, information from the cookie was transmitted to the Web site, again without the user's knowledge. With browser upgrades users may be alerted when they are being offered a cookie, but the formatting of the information may tell the user little about what is actually being stored. It is often difficult to determine what information will be stored in cookies even if the user is alerted that cookies are being used. In addition to the difficulties in understanding the content being captured by cookie alerts to users, it is also not always clear where the cookie is coming from.

Cookie Application Development Vulnerabilities

The security of personal information stored on a user's hard drive has also been a concern associated with the use of cookie technology. Concerns have been raised about the possibility of cookies being written that would allow access to other information that the user has stored. An upgrade to the Internet browser Netscape Communicator was plagued with a bug that would allow a Web site access to the information that was passed between that site and the cookie file, including credit card numbers and passwords that had been entered into files. While this bug was subsequently fixed and did not allow access to the user's hard drive, it was still a serious breach of cookie security. Further concerns have been raised about the possibility of Web sites gaining access to cookies placed by other sites, but it is being debated whether or not this is practicable. Another issue regarding cookies is that they may contain viruses that would be transferred onto the user's hard drive. While it is possible that a malicious program might be transmitted and allowed to execute by a bug in a browser, it is not a strong concern. Cookies are routinely stored only as text files, and so are not executable. A more serious worry could be the possibility that a cookie might be developed that could browse a user's hard disk looking for information like bank account numbers, Social Security numbers, and other commerce-worthy data.

Cookies and Internet Privacy

The most significant issue concerning cookies is the concern for user privacy and the potential for abuse. Advertisers and Webmasters are currently using cookies to develop detailed profiles of users and their browsing habits. Each click on a particular type of advertisement or page in a Web site is added to the profile maintained by the maintainer. For the time being, this information is primarily used for Web site design and the placement of banner advertisements, but the possibility also exists for these profiles to be sold to other e-tailers and commerce-focused businesses. This could lead to deeper incursions into personal privacy, because if any one of the cookie maintainers links a user identity to their cookie ID, then that information could also be resold.

Although this might at first seem to be only a nuisance, which would probably lead only to a serious increase in "targeted" junk paper mail or e-mail, there are more serious concerns for potential abuse. In addition to extensive information on personal interests, those individuals who do online research on controversial subject matters such as religion or gun control issues might be harassed by groups that have opposing views to theirs. The possibility of such abuse of information is not nonexistent, especially for researchers who frequently utilize search engines employing cookies. By matching the cookie identification with a user profile, the user's past search history can be accessed by the Web server. If these search profiles were to be resold or otherwise accessed, the user's patterns of research would be immediately apparent. If any form of identification were linked to these profiles, it might prove to be a serious invasion of user privacy, not unlike the records of public library patrons. A closely related possibility is that user information could be resold to nonadvertising entities, and possibly used in ways that advertisers had not intended. For example, let's say that an Internet user consistently is found to be searching and reaching Web sites that deal with increasing the performance and speed of an automobile. Next, let's say that cookie information showing this trend is captured by the insurance company currently providing automobile protection for this same user. Is it possible to think up a scenario where that insurance company might raise the rates of this user on his automobiles because there is implied risk based on the fact that this user obviously desires to drive faster? Another potential scenario has to do with the federal government. Whether the issue is gun control, tax law, or abortion, government agencies may have the ability (someday) to quickly assess those in America and elsewhere who do not support a current policy or position based on the sites they access and search for on the Internet. The other privacy risk is that information is inaccurately accounted for and propagated to other Web sites . . . plus underlying data warehousing environments. Internet users could be harassed, targeted for commerce advertising, and possibly harmed based on inaccurate information. This scenario is analogous to an inaccurate credit report.

Information collected through the use of cookies can also cause unwelcome burdens and hassles for Internet users. A recent occurrence, relevant to this discussion, happened to Steven Shaffer. After visiting a Web site and filling out a form expressing a slight interest in getting into a "home-based Internet business" and indicating the ability to fund such a venture, this author was bombarded with "snail mail," e-mail, and phone calls soliciting the author to fund and start his own entrepreneurial home business. (In the author's nearly 40 years, he had never seen a more focused, organized, and aggressive campaign to seize his business.) In addition, the bombardment started less than one week after visiting the site. It was obvious that specific information was captured about the author and sold to other organizations selling similar business concepts. Proponents of Web commerce, Web advertising, and other Internet-centric services should note that it is important that this type of experience does not happen to other Internet surfers. (The author is still responding to e-mails and phone calls, and receiving solicitations through regular mail. By the way . . . he was never asked if cookies could be used, or informed that they were being used, during his initial session!)

Another possibility for cookies to pose an active threat to users would be in the case of law enforcement. User profiles, compiled via cookies, can be used by law enforcement, and possibly used as admissible evidence. Computer files, like other documents, may be seized as evidence with proper warrants, and since the cookie files exist on the user's hard drive, they would be retrievable consistently with other files.

It should be noted that the Internet was insecure before the widespread use of cookies. Without cookies, Webmasters can obtain information about the user's IP address, browser type, last pages visited, and more depending on the user's software and the program being executed. Cookies are the preferred method of collecting user profile data because the information persists from session to session, and allows the Web server to recognize a user as having visited from the same computer as before. This is what allows the compilation of complex user profiles and large amounts of relevant user profile data.

The Conflict between Web Advertising and Privacy

Request for Comment (RFC) 2109 was a proposal before the Internet Engineering Task Force that set forth guidelines for cookie use by Web sites. When RFC 2109 was released to industry, many Web advertising firms and organizations took exception to its content and general restrictive direction because it limited the use of cookies on the Internet. RFC 2109 suggested tight controls on how cookies could be set and the information transferred. In addition to requiring notification of the user, RFC 2109 also suggested that circumstances be defined under which cookies could be set and what information they could contain. One item of particular concern to advertisers was Point 7.1 of RFC 2109, which stated:

> An origin server could create a Set-Cookie header to track the path of a user through the server. Users may object to this behavior as an intrusive accumulation of information, even if their identity is not evident . . . This state management specification therefore requires that a user agent give the user control over such a possible intrusion . . .

In the end, RFC 2109 was not supported by browser designers. Where the browser manufacturers had been asked to redesign their software to reject cookies automatically, Netscape and Microsoft Internet Explorer instead included options for users to reject cookies if they so chose. Browser defaults were still set to accept cookies, since it was felt by the designers that if cookies were disabled that some existing content on the Web would no longer operate.

Since cookies are still accepted by the popular browsers, there has been increasing information given to users on how to control or eliminate cookies. In addition to advice in many technical publications on the proper methods of deleting cookie files, add-on software packages have been designed that automatically delete or reject cookies. An example of this approach is a piece of no-cost PC software called the Cookie Crusher that automatically accepts or rejects cookies from user-selected sites. A free program for Macintosh users is the Cookie Monster program, which automatically deletes the MagicCookie and cookies.txt files at each start-up. There are other low- and no-cost software packages available for users who have privacy concerns about receiving cookies.

Cookies—Where Are We Going from Here?

Netscape and Microsoft, and over 60 other companies, have agreed to a new proposed system of collecting user information on a strictly voluntary basis. The Open Profiling Standard (OPS) proposes to allow computer users to create their own profiles, including their names, e-mail addresses, hobbies and interests, and any other information that they wish Web sites to have. OPS gives users control over their personal profile and the ability to manage which personal information gets disclosed or withheld from a particular Internet site. As a result, individuals can respond to requests from Internet sites for personal information with all, some, or none of the requested data. The main purpose of OPS is to protect user privacy while still allowing for the individualized Internet advertising that cookies are designed for. As an additional safety measure, user information is to be encrypted to protect privacy. Many advertisers and marketing consultants have based a great deal of their marketing strategies on the use of cookies, but may be forced to adapt to OPS as cookies are increasingly rejected by users. Likewise, the privacy and security issues will still remain, and it will be up to the OPS developers to ensure that it will not be met with the same media suspicion that cookies created.

The awareness of computer users about cookie files is increasing with media coverage and public discussion. Although advertisers and privacy groups remain at odds over the potential value of cookies, they remain in wide usage. Options for rejecting cookies are now readily available to most users, as well as a variety of add-on programs that will eliminate cookie files altogether. Some users may not mind having cookies used to make their Web browsing more convenient, while others may consider their privacy concerns of greater importance than the time it takes to enter a password or fill out a form.

The Open Profiling Standard may ultimately render cookies meaningless, or cookies may remain and become a standard part of the Internet landscape. What is clear is that Internet businesses should be aware of these concerns and be in a position to address privacy issues and potentially change directions if required. Until consistent Internet privacy standards are adopted, an informed decision is the best option.

Platform for Privacy Preferences Project

Web sites that violate user privacy will encounter increasing public scrutiny and legal ramifications. The perceived use of cookies in "covert" ways has created a wave of privacy concerns. Out of these concerns has come the *Platform for Privacy Preferences Project,* or P3P.

Developed by several companies and privacy advocates in conjunction with the standards-setting World Wide Web Consortium (W3C), P3P will alert Web users whenever they encounter Web sites that seek to collect more data than the user wants to share.

Here's how P3P works. As soon as someone using an application equipped with P3P technology accesses a Web site, the technology scans the page's P3P privacy policy. This machine-readable policy, written in the special Web language known as Extensible Markup Language (XML—see Chapter 7), strictly defines what information the site collects from visitors.

A user agent then issues color-coded warnings about any sites that follow data collection practices that go beyond the boundaries of personally defined limits. Users will be able to configure their agents to notify them when they visit sites that do not support P3P. The assumption is that Web sites that do not want to attract negative publicity will pay more attention to guarding user privacy. Some privacy proponents are also suggesting that P3P could be used to set off a special sound, song, or noise to alert the user to privacy problems with the site.

It is important to note that P3P is not a tool or countermeasure that provides anything more than awareness of the data that the site intends to collect. P3P does not provide any safeguards, authentication, or security provisions other than a "heads up" as to the privacy policy implemented on the particular site being surfed. Once the user is alerted that the site does not reflect the same privacy policy that they have established for themselves (Red Light), then the user can choose to terminate the session and move on. If, on the other hand, the site's privacy policy is consistent with that of the user's (Green Light), then the user would likely "stick" on the site. P3P is entering the market at a time when Internet companies are under increasing pressure to balance the conflict between customer demands for privacy and commercial interests in building customer profiles.

A report released in late May by the Federal Trade Commission found that only 20 percent of sites offered privacy polices that honored all of the so-called fair information practices established by the government. These include offering notice about the collection and use of information; a choice in how that information will be used; reasonable access for consumers to the information collected about them; and adequate security to ensure proper handling of consumer information. This is a far cry, apparently, from what consumers are demanding. A survey published in October 1999 by market researcher Forrester Research Inc. reported that almost 9 out of 10 consumers want to control what companies are allowed to do with their information.

Internet Aggregation Services

A growing trend in the virtual world is called aggregation services. Aggregation services work on behalf of an end user or a business to consolidate Internet-based information into a single presentation for the user. The purpose of aggregation services is simple: ease of use. A given end user or business may find themselves needing 15–25 bookmarks to keep up with all of their personal information (bank, insurance, credit cards, schools, stocks, bonds, mortgage, church, weather, news services, phone bill, cable bill, utilities, bonus-mile accounts, etc.). An aggregation service brings all of this information together into a simple, easy-to-use presentation for the user. In most cases, the end user is able to access all information through the use of a single password. In effect, the end user is handing over his or her privacy and security rights to the aggregation service, and the service does all the connection and access to get the information. This approach offers tremendous efficiency, but at a potential big cost.

The aggregation process also raises legal and competitive concerns. These services provide what is commonly referred to as "screen scraping." Screen scraping, in this context, refers to the process of gathering information without first being given permission from banks or other institutions whose information they collect and organize. Instead, the end user provides the aggregator with their user IDs and passwords, and the aggregators send automated processes to pull and update customers' financial data. Because the aggregation service is serving as a "middleman," the bank or other business loses the touch point with the end user. Therefore, banks and other institutions see aggregators as potential competitive threats to their business and to their customer relationship management practices and strategies.

Along with security concerns, the process of aggregation also has privacy groups up in arms. The consolidation of private information into a single place provides a wealth of targeting data for any "would be" e-tailer or bank trying to sell credit cards or other financial instruments. Several large banks are teaming with aggregators for just this reason. Armed with information about someone, the bank can dangle lower mortgage rates, lower-rate credit cards, and great opportunities for equities or bonds based on "real-time" information. Table 10.3 presents some of the most common aggregation services.

Access to Government Information

There are also many "formal" ways to gain access to information. The federal government can be used to access most information through the following acts of law:

- The Open Records Act
- Access to Public Records Act
- Freedom of Information Act

Privacy—Where Do We Go from Here?

The acceptance and use of the Internet, coupled with the mass proliferation of information and search technology, make the protection of personal information nearly impossible. It is likely that we, as a society, will need to reassess our views of privacy and the laws that govern privacy and reintroduce new approaches and

Table 10.3 Aggregation service providers.

Service	Description
1viewnetwork.com	Focuses on investors. Users can download information to Excel spreadsheets. Financial advisors have access to the numbers. e-Mail is sent to alert user when account balances are low or if stock prices hit predefined levels.
Calltheshots.com	Web users choose from predefined content items and categories or visit any Web site and select images or text to be used on their "personalized" Web page.
Ebalance.com	Offers less overall aggregation than many services, but provides a more focused offering and set of services around financial management, financial calculators, and investment research.
Ezlogin.com	Unique offering of this service is that users can set up multiple profiles to look at things differently and at different times.
Moreover.com	Aggregates news and information from more than 1,500 Web sources in near real time. The service then assembles Web feeds in more than 2,000 categories.
Octopus.com	Provides the services necessary to allow users to "cut and paste" from any other Web site to create their own personal view.
Onepage.com	Users create "their own" consolidated page by previewing and selecting from a series of options and choices.
Paytrust.com	A leading service that allows consumers to receive, analyze, pay, and organize all of their personal bills online.
Verticalone.com	Focuses on the capture and presentation of financial information, e-mail data, and bonus-mile accounts.

strategies for protecting information that is considered private. Currently, laws and approaches to privacy will simply not scale or support the future of e-commerce and Internet technologies.

Security for e-Commerce

One of the most pressing issues in today's digital economy is security. Security and privacy concerns continue to be one of the most commonly used reasons for not adopting or embracing the Internet for business. The news is full of reports and stories that characterize the Internet as a security nightmare, full of holes and vulnerabilities. It seems that every week there is a new story about hackers or a new virus. Nevertheless, those choosing not to use the Internet, in some form, to conduct electronic business are fading away rapidly. So the question to data warehousing architects and strategists focusing on e-commerce needs becomes "How can we effectively protect the integrity, content, and privacy of the information we receive, consolidate, and disseminate?"

There are several reasons why security over the Internet is such a complex problem. First, everyone on the Internet "looks the same." By design, e-commerce is set up to conduct virtual business. This approach allows most users and consumers to remain anonymous and to not "look like anyone in particular" (i.e., be identified as the individual who he or she really is).

Next, the legal framework for swift and exacting punishment for Internet crime is still evolving. Governments are starting to provide additional legal substance in this fight against electronic crimes, but there is still a long way to go.

Finally, security cannot be provided by technology alone. Most security breaches are not caused by technology, but occur because the person or process responsible for managing security forgot to do something. Security is broken consistently by perpetrators who understand that attacking the weakest link is always the fastest way to achieve their goal. For security, the links are many and the chain is long. Moreover, security involves technology, procedures, operations, policy, human interaction and intervention, and many other disciplines that create many cracks and opportunities for penetration. Even if a company were able to implement a perfect security system on the Internet, they would still be vulnerable to an "inside" attack. An inside attack is very common and involves personnel who are authorized and approved for access using their privileges to exact a crime or to create a vulnerability. It is nearly impossible to protect against this type of attack. So given the overwhelming challenges associated with protecting the integrity and content of information on the Internet, it is no wonder that many businesses are concerned and spend a substantial amount of time and energy putting together a corporate Internet security strategy.

Developing an E-Commerce Security Strategy

Before even beginning to think about security for an e-commerce data warehousing environment, an organization's strategists and architects must focus on an overall e-commerce security strategy. When properly planned, architected, and deployed, an organization's overall e-commerce strategy will dictate the specifics of accompanying data warehousing environments. And, when adequately adhered to (i.e., not disregarded as a result of project budget cuts or schedule delays), those data warehousing security specifics will form a viable foundation for protecting information privacy and ensuring that data-warehousing-enabled business intelligence doesn't become an organization's weak link in its overall security architecture.

Security Policy

Every organization involved in the information age should have a security policy. A security policy provides the business information required to make good decisions on which information to protect and how it should be protected. A security policy is the logical first step in the creation of an overall e-commerce security strategy.

The first step in creating a security policy is to identify all information assets within the business that need to be protected. This includes not only data but also applications, servers, printers, facilities, and so on. Once all assets are defined and categorized, then each must be assigned a relative value. These values will later be used to determine how much security protection should be applied to protect them. The security policy is also an important document to define all security processes. Processes should include physical security (who has access to the facility and information assets), information access profiles (who has access to what information based on responsibility), back-up and recovery processes, off-site storage, and so on. The security policy is designed first and foremost as a means to allow management to make good, informed decisions about how much money to spend and where to spend it on security. Too many times, organizations spend money to protect assets that should not be protected and not enough in areas that should be protected. In addition, the security policy lays the initial foundation for the definition of security processes and procedures. Over time, the security policy document must evolve with the business to reflect additional systems, applications, and threats.

Risk Analysis

Once a security policy is created, the next step is to conduct a risk analysis of the business. The purpose of a risk analysis is to understand what likely threats exist and how they may manifest themselves through vulnerabilities in the systems and applications that have been implemented. It is also worthwhile to assess the impact of specific threats to determine which ones should be taken seriously and which ones would have the most severe impact on the business. Figure 10.1 describes the steps necessary to conduct a risk analysis.

A risk analysis serves several purposes:

1. It provides additional information to management to help direct expenditures to protect information assets.

2. It provides insight and understanding to help prepare the organization for threats and resulting risks. The understanding and awareness that comes

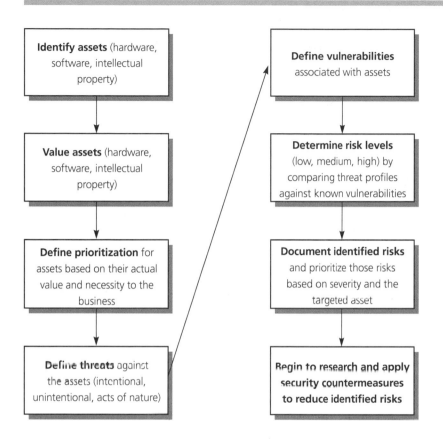

Figure 10.1 Risk analysis process.

from conducting and documenting a risk analysis is worthwhile in preparing the organizations for events that may occur.

3. It provides the catalyst and justification for putting processes and procedures in place to deal with security events that may disrupt or damage systems and applications.

e-Commerce Threats

The Internet and the thousands of organizations using the Internet for conducting business create a wonderland of opportunity for the would-be hacker. Figure 10.2 illustrates the threat environment for e-commerce data warehousing applications. Security threats can be grouped into three major categories:

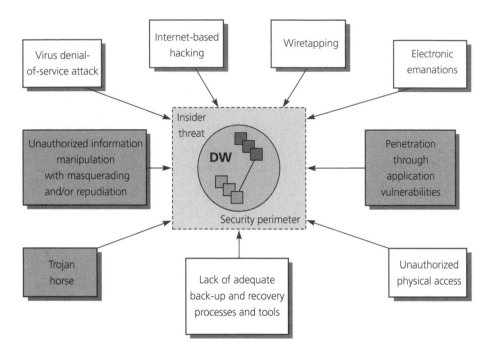

Figure 10.2 e-Commerce data warehousing threat environment.

1. **Loss of data secrecy** - Information is accessed by individuals without authorization.

2. **Loss of data integrity** - Information is modified, created, or deleted by an unauthorized individual.

3. **Loss or denial of service** - Information, applications, or services are degraded or made unavailable by an unauthorized individual.

The Internet took a humbling step in February 2000 when some of the Internet's largest sites were attacked, penetrated, and disrupted all in a single week These sites included Amazon, Yahoo, eBay, and E*Trade. These security attacks were categorized as "denial-of-service attacks" as they were designed to disrupt and degrade service. Denial-of-service attacks can be very complex and can also be very damaging to Web sites that are trying to attract new consumers to their site.

Online banks and stores are popular sites for hackers today who attempt to transfer money or steal merchandise without paying for it. Some online sites record thousands of unauthorized attacks in a single day! The threat profile for a particular environment varies depending on the systems, network components, and applications being used. Each of these components must be analyzed and continuously updated, as vulnerabilities are discovered, to stay free of obvious and simple attacks. As vulnerabilities in applications and protocols are discovered, they are immediately made available on the Internet by the hacker community. Organizations must be quick to respond to fix such vulnerabilities before hackers have a chance to penetrate them.

Attack Methods

Hackers and intruders are constantly trying new ways to penetrate systems and overcome the latest security technology. Some common attack methods include the following:

- Monitoring communications - This attack involves "listening" and intercepting communications between two parties. The purpose of this attack is to capture secret information (like user name and password) to be used later by the intruder to break into systems. An intruder that intercepts traffic can also change or modify the information, creating loss of integrity of the communications.

- Overloading systems - This attack is intended to degrade or cause denial of service for a particular site or service. Hackers have been known to create programs that create repeating requests to a particular site that ultimately bring the site to its knees. Another common attack to create a denial of service is to exploit a known vulnerability within operating systems or applications.

- Electromagnetic emanations - This attack is designed to steal unauthorized information during communications. With relatively simple equipment, it is possible to pick up signals and communications from monitors and computer systems from distances of hundreds of yards. Once this information is stolen, it can be used to break into systems.

- Physical security attack - These attacks are designed to break into facilities by eluding physical security controls (badges, locks, etc.) and gaining access to systems, applications, and services. Once an intruder gains unauthorized access to a computer system, data center, or point of presence (POP), there is untold damage that can be manifested.

- Spoofing/masquerading - This type of attack occurs when an intruder masquerades as someone he is not in order to gain access to systems, applications, services, and data for which he is not authorized. The most common way to masquerade is to "borrow" someone's user ID and password. Normally, authentication is based on a single piece of information and is consistently something that "the user knows." This approach for authentication is broken easily. A more effective approach is to secure systems and applications through the use of authentication approaches that include something a user knows and something a user physically possesses (e.g., a smart card). Many smart card technologies change the content of the information based on time and date to keep the information even further secure. For B2C and even B2B applications, distributing smart cards or other stronger authentication approaches may prove impossible or too expensive because of the number of potential customers. Another common approach is to masquerade as a legitimate IP address. Many systems and services are configured to allow a certain subset or range of IP addresses access to their services. By masquerading as a legitimate IP address, an intruder can possibly get through the first layer of security and gain access to information that may aid in gaining further access into systems and applications. Another type of attack is Domain Name System (DNS) spoofing. DNS spoofing is a threat where hackers attempt to redirect users accessing the system to another server while capturing sensitive customer information. To ensure that the server that a customer is accessing is the correct one, it is necessary to implement server-side authentication. Server-side authentication can be implemented through the use of digital certificates on the server, which is uniquely configured for each domain name and IP address.

- Trojan horses and logic bombs - A Trojan horse is a piece of executable code that hides itself within a legitimate application so that malicious code executes without the user or system administrator being aware of its execution. The power and threat of a Trojan horse is that it is designed to do its damage behind the scenes without being noticed. If properly implemented, a Trojan horse can exist for a long time without being discovered. The intruder responsible for the implementation of a Trojan horse typically arranges a method to allow the Trojan horse to manipulate data or to communicate data in a covert manner to the intruder. A logic bomb is also a piece of executable code that is "planted" into a legitimate application and is designed to "explode" or execute based on a predefined activity, threshold, or action. Logic bombs can be designed to cause denial of service or to erase or modify data. Trojan horses and logic bombs are typically more sophisticated and complex attack methods that require significant expertise and technology understanding.

- **Repudiation** - One challenging security threat to Internet business today is the repudiation of messages. Repudiation (in terms of security) means that a user, system, or application falsely denies receipt of a message or piece of information. Repudiation can also be used to falsely deny that a message or report was ever sent. Repudiation is often used for business transactions, such as online ordering and payment systems. For B2C applications, users may order merchandise and then deny that they ever ordered the items. For B2C and B2B applications, it is essential that the risks associated with repudiation be dealt with in the architecture of the systems, networks, and applications. One common way to minimize the risk of repudiation is through the use of digital certificates, which identify a customer or user in a very secure way.

- **Information/data modification** - Information integrity is very important for Internet-based commerce and businesses to continue to flourish and grow. Of even greater concern is the malicious modification of information to convey a transaction, state variable, or condition for which a hacker illegally benefits (e.g., that the hacker had purchased and paid for goods that are overdue for shipment to him or her). To minimize this risk, a message hash can be added to a message or a transaction. The encryption of messages or transactions helps to prevent eavesdropping on confidential and secret communications. Encryption makes it nearly impossible for a confidential or secret message between two or more parties to be intercepted, read, and modified en route.

- **Personnel security attacks** - For Internet, computer, and consulting companies today, the job market is very fluid. People with the right skills can get a job anywhere they want to and ask for anything they want in salary and in perks. Many companies feel forced to make outlandish promises to attract new employees. Many promises that are made are not kept, and employees leave on bad terms and disgruntled. Other Internet and dot-com start-ups lose their funding and investment and end up laying off many technical people. This situation has happened over and over again. Many of the technical people leaving companies because of broken promises or cutbacks in investment are in a perfect position (if they have the resolve) to hack back into these businesses and cause havoc. Disgruntled employees cause a lot of harm to computer systems. The fluidity of the market and also the rapid growth and changing technologies present in today's companies make it very difficult to keep pace with employee changes. Lack of attention to detail makes personnel security a very real risk in today's environment. The age-old approach of bribing employees is also common, along with gathering research and even garbage to find clues about ways into the computer systems of the organization.

The computer crimes that make the headlines consistently involve the use of sexy technology or a computer virus implemented by a 15-year-old youngster in a different country. In reality, many computer crimes and attacks are much less sophisticated and involve much easier routes than taking advantage of a bug in a software application. The human link is consistently the weakest link in the security chain.

The "Insider" Threat

Most organizations using e-commerce technologies spend the overwhelming majority of their time defining a security policy and strategy that protects them from outside forces. However, it is also productive to think about and plan for attacks from within the company. This is particularly true for supporting data warehousing environments, given the one-stop shopping available to malicious internal users via the consolidated set of highly valuable, highly sensitive data that has been built.

The insider threat is defined by risks that are introduced to the business by employees, contractors, and investors who are authorized to have access and permissions to the e-commerce systems of the company.

There have been numerous studies over the past 20 years that highlight the risks associated with the insider threat. Many of these studies showed that insiders accounted for 80+ percent of all security breaches. These percentages are decreasing as e-commerce systems provide a much broader channel of access from external would-be perpetrators, but a company using e-commerce technology would serve itself well to take a hard look at policies and procedures that can minimize the risk and impact of the insider threat.

Security Countermeasures and Approaches

This section describes security countermeasures (tools and technologies), along with approaches and strategies to keep your systems, applications, and services as secure as possible. Though applying these techniques to the e-commerce transactional environments should be considered as the first line of defense, it is equally critical to ensure that they are also applied to the underlying data warehousing environments as well.

As described previously, a security policy is a critical first step in defining assets, their relative value, and what specifically should be protected and why. Once the policy is defined, it then becomes a process of design, implementation, and operational management to find the right balance of security compared with the risk inherent in the business. Finding this balance is important. Remember that no system is totally secure, and at some point, adding another security tool, countermeasure, or procedure may actually make the system less secure because it may overwhelm the administrator who has to ensure that it is properly maintained and configured.

Security Administration

Selecting the right people to manage security countermeasures within the organization is a very important decision. Often a good choice means selecting individuals who are extremely paranoid about security and have a keen interest and urgency to protect systems, networks, and information. These individuals normally create problems for sales, business development, and product managers who like to "shoot from the hip," make quick decisions, or get something to market quickly. These fast-moving business types tend to overlook security or may even view security as a barrier to success. Competition and balance between these two forces is healthy. Be careful about who you choose to manage security administration and management within the business. These individuals will set the tone and be the ones that will ensure that countermeasures are properly configured and stay that way. Attention to detail is a must.

Security Processes and Procedures

Common sense will prevent more security breaches than anything else. There will always be the ingenious attack that no one ever saw coming, but in most cases, security breaches are enabled because someone forgot to do something very simple. The establishment of security procedures, and a willingness to uphold and manage these procedures, is a great approach to minimize many common security vulnerabilities. Security procedures can include the following:

- User authentication procedures - How a user gets a user ID, password, password update criteria.

- User profiling - Defining the access requirements determined to be essential for performing your duties—and nothing more.

- Buddy system - Procedures that ensure that key security processes are checked by a second party to ensure that a "bad apple" can't run amuck without another person or group having visibility into their activities.

- Security logs - Procedures designed to review audit trails and audit logs are a good and consistent practice that should be used to minimize risk. These logs can reveal security threats and attack types and trends. Review your logs!

- Physical security - Procedures for access to facilities, systems, and various information sources should be managed.

- Back-up and recovery - Processes and procedures for backing information up and having a plan for disaster recovery are essential. Anyone who has been hit hard in this area will never make the same mistake twice. The pain is too great.

- System upgrades and bug fixes - Any operating system or application used by the business will require updates periodically. These activities should be monitored to ensure that new vulnerabilities are not introduced with the changes. Moreover, the upgrades should be tested to ensure that the current security policy (implemented through configuration and countermeasures) remains intact with the changes. Well-defined procedures and test plans can make this a fast and worthwhile activity.

If your organization is operating in an ad hoc fashion regarding security, consider replacing the people administering and managing your security controls and insist on putting well-documented security processes and procedures in place immediately.

Security Education

Any business should periodically spend the time and effort necessary to train system users and business managers on the need for security. For rapidly growing e-commerce-focused organizations, security awareness and training is often an afterthought. Surveys have shown that a commitment to security awareness and training helps reduce the most common threats and risks to information systems. Security training provides users and managers with a more complete understanding of the importance of security and also the common types of attacks that exist in our e-commerce economy. In many instances, security awareness training provides the forum for users and managers to talk about security attacks that they themselves have experienced. In some cases, these individuals may not have realized that they were attacks or attempted attacks when they happened. Using a security consultant to conduct this type of training is a good option to pursue.

Encryption

Various forms of encryption provide protection against specific risk types including information compromise and information integrity attacks. The use of encryption is important in any discussion on privacy or information security because it provides a nearly sure-fire way to ensure privacy and secrecy in specific instances and applications. The use of strong encryption, for example, allows users and businesses to transmit confidential information and documents by e-mail or save similar information on computer systems or mobile laptops with less concern of compromise.

Encryption Overview

Encryption is used to scramble the visible/readable content of a message or document so that if the information or document is stolen or intercepted, it will not communicate any intelligible or meaningful information to the perpetrator. The use of encryption or cryptography is nothing new to data communications and information security. Cryptographic algorithms have been used throughout history, mainly to keep communications private. The private sector first started using encryption in the financial services industry to protect secure electronic transfers. The common encryption algorithms used by banks connecting branch offices to central mainframe computers was the Data Encryption Standard (DES) developed by IBM in the 1970s. DES was a less secure encryption method than the algorithms used for military communications. DES was mass-produced and became very popular within the commercial sector for point-to-point communication networks.

Today, the most prominent Internet applications requiring the use of encryption for protection are also online banking and online payment systems. Internet users and consumers are very concerned about providing personal financial information like credit card data and bank account information. For this reason, all Web browsers support some type of encryption for documents. Some of these browser encryption algorithms only use a 40-bit key, which is not considered very secure. For applications requiring secure communications and special attention to privacy concerns, this level of protection may not be sufficient.

Types of Encryption

There are two primary types of cryptography being used today—secret key and public key.

Secret key encryption, also referred to as *symmetric cryptography*, is the traditional form of encryption used to protect point-to-point (link) communications. The common algorithms used for secret key cryptographic systems are stream ciphers and block ciphers. Stream ciphers enable high-speed communications. Stream ciphers achieve high-speed communications by operating on small units of plain text. Normally, stream ciphers operate at the bit level. A key stream, which consists of a sequence of bits, operates on the plain text using a bit-wise exclusive-OR operation. The encryption of each bit depends on the previous bits. A block cipher, on the other hand, is used to manipulate a block of plain text with a predefined length (such as 56 bits) into a block of cipher text with the same length.

For secret encryption, a single secret key is used to encrypt and decrypt messages. For secret key cryptographic systems to be effective, the secret key must be distributed in a highly secure manner to all parties involved (or potentially involved) in communications. The protection of the key becomes the most important security measure for systems employing secret key encryption. For this reason, it is very unlikely that the secret key is ever communicated over the same medium for secure communications. Normally, secret key material is communicated via a different method to each of the sites receiving and communicating secure communications. Secret key cryptographic systems are effective in providing strong security for point-to-point communications, high-speed communications, and single-user information security.

Public key encryption, also referred to as asymmetric cryptography, is a more recent development in the protection and security of information communications. Public key encryption has a major advantage over symmetric cryptography because it does not rely on a secure process and method to exchange keys. Systems using symmetric/secret key cryptography must agree on the use of the same key and must use that key to encrypt and decrypt messages. Moreover, symmetric encryption systems must define a process and method for communicating these "secret" keys in a secure fashion. If the key is compromised, then the communications that are protected by the use of the key can also be compromised. For symmetric encryption systems, each end point must be known in advance so that the "secret" key can be securely communicated to that end point. The Internet has created an environment of temporary, sticky, and one-time relationships that require security and protection. For these environments and business models, it is impossible to distribute keys to every potential consumer or partner in the world.

Public key encryption systems, on the other hand, do not have the same restrictions. Public key systems utilize two keys for each secure communication session and can operate effectively over nonsecure networks—like the Internet. The public key system generates two distinct keys (initially) for each user. One of these keys is defined as the public key. This public key can be freely distributed over a nonsecure network to anyone using any method. This public key is not used to decrypt (descramble) any message. Rather, the public key is only used to encrypt messages that can be sent to the owner of the public key. The owner of the public key has the ability through the use of his private key to decrypt the messages that were encrypted with his public key. Many mathematicians have attempted to break the public key algorithm through brute-force methods. While a brute-force methodology can theoretically be used to decrypt public key encrypted messages, it is not feasible to do this if the public key is of a sufficient length.

The RSA public key implementation algorithm was invented in 1975 by three professors at MIT for which the algorithm was named (Rivest, Shamir, and Adleman). In the vast majority of cases, the RSA algorithm is not used to encrypt communication messages because of the computational overhead required. For most business applications, the use of RSA is not feasible because of the time that would be required to encrypt and decrypt messages. RSA is used, however, very effectively to encrypt (thus protect) the symmetric key, which is used to encrypt messages in a public key system. The Secure Socket Layer (SSL) standard, which is used to encrypt Web pages, uses the RSA algorithm to protect the use of symmetric keys. Note that URLs that use SSL are annotated with "https://" instead of "http://." In the combined RSA/SSL implementation, the key is generated on the Web browser and then sent to the Web server. Without public key cryptography a user, or system/application action on behalf of a user, would need to send the key without protection over the Internet. To secure the transmission of the key, the Web server sends its public key to the Web browser. The Web browser then determines the use of a symmetric key and encrypts the message with the public key of the Web server and sends the encrypted message back. The Web server is the only system that can decrypt the public key with its private key. The RSA key is used as a secure "wrapper" for the symmetric key. From this point forward, the symmetric key accomplishes the encryption, which is dramatically faster than public key encryption.

The security of this approach is further enhanced by the participating systems randomly selecting which symmetric keys are used. If a would-be perpetrator is able to break in and capture an encrypted message en route, one message will not give evidence about the keys used for previous or future messages. e-Mail messages can be secured by using multiple public keys to encrypt the same message. Each public key used in the encryption process belongs to one of the recipients of the message. This approach provides for multiple secure "wrappers" around the message and allows the message to be sent to multiple recipients who can each decrypt the message. This approach for secure e-mail messaging has been used in Pretty Good Privacy (PGP) and SSL encryption on the Web. PGP is a very effective and safe form of encryption for e-mail. PGP uses a public key algorithm that has proven to be unbreakable. PGP source code has been open to industry critique for years and has resisted all attempts to break it. PGP requires the end user to install a separate piece of software on their computer.

Secure Multi-purpose Internet Mail Extensions (S/MIME) is much easier to install and set up than PGP. Netscape's Communicator and Microsoft's Internet Explorer natively support S/MIME. In other words, no other software is required to use S/MIME. All that is required to utilize S/MIME is a digital certificate, which can be obtained from various sources, like GTE (*www.gte.com*) and TrustCenter (*www.trustcenter.com*). S/MIME uses a similar approach to PGP. S/MIME uses asymmetric encryption as a secure "wrapper" to send a key to be used in the symmetric cipher that encrypts the message. S/MIME is far less secure than PGP because it uses a far lower bit rate for the key outside of the United States, and the source code was not public until recently, when Netscape opened the Mozilla Web site and gave away the source code of its browser.

The most compelling advantage of public key cryptographic systems over secret key systems is that the private keys are never sent out over a protected or non-protected medium. This simple fact makes this type of encryption more secure, easier to use, and easier to manage. In a "secret" key environment, keys need to be communicated to each end system and thus pose a significant security risk while en route. With secret key encryption systems it is also very difficult to implement any type of strong authentication. A digital signature using a public key environment is very simple to implement, but in a secret key environment secret information needs to be communicated. In order to prevent systems from repudiating specific actions, it becomes necessary to have a third party involved to verify authenticity. The most compelling advantage of secret key cryptographic systems is efficiency and speed. Combining public and secret key systems can leverage the best of both worlds. In such a combined environment, the message is encrypted with a secret key, and the secret key is associated with the message, but instead is encrypted with a public key. This strategy provides the flexibility and scalability inherent in public key systems and the speed and efficiency associated with secret key environments.

e-Commerce Data Warehousing Implications

Before wrapping up this chapter, it's important to consolidate our discussion of security and privacy and discuss the implications for data warehousing environments constructed for e-commerce.

Privacy

Requirements on the part of businesses to aggressively maintain the privacy of their customers will certainly increase, in part due to the backlash on the part of the consuming public at large, and also because of the likelihood of privacy-oriented legislation in most U.S. states.

Many pure-play B2C companies' business models are (or increasingly "were" as dot-com bankruptcies and consolidations began to occur by mid-2000) built primarily around the acquisition of and the sale of large volumes of personalized consumer data. Constructing a "whole-customer" or "whole-prospect" view is typically dominated by use of cookies, clickstream data, and personalization information.

Business models based solely on the exchange of this type of consolidated information (along with the sale of advertising on a company's Web site) will increasingly become archaic as these companies fall by the wayside. Even without the survival-of-the-fittest marketplace Darwinism, the combination of public outcry and prospective legislative prohibitions should lead forward-thinking companies to take their e-commerce business models—as well as their transactional systems and, very importantly, their underlying data warehousing and business intelligence environments—away from being dominated by collections of information about Internet behavior.

This is not to say that an e-commerce data warehouse should not contain information about cookies, clickstream data, and information gleaned and categorized as a result of consumer personalization. Rather, as we discussed in Chapter 2, such content is an *essential* component of a high-value data warehousing environment that can build new levels of long-lasting customer relationships through a variety of channels, on the Internet as well as otherwise.

What's essential, though, is that this content itself should not be viewed as a primary component of the company's revenue generation models, but rather part of a holistic set of tools. Companies should, then, do the following:

- Be very cautious about buying large volumes of prospecting data built from people's Internet behavior, given (at best) the likelihood that the overwhelming majority of those individuals will have no interest in the company's products and services when cold-called (or "cold e-mailed"), and—at worst—will actively promote or participate in a backlash against the company because of the perceived intrusion on their privacy.

- Be likewise as cautious about selling consolidated sets of data about their own customers to others, given the likelihood of a backlash against the company for not maintaining confidentiality. This goes beyond failing to adhere to posted privacy guidelines and selling information that the company had promised wouldn't be sold; increasingly, consumers are becoming very protective of their privacy, and even information selling within legal and company-specific guidelines is likely to have as much downside as financial upside.

- Emphasize the collection of cookie, personalization, and clickstream data from activity within the company's own domain (i.e., its Web site as well as non-Internet channels), with the intention of building better, more productive relationships with the company's own customers rather than brokering that information to others.

Security

Those responsible for planning and architecting an e-commerce data warehousing environment need to go to extra lengths to ensure that they don't wind up creating a weak link in their company's e-commerce model—or their company's business operations as a whole. This means that attention must be paid to the security policies and architecture of

- the database(s) that comprise the data warehouse

- all staging areas, temporary databases and files, archived databases and files (including external media such as CD-ROM, optical disk, tape systems, etc.)

- all extraction/transformation/loading (ETL) processes into the data warehouse, from Internet-based transactional applications as well as non-Internet transactional applications

- all "front-end" user-side functions, such as creating and maintaining report and query formats, historical reports and queries, transmitting data from the data warehouse's database to the user(s) requesting the information, and so on

- all system-generated standard reports (e.g., regular monthly production reports) produced not by the actions of a user but by logic programmed into the data warehouse itself

- all "feedback loops" through which content from the data warehouse is transmitted to applications or system components within the company's enterprise

- all cross-enterprise flows of data, such as those applicable to a supply-chain-oriented B2B environment in which data-warehouse-resident information is exchanged

- all system management functions, such as backing up databases

The following security-related capabilities should be considered in any e-commerce data warehouse architecture:

- A detailed log of all requests against the data warehouse should be maintained, particularly those that come in via the Internet from outside the enterprise (e.g., customer self-service to limited data warehouse content—see

Chapter 2), as well as some indication of the results sent (e.g., time to complete the query, number of rows of data sent as part of the results set, any particular anomalies, etc.).

- In addition to login-password user authorization, authentication of all users—inside the enterprise as well as outside—should be mandatory.

- Database security equivalent to that of the company's transactional environments (e.g., using the lowest granularity of database security available, even if that means some ad hoc queries will be initially denied as a security violation) should be an inherent part of the data warehouse's database environment.

- A *full-time* data warehouse security manager should be assigned for medium-sized environments, and more than one individual assigned to large-scale environments. For small, departmental-scale "e-commerce data marts" it may not be necessary to have a full-time security manager, but security must be part of the job functions of whoever administers the data warehousing environment.

- All data warehousing operations should be regularly and frequently reviewed, looking for potential security violations.

- Encryption and other network/communications security methods should be applied as much as possible to "data on the wire" in and out of the data warehousing environment.

Summary

Privacy is a significant concern for anyone who uses the Internet, for any purpose. Business would be prudent to consider privacy issues from the very beginning when designing their e-commerce environment and when they build data warehouses—or, for that matter, any of the transactional systems (e.g., e-CRM) that will provide content to the data warehouse. The current trends in privacy policy seem to be heading in the direction of protecting the end user/consumer. These changes in policy direction will force e-commerce to communicate their privacy policies openly to anyone visiting their sites or using their systems.

Internet security presents many challenges, several of which are not new, but the amount of damage and collateral damage that can be caused by a malicious hacker has dramatically increased with the Internet. Moreover, the Internet serves as a target-rich environment with thousands of systems available and waiting for attack. Businesses engaged in e-commerce would serve themselves well to take the time to define their security policy, their security plans and strategies, and to educate their personnel on the risk and need for security. You will find it easy to skimp on security, but don't do it—not in the world of virtual commerce. The consequences are severe.

Endnotes

1. Mary J. Culnan, Georgetown Internet Privacy Policy Survey—Executive Summary, Management Department, Bentley College, Waltham, MA.

11

Solutions Architecture Case Study

In this chapter we bring together many of the topics we've discussed in previous chapters—B2C and B2B e-commerce models, technology and product building blocks, security, and data quality and integrity—into a single solutions architecture case study. The fictitious company that is the focus of our case study—Acme Computer[1]—is currently an "old economy" brick-and-mortar high-tech manufacturer of computers with no Internet presence, either customer-facing (B2C) or in its internal cross-enterprise operations (B2B).

As we've noted throughout this book, recommended best practices with regard to e-commerce data warehousing demand that an organization focus its initial efforts on developing a comprehensive strategy that takes both the transactional and business intelligence sides of e-commerce into consideration to prevent unhealthy barriers between business processes from developing.

Therefore, our case study in this chapter will take you from the up-front strategy work, including assessing the company's current situation with regard to e-commerce and accompanying business intelligence and creating a road map from their current state to the desired future state. A healthy dose of existing systems migration and integration architecture is also part of the scenario, since real-world development rarely occurs without needing to consider the integrate-or-migrate problem. (Except for brand-new dot-com companies, that is, and we saw how that played out during 2000.)

Finally, we map the strategy and conceptual architecture into implementation-specific architecture and technology selection as we bring other topics from this book into the scenario.

The Current (Pre-e-Commerce) Acme Computer Business Model

Acme Computer Inc., a publicly traded company based in Denver, Colorado, assembles and sells personal computers to consumers. They have been in business since 1988, following the first manufacturer shakeout in the PC marketplace of the mid-1980s, and since then have established themselves as a major player in the PC business segment. Acme is a midsized player in this space, nowhere near as large as Dell, Gateway, Compaq, or other market leaders, yet to date they've been able to survive subsequent shakeouts and consolidation and retain a loyal customer base primarily due to value-added features that are part of their various PC offerings.

However, because of the constant downward price pressure on PCs and the ever-demanding consumer (More functionality! More features! Lower prices!), Acme has started to stumble in the market. They are losing market share to the competition, and various marketplace surveys show them slipping in key customer "mindshare" ratings. On the financial side, their stock price has trended downward for the last five quarters despite an overall upward trend in most stock market industry segments, including PC manufacturers. Nevertheless, the company's overall financial picture is still fairly healthy because the company has been very conservatively managed during its lifetime and a significant "war chest" of cash and unused but available credit exists.

So far, the company has resisted pressure from its stockholders and others to undertake a "go for broke" e-commerce strategy. To date, Acme's Internet presence has been little more than billboardware, posting marketing material, technical specifications, and other noncommerce content on their Web site, but they are not selling PCs directly to the public at all, nor using the Internet for supply chain optimization or any other B2B functions.

Company management has considered—and so far rejected—suggestions ranging from selling PCs online at cheaper prices than available through retail outlets (something the company believes will cause a channel conflict situation) to scrapping all non-Internet sales and selling online only through B2C capabilities. Concerned about the downturn in Internet-related stocks in the spring of 2000, Acme wants to proceed very cautiously with regard to its e-commerce strategy, since management realizes the company is very much at a critical juncture in its life cycle. Embracing e-commerce seems to be a must, and doing so successfully can jump-start the increasingly stagnant company. e-Commerce failure, however, will likely mean disaster.

Acme's Business Operations: Current and Desired States

Among the first activities that need to be accomplished when conducting the necessary strategy work is to review the state of existing business operations, followed by establishing a vision and direction for the future state of those same operations. From an e-commerce data warehousing perspective, it's essential to examine these operations and not only look for places in which e-commerce capabilities can be inserted, but also to identify serious gaps in how the company currently uses its wealth of stored data for

- information-based decision making

- building and maintaining customer relationships

- improving internal operations

- improving the productivity of mandatory reporting functions (e.g., regulatory agency reports that must be filed)

Sales and Marketing

Current State: The sales and marketing group is currently responsible for developing all advertising campaigns for Acme Computer as well as coordinating sales promotions with their channel partners. Channel partners include large electronic warehouses and several small specialty stores. Acme does not currently sell directly to consumers.

The sales and marketing group also is challenged by the fact that they do not have access to detailed, high-quality data for assessing their marketing campaigns and sales promotions. For example, in the previous year Acme spent a large amount of money for the Christmas holiday season, but could not with any certainty assess the effectiveness of that campaign relative to their August and September "Back to School" campaign. The information that the sales and marketing group does have is all in Microsoft Excel spreadsheets scattered among a variety of office servers, desktop PCs, and laptops; the result is the usual lack of consolidated information with very labor-intensive and error-prone cut-and-paste processes needed to achieve any degree of sales and marketing data integration.

Another major challenge they have is that Acme knows very little about the consumers that buy their computers. This is largely because they sell their product through channel partners, and to date they have not implemented any type of Internet-based warranty registration and consumer data gathering engine. (On occasion they do receive letters or e-mail messages from customers regarding their product; however, these communications usually contain product improvement suggestions or complaints about their product rather than any type of consumer demographic information. Most of these letters and e-mail messages are just filed away following Acme's response without any transfer of the content into an encoded, database-storable format.)

Desired State: Previous to the current e-commerce initiative, leadership in the sales and marketing organization has identified a number of key initiatives, all of which (after further consideration) are still very much on that organization's wish list. These initiatives include

- Partner relationship management (PRM) - To help Acme better manage their sales channels. Today they have only the most rudimentary—and surprisingly sporadic—data about the effectiveness and profitability of their various partners. The desire is to know *why* certain partners are performing better than others and to what degree, and what partners are costing Acme in terms of marketing funds and advertising campaigns. This information would then be used as part of future negotiations with existing partners to help Acme maximize high-value relationships while possibly discarding lower-value ones.

- A data warehousing environment - For comprehensive reporting and analysis related to their sales and marketing activities. This would include partner sales information, information about their customers, and information about product enhancement requests or issues that would be useful in marketing-related business processes and the sales cycle.

- A direct sales channel - The sales and marketing leadership believes that Acme should break tradition and start selling directly to customers, despite the potential for channel conflict with partners. They believe that being disconnected from the customer because of sales being conducted exclusively through channel partners has hurt their ability to "know" the customer, which in turn has a direct impact on every other aspect of the business from product development to production to customer support.

  As with the rest of the company's management, there is somewhat of an uneasiness about proceeding with Internet-based direct sales through B2C e-commerce, given the almost universal lack of profitability of most e-tailers. Nevertheless, there is a recognition that there actually is some merit to online direct sales beyond the "everyone will get rich on the Internet" hype that has now worn off.

- A dramatically enhanced Internet presence - Moving beyond the current billboardware toward online sales (if approved as part of the company's overall e-commerce strategy), online customer support, community building among customers, and so on.

Finance and Accounting

Current State: The finance and accounting group is currently in the midst of migrating to a new SAP environment. However, there are still very manually intensive processes for purchasing, accounts receivable, inventory receiving, and purchasing approval that have not yet been addressed by the SAP migration.

Another significant problem that Acme is experiencing is that their "cash to cash" conversion cycle (the time it takes for Acme to actually receive payment on a PC that they produced) averages just over 140 days, a metric that is extraordinarily high in an era of just-in-time manufacturing. They also average only four inventory turns per year. Consequently, inventory holding costs are unacceptably high.

Additionally, many of the workers responsible for accounts receivable spend a large amount of time on the phone with sales channel partners manually synchronizing their information in their personal tracking spreadsheets so that Acme can be accurately paid. There is also a lot of time seemingly wasted on processing the paperwork from the inventory receiving department that identifies when parts have arrived, where they are stored, and other pertinent receiving-related data. There have been many instances where parts have to be reordered because they have been "lost," only to have the supposedly lost parts show up later in some overlooked corner of the production facility. This has been especially problematic since some of these parts become obsolete very quickly (e.g., disk drives, processors, memory chips, etc.) and may very well have become unusable in the time it has taken them to resurface. Consequently, waste products (by accounting terminology) are unacceptably high, and overall the company's financial ratios and other measures of financial health are steadily worsening.

Desired State: The finance and accounting leadership believes that they can improve greatly in a number of areas including the following:

- Further integrate SAP into their business operations beyond the current project - The opportunity here is to electronically bond SAP with Acme's suppliers and sales partners.

- Increase the inventory turn average - Acme believes that they should be able to obtain an annual inventory turn rate of about eight, twice where they are currently.

- Decrease the "cash to cash" conversion cycle - Acme needs to initially—and dramatically—decrease this measure from the current 140 days to about 60–70 days, but they also believe there exists the opportunity to drive this measure even lower.

- Reduce the time spent reconciling with partners and suppliers - Accounting staff members and analysts spend about 30–40% of their day reconciling payables and receivables with suppliers and sales partners. They should be able to reduce this to 20% to enable more productive use of time by all members of the accounting team.

- Obtain more competitive prices from parts suppliers - Aggressive as they are with regard to pricing negotiations, Acme's CFO strongly believes that they can obtain better prices from their suppliers. Though they don't know much about the subject yet, they believe they would like to utilize some of the online auction sites that bring buyers and suppliers together as part of their overall strategy to reduce prices they pay for components.

- Dramatically increase financial reporting and analysis, courtesy of a finance and accounting data warehousing environment - Acme's accounting legacy applications had traditionally been the vehicle through which required financial reporting (e.g., SEC quarterly reports) had occurred, and Acme's management simply used those same reports as the sole source of their own "How are we doing?" analysis. Though the initial approach had been for Acme to migrate that reporting from the legacy applications to SAP, the CFO and the CIO have jointly decided that a better direction would be to build a finance and accounting data warehouse that would not only produce required regulatory reports but also provide much more comprehensive analytical and internal reporting capabilities than had ever been available at the company.

- Prepare for selling directly to customers - Selling directly to customers is certain to present many challenges such as how to handle e-payments, customer credit card payments, returns and refunds, and many other consumer-facing finance and accounting functions that Acme has had little or no exposure to in the past. Consequently, the CFO wants to ensure that all of the internal accounting and finance processes are equipped for the new direct sales era (including B2C e-commerce, if that's what the company decides to do) far in advance of when such services will be needed.

Customer Support

Current State: Today, Acme's customer support is largely made up of a single call center. When customers have any issues with their purchased PC, they call the center and talk with a representative. As might be expected, there is a short list of "favorite" questions and problem reports that surface repeatedly.

When a software fix to an Acme PC is required, the call center agent takes the customer's information and orders a diskette or CD-ROM containing the software fix to be shipped to that customer. Customer support is responsible for managing the inventory of CDs and diskettes for those software patches, which are created by an outside vendor.

One nagging problem Acme is having in the customer support area is their ability to resolve an issue with a single phone call. Often the customer calls back since the resolution to a problem was either incorrectly stated or, perhaps, incorrectly applied by the customer. Another common situation is when one agent needs to have another agent call the customer back because the first agent doesn't have the background or knowledge to personally resolve the issue.

Though the customer support VP's objective is to achieve much higher levels of one-call resolution than currently exist, efforts in this direction are constantly thwarted by attrition rates among call center staff running about 30% annually. There is a long training cycle for a new call center agent to become sufficiently skilled to handle the many types of calls he or she is likely to receive, even just among the list of "favorites." Consequently, agents who have a great deal of experience find themselves working a great deal of overtime, which in turn leads to morale problems and retention issues, which in turn leads to newly qualified staff needing to work substantial amounts of overtime shifts—all part of an unfortunate circle of cause-and-effect events.

Desired State: The customer support VP and management have identified the following components to their business strategy:

- Expanding the company's Internet Web site to include customer support functions - Doing so would likely reduce the number of calls that come into the call center; provide a higher degree of consistency to Acme's problem resolution processes; improve morale and retention (and consequently customer service) among the current support staff; and be a key piece of a multichannel support environment.

- Implementing a knowledge management system and accompanying portal - Much of the information needed by customer support processes, whether managed in the call center or online via the Internet, involves the use of unstructured data: diagrams, documents, audio and video clips, and so on. To date, this unstructured content is almost all paper-based, following a failed attempt in the mid-1990s at implementing an online document management system. The customer service VP has a vision of mimicking the interaction model between an Internet user and the myriad of content he or she can obtain via the Internet to bring search engines, directories, and online multimedia information into the realm of Acme's support organization.

- Relating relevant customer support data to other business processes, such as manufacturing and procurement - Despite the presence of first-generation call center management software within the customer support organization, usage and analysis of data captured and managed by that software has remained exclusively in the customer support domain through a sort of data mart—a database populated each month by statistics from the call center application that produces reports on which problems occurred the most frequently, how many one-call resolutions there were, how many hang-ups resulted when all customer service agents were busy, average on-phone wait time, and so on.

  The customer service VP realizes that the data collected within the call center—and, eventually, from Internet-based online support—would not only be of value to product development, manufacturing, and procurement (and most other organizations within Acme), but could also lead to a reduction in the number of support requests because of problems.

- Reducing the number of agents required in the call center - Acme's customer support organization has almost twice the industry average number of customer service agents for a company its size, and they would like to reduce headcount.

Distribution

Current State: Acme's distribution department feels they are well equipped. They have implemented the SAP system and feel they have shaken out many of the processes and issues. In fact, the distribution group has often told management that they believe they could handle shipping directly to customers with just a few enhancements.

Desired State: To build upon their current abilities and prepare for selling directly to consumers, distribution believes the following capabilities should be studied and implemented:

- Integration with shipping carriers - Integrate tracking numbers with shipping carriers (e.g., FedEx, UPS).

- Enhance the capabilities of handling returns - Since direct consumer returns (as contrasted with returns coming via a limited number of channel partners) could greatly increase, a system will need to be implemented to help walk consumers and customer support agents through the process.

Manufacturing

Current State: Acme's manufacturing—actually, assembly—of the PCs is rather straightforward today. Sales partners are given a rather limited configuration of PCs that they can order, which keeps the process complexity low, even given Acme's traditional strategy of differentiation via value-added features. Problems sometimes arise when inventory gets out of lockstep with what is being ordered, as was noted earlier with regard to financial performance. However, the implementation of the SAP system has helped prevent unintended manufacturing shutdowns due to lack of parts, even if the inventory overage problem is still a concern.

Desired State: Acme's desire to sell directly to customers means that manufacturing will likely have to equip themselves to build PCs with configurations that are outside their traditional narrow set of choices. There is great concern over this since there are configurations that might be specified by a customer that, in actuality, aren't buildable. For example, a customer might order a PC running the Microsoft Windows NT operating system with a particular sound card only to find out that the sound card is not supported by Windows NT. Such an issue warrants the following requirements:

- Implementing a configuration management system - This system would be a rules-driven application that would assist the consumer or an Acme customer support agent in specifying a buildable PC configuration.

- Implementing an underlying configuration management data warehousing environment - This data warehouse would capture and make available for analysis all applicable detailed data about the product configuration process: what combinations are the most popular; what configurations were put together by consumers only to be discarded (and attempting to determine the reason for discarding a particular configuration, such as price); identifying whether a customer seems to be comparison shopping (e.g., a configuration is put together and not ordered at that time, but then is subsequently ordered, perhaps several days later); and so on.

Internal Information Technology

Current State: The internal IT organization currently supports the SAP environment, other internal applications, and all of the PC desktops that are used by everyone in the company. These PCs run various Microsoft operating systems (mostly Windows

NT) and connect to servers that also run Microsoft software, including e-mail, file services, and so on. The company standard for desktop software is Microsoft Office.

Acme has Internet connectivity through a T1 leased line into an Internet Service Provider. This provides all employees access to the Internet as well as e-mail services.

Desired State: Like most corporate IT organizations, Acme's is stretched rather thin with regard to its support requirements. They had implemented SAP using in-house staff with only minimal outside contracting assistance. Currently, the support staff for Acme's Internet site consists of a single part-time Webmaster (she is also part of the support staff for the call center application).

An enhanced Internet presence *will* come to Acme. The CIO (who spends a great deal of his own time doing hands-on systems support and troubleshooting) knows that even though the internal IT staff is collectively very Internet literate from a user perspective, they also collectively have very limited knowledge about Internet architectures, Web servers, and other technologies.

To date, all reporting and data warehousing environments have been built in-house by Acme staff, but all of these initiatives have been relatively small scale (low data volumes, simple reporting functionality, etc.). The current list of requested data warehousing capabilities that has resulted from the consolidated Acme business strategy effort—data warehouses for customer support, manufacturing, finance, sales and marketing, and product configuration—has the CIO facing two key questions. First, should each of these data warehousing initiatives be a point solution itself, or should they be part of an overall Acme enterprise-wide data warehousing initiative? Second, how does the likelihood of Acme entering the world of B2C e-commerce— and possibly B2B e-commerce operations as well—affect what should be done in the data warehousing space?

The decisions made by the CIO based on these concerns include

- Outsource where possible - The difficulty in finding adequate staff to support and maintain these many new initiatives gives reason to strongly consider using application service providers and other outsourcing units.

- Plan for high-availability systems - Online commerce will result in 24 × 7 customer-facing operations. Correspondingly, Acme's infrastructure—hardware, networking, and systems software—must be upgraded from its current state to components that comprise a high-availability environment.

Human Resources
Current State: Acme's human resources (HR) department has operated in a very traditional manner, largely because the company's workforce has always been on the

smaller side (under 1,000 employees and temporary contractors). Benefits, enroll-ment, payroll, and other HR functions are largely handled through either paper means or point-solution HR software. Even the recruiting process has yet to leverage the Internet. In addition, training expenses are fairly high for the company, espe-cially (as noted earlier) in customer support.

Desired State: The HR department would like to automate many of the processes they have today. Requirements that will help include

- Move toward an employee self-service model - Most likely by implementing some type of Web-based solutions, the objective is for the HR department to be-come less labor intensive and significantly less "in the middle" of many HR-related processes. HR would become more of a planning and problem resolu-tion organization, with repetitive and routine functions being handled by the employees themselves.

- Implement automated training - The company would benefit greatly by using computer-based training, perhaps provided through courses they purchase (typically on CD-ROMs) or perhaps over the Internet. Training-related data (courses completed by each person and when, etc.) would then be-come an integral part of an overall employee profile within the HR environment.

- Implement Web-based recruiting - If Acme's e-commerce business strategy is suc-cessful and the company begins to grow again, it's expected that the work-force could grow by as much as several hundred people per year, even with improved productivity throughout the organization. Given the seemingly endless robustness of the U.S. economy, the competition for skilled workers seems to get more desperate every day. Acme needs to make recruiting far less labor intensive and to use the Internet as a key component of its workforce expansion efforts.

Strategy Decisions

Acme's executive management huddles during a weekend retreat in late Septem-ber to review the results from the information-gathering phase of the busi-ness strategy effort. By the end of the weekend, the following decisions have been reached:

1. First—and most importantly—Acme will move away from its traditional strategy of partner-only sales and begin selling directly to consumers. Two sales channels for direct customer sales will be implemented: the Internet

and through the Acme call center. A B2C e-commerce initiative will be funded and will commence immediately.

2. Consequently, Acme's Internet presence will undergo (from a business sense) a total makeover. The billboardware (i.e., marketing material) will still exist but will be tightly integrated into other portions of the company's Web site dedicated to sales, customer support, communities, and so on. The makeover will be far more than cosmetic: the entire infrastructure will be redone from scratch.

3. Because the topic of data warehousing was raised almost universally by Acme's functional organizations, the executive committee has authorized the CIO to "go build a data warehouse." The architectural and technical details will be worked out later; the rationale, though, for proceeding with this initiative (or set of initiatives, as will be determined by the data warehousing strategy effort) is to help make business intelligence an integral part of *every* Acme Computer business process. Every decision maker in the company knows that maintaining the status quo of sporadic reporting, manually intensive and error-prone data integration, and other hallmarks of the way business is conducted currently is unacceptable.

4. Internet technology will also be used to reengineer non-customer-facing business processes, such as procurement, distribution, and manufacturing. Therefore, a B2B initiative will be funded and will also commence immediately.

5. Internet technology will also be applied to internal HR functions. Where applicable, links will exist between functions and the B2C and B2B initiatives, but it's expected that the links will be primarily in the infrastructure realm rather than sharing information. This will be determined as part of the data warehousing strategy and subsequent data-warehousing-related specifications and architecture work.

6. Acme's financial picture is still strong enough in terms of cash on hand, available credit, and other instruments to finance the other application environments that have been requested (e.g., the partner management system, the product configuration management system, etc.). No outside investment (e.g., additional stock sales or obtaining a new line of credit) is necessary at present.

7. Addressing the issue of potential channel conflict once direct consumer sales begin, the enhanced Acme Web site will prominently feature links to the Web sites of their channel partners with no click-through fees. However,

click-through statistics will be captured and stored in the data warehouse for internal analysis as well as supporting the partner negotiations process.

The meeting concludes, and the executive management team gets to work.

Acme's e-Commerce Data Warehousing Strategy

The CIO hands responsibility for the data warehousing portion of the company's e-commerce strategy to his long-time deputy IT director. Since she had been responsible for building Acme's existing data warehousing capability and is fairly up-to-date on trends in the data warehousing realm (architecture, products, etc.), there is a high degree of confidence that a top-notch data warehousing strategy will be developed.

After studying the decisions from the company's executive management off-site, examining the current and future transactional initiatives, and performing substantial amounts of additional research, the following recommendations are made:

1. A single integrated data warehousing environment will be developed for Acme's "core operations" - Leaving aside support functions such as HR, the increased levels of integration among Acme's organizations—sales and marketing, product development, finance, customer support, distribution, and so on—seem to indicate that no logical demarcation can be made among these organizations to justify function-specific data warehousing point solutions. The existing data warehousing environment such as the call center's "sort of data mart" will be studied and a determination made as to whether those systems can be retrofitted into the new integrated data warehousing environment or should instead be retired, their functionality replaced by the new data warehouse.

   One concern is whether or not such a comprehensive cross-organizational data warehousing environment can successfully be built. For more than a decade, the industry trade magazines have been filled with stories of failed large-scale data warehousing efforts that exhibited the same breadth of organizational involvement that Acme is attempting. However, several mitigating factors indicate that Acme won't face the usual stumbling blocks in trying to implement enterprise-scale data warehousing:

   • The company has never acquired any other companies, so the data source environment is relatively straightforward: only one finance and accounting system, one inventory control application, and so on.

   • Unlike a Fortune 1000–sized (or even Fortune 2000–sized) company, Acme doesn't have multiple divisions producing different types of products (i.e., one division for PCs, another for personal digital assistants); there is only one sales force, and so on, so the organizational structure isn't very complex.

- The project has sponsorship and full support from the entire company, from the top down, to build that data warehouse. There are also some very clear business objectives behind the project.

2. The data warehousing environment will support online e-commerce as well as non-Internet operations - Related to the single-warehouse decision, the mostly "green field" situation facing Acme provides a green light to build a single environment and avoid the particularly troublesome cross-data-warehouse exchanges of information faced by click-and-mortar organizations when one data warehouse supports e-commerce operations and another supports more traditional forms of business intelligence.

3. B2C and B2B functions will be integrated where appropriate - Enough anecdotal points have already surfaced with regard to the types of questions that will be asked of the data warehouse and overall business intelligence functionality to justify some level of commonality among the B2C and B2B sides of e-commerce operations. For example, the CEO has already indicated that a key decision driver for Acme in the future is how B2B supply chain operations affect customer satisfaction ratings, the number of problem reports, and other customer-facing metrics. Rather than build separate data warehouses tied to the different transactional environments that will be put in place for B2C and B2B—and then be faced with ever-increasing needs for data exchange between the two—a single environment is indicated.

4. The data warehouse will support after-the-fact business intelligence and information-driven customer-facing operations - The entire spectrum of classical business intelligence functionality will become an integral part of Acme's future operations: simple reporting, OLAP, EIS, data mining, and geographical information systems (GISs). But additionally, the integrated data must be used for operational functions such as shopping-time customer dialogs, batch-oriented campaign management, real-time dialogs (whether system-to-system or system-to-person) in the B2B realm, and possibly other uses. The traditional view of a data warehouse as being focused solely on after-the-fact reporting and analysis is outmoded for how Acme plans to use its enterprise data as a key corporate asset.

5. The transactional and data warehousing environments will be architected in concert with one another - Even though a number of separate project teams will likely be

assigned to each transactionally focused project and to the data warehouse development project, regular information exchanges—end-to-end design walk-throughs, for example—will occur throughout, from the commencement of the architecture phase until the systems are deployed and in operation. This way, unpleasant surprises such as scalability issues and networking bottlenecks will hopefully be avoided.

e-Commerce Solutions Architecture

The following sections contain the details of Acme Computer's solutions architecture put in place to meet their e-commerce needs. As we've noted throughout this book, the necessity of a close relationship between the transactional and business intelligence sides of e-commerce typically requires that, even when separate projects are at hand, the architectural efforts of each be closely coordinated.

Infrastructure Architecture

Considering the requirements and direction of Acme's IT department and given a determination to use Broadvision as an e-commerce platform (discussed in the next section) Acme investigated and selected an application service provider (ASP) to provide the Broadvision functionality while supporting the application. As part of the contract negotiations, they factored in the requirements for high availability (24 × 7) as well as connectivity back to Acme's own data center, with the SAP application to remain hosted. Figure 11.1 illustrates the resulting infrastructure architecture.

The overall infrastructure environment is actually divided between two different physical locations: Acme's data center, located in their headquarters building, and the off-site ASP location. Within Acme's own location will be its existing platforms—for SAP and office and file services—plus the data warehousing environment (currently targeted for a single Oracle database, though capacity or performance issues could force the company into a multiple-database data warehousing environment), plus the knowledge management portal. Hosted at the ASP site will be the Broadvision application along with the necessary Web servers, firewalls, load balancers, and the other necessary Internet environment components we discussed in Chapter 7. Given the requirement for high availability, redundancy is factored into the ASP site architecture.

Between Acme's data center and the ASP site lies the networking and communications infrastructure. Based on a networking analysis that included the data flow needs to and from the data warehousing environment as well as the transactional applications and platforms, it was determined that the single existing T1 line would

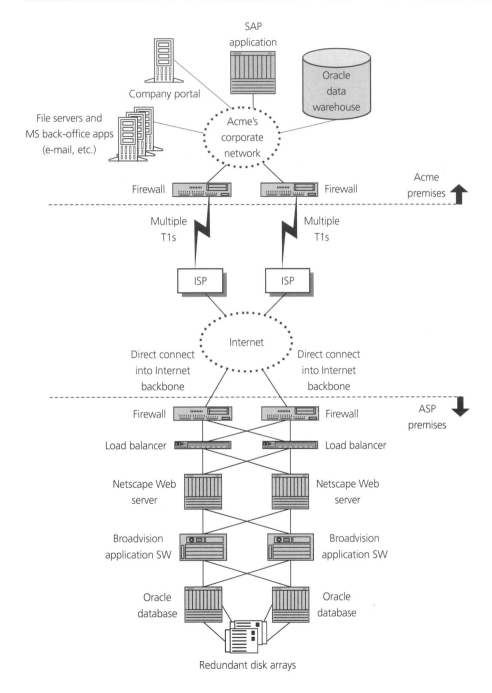

Figure 11.1 Overall Acme Computer e-commerce infrastructure architecture.

not support the high-availability requirements of Acme and the need for consistent access from the systems that will be supported by the ASP, nor the anticipated traffic loads. Further, the requirement for high availability leads to a concern that even when the networking environment is upgraded to the multiple T1 lines and the multiple paths shown in Figure 11.1, a single point of failure might still exist should all communication paths flow through a single Internet Service Provider (ISP).

Consequently, two different ISPs and two separate carriers of T1 lines need to be identified and selected as part of the implementation-specific architecture to ensure that the required levels of redundancy and the necessary back-and-forth flow of data can be achieved and supported. Redundant firewalls are also part of the architecture.

Note that many of the additional pieces of the networking infrastructure aren't shown in Figure 11.1 because of the very low level of detail; an in-depth discussion of networking architecture is beyond the scope of our topic (and usually outside the realm of responsibility of a data warehousing architect). For completeness and purposes of reference, though, these are listed below:

- Ethernet connectivity - Ethernet is the network used throughout.

- Routers/switches/gateways - These devices are necessary to establish the appropriate connectivity even though they are not explicitly shown in the figure.

- TCP/IP - This is the protocol that is used throughout the entire architecture since there are no other legacy networking environments (SNA, DECnet, etc.) with which integration is needed.

- Domain Name System (DNS) - Acme has to implement a DNS in order to effectively communicate with the various systems.

- Other servers - FTP servers, SMTP servers, POP servers (see Chapter 7 for details).

B2C Software and Applications Architecture

After evaluating a number of products, Acme chose Broadvision (*www.broadvision.com*) to be the foundation for building its B2C e-commerce applications. A major decision point was Broadvision's ability to integrate with Acme's SAP application with very little custom integration work.

All databases—transactional as well as data warehousing—will be hosted on database management system software from Oracle. Completing the rest of the software infrastructure is the need for a Web server; in Acme's case, Netscape Enterprise Web Server was selected.

On the transactional side of the B2C environment, a number of new or up-graded applications will be developed, including the following:

- The core "Acme Direct" Internet-based application for direct customer sales, based on Broadvision with links to SAP to ensure that the product catalog is synchronized across applications (using Oracle database triggers to coordinate the replication, in this case).

- The product configuration management system, through which online customers will, with assistance, configure their PCs as desired. Given the conversational nature of this application and the Internet foundation, Acme decides to use Revenio's (*www.revenio.com*—see Chapter 8) dialog marketing environment as the application foundation, with custom-developed links as necessary to the ASP-hosted Broadvision application over the T1 lines.

- Intelligent customer profiling and personalization using the Broadvision application, which will be equipped to track customers' preferences and transfer that information to the data warehouse. The application itself will be set up to track user activities while on the Web site. And, using cookies, it will also track customers that return to the site and combine that information with other content from the data warehouse—such as the results of the customer profiling—for personalized shopping-time one-to-one marketing.

  Because of Acme's stated strategy to use its data assets operationally as well as for behind-the-scenes analysis, a real-time, message-enabled interface will be built between the Oracle data warehouse and the Broadvision application. This will enable the Acme Direct application to request content from the data warehouse—purchase history information, for example—and combine that information with other data from that particular session; perform on-the-spot analysis; and then further personalize the shopping experience.

  Additionally, the Broadvision application will send messages back to the data warehousing environment on a near-real-time basis (e.g., when a user finishes browsing and leaves the site) and, should the online shopper return to the site shortly afterwards, the data-warehousing-resident "whole-customer view" is up-to-date, including information about the most recent visit that may have been only hours—or even minutes—earlier.

- Online sales, initially using credit cards only (rather than other forms of e-payment). Credit card authorization will be handled by Broadvision connectivity to a credit card authorization service, which in turn should minimize the amount of fraud from online sales. In the future, however, Acme plans to offer other payment options including financing. Consequently, links will be established within the environment to pass payment information into the data warehouse in preparation for the day when multiple payment options are available and Acme wants to analyze how many customers are using which methods, what the trend lines indicate, fraud and other problems categorized by payment type, and so on.

- The "Ask Acme" knowledge management system and portal, which will serve both internal and external users. The knowledge base will be comprised of links to applicable content available over the Internet, internal "unstructured" content (such as product diagrams and documentation, audio and visual support-related material, and similar content that today is just floating around Acme's various computer platforms), and structured data stored in the data warehouse (product specifications, statistics from the call center and the to-be-deployed Internet-based support application, etc.). The portal will feature a link directly into a front-end data warehousing query tool, which in turn hooks into the data warehouse's Oracle database(s) from which pertinent information will be accessed and presented on demand.

- To reduce the amount of time and money spent sending out CD-ROMs and diskettes, software patches that are downloadable patches right from the Acme Web site. Structured information about the patches (e.g., requesting user and identifying number; session start and end timestamps, etc.) will be fed into the data warehouse, with applicable links into the knowledge management system. The knowledge management system also links directly into the patch management system so that when a customer asks a question that results in the resolution being a software update, that person can be directed immediately to the section for downloading the appropriate patch.

Other applications will be built and deployed as necessary in concert with Acme's e-commerce business strategy. The key commonality among these applications is that

- whether packaged software or custom code is used;

- whether the application is directly customer-facing or if it handles behind-the-scenes aspects of B2C e-commerce such as bill paying; or

- whether its users are internal Acme employees, external prospects and customers, or both;

appropriate linkages *to and from* the data warehousing environment will be architected and built from the outset.

More about the Acme Computer Data Warehousing Environment

Elaborating on the previous discussion points about the data warehousing environment, Figure 11.2 illustrates the environment through which data flows into and out of the data warehouse will occur.

Points worth noting about the data warehousing environment include the following:

- A combination of batch-oriented ETL processes and real-time messaging - Though real-time messaging becomes a necessity for a data warehousing environment to support shopping-time B2C dialogs, there still exists a role for classical batch-oriented extraction, transformation, and loading (ETL) processes within the architecture. Specifically, source applications in which one-by-one changes in the source data don't have real-time importance to business intelligence (i.e., adding each piece of newly stored source data into the reporting or analytical processes is irrelevant) are better integrated with the data warehouse through classical batch ETL processes, whether implemented via a tool or custom code.

- A staging area for B2C e-commerce data - Performance and response time become very important concerns in a data warehousing environment that will be communicating in a real-time manner with an operational application such as the Broadvision-based Acme Direct system in this example. Very likely a separate staging area needs to be built to serve the transactional dialog needs. For example, when a given user online session commences, relevant information is extracted from the "main" data warehouse and staged in the separate area; ongoing dialog activity, including the receipt of shopping-time information and the associated processing logic to merge that just-received data with existing data, would occur within the staging area. Should the logic of the staging area determine that additional content that had not already been loaded into its domain be needed, the staging area at that point would request the additional data from the data warehouse. (Note that this is conceptually the same paradigm as caching; if the content exists within the cache it's used, otherwise new content is requested from the underlying environment—operating system, file, the Internet, etc.)

  At the completion of a session, the information is "written back" to the data warehouse's database, including newly obtained information, and that

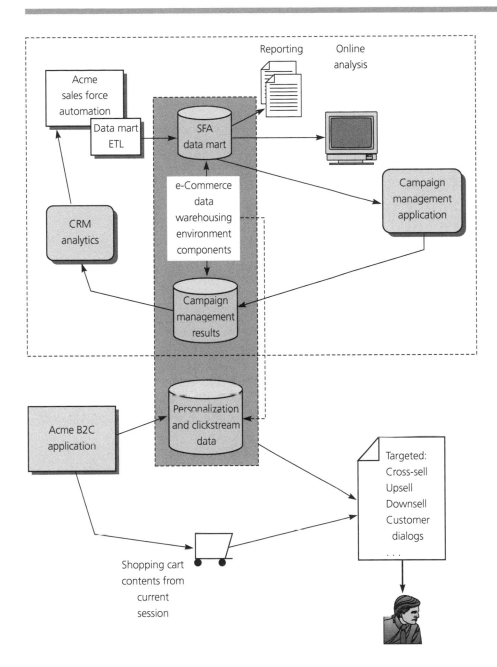

Figure 11.2 Acme Computer data warehousing environment.

portion of the staging area is flushed (the portions managing other dialogs are retained until they complete).

The staging area is still part of the data warehouse's domain rather than being an extended part of (in this case) the Broadvision application. The reason: it's possible that the staging area needs to support more than one application with real-time access to, and transmission of, data warehousing content. Therefore, the staging area needs to be architected and implemented as a separate entity from any of its customer-facing (or other) applications.

- Support for intrasession dialogs - The example above reiterates the fundamental premise of the data warehousing environment as an active participant in ongoing operations. Not only does content come into the data warehouse via batch-oriented ETL processes and real-time messaging, but content must flow *out* of the data warehouse as well in a manner other than through a front-end reporting or query tool. Consequently, the database must be appropriately tuned and structured to support not only large-volume data requests (as typical in reporting and analysis business intelligence situations) but small-volume requests that, essentially, are the same as if the database were exclusively for transactional purposes. If necessary, redundant data structures may be part of the database (i.e., dimensionally oriented content for reporting and separate normalized or lightly denormalized tables with the same data for the transactionally oriented requests). Over time, it's expected that leading relational DBMS engines will evolve to better support a mix of transactional and data-warehouse-like access against the same data structures through enhanced query optimization and transaction planning engines.

- Continual intra-data-warehouse logic - Traditional data warehouses are very passive environments. Data comes in, courtesy of logic outside the realm of the data warehouse itself (e.g., the ETL processes). However, once within the data warehouse, the data typically serves only one purpose: to be available when requested by a front-end tool via a direct SQL call or some other mechanism.

The examples above made reference to an e-commerce data warehousing environment taking a much more active role with regard to processing logic. Whether implemented via the DBMS's stored procedures, some form of application sitting on top of the data warehouse, or some other mechanism, the days of the data warehouse as solely a passive entity are past. Processing capability must be used to process incoming data as quickly as possible and present not only the raw data but some type of value-added functionality (i.e., a recommendation) for use in e-commerce functions such as real-time, information-based dialogs with online users.

B2B Architecture

The overarching strategy for Acme in the B2B space will be to implement an online "Acme Partner Portal" through which interaction with suppliers and sales partners will occur. Components of the "Partner Portal" include the following:

- The partner relationship management (PRM) system - The PRM solution will be deployed using Broadvision's functionality and provide a portal for sales partners and suppliers to interact with Acme. Services include tracking orders (e-tracking), online bill presentment (e-billing), and e-payment. All applicable information will be captured and stored in the data warehousing environment, appropriately linked with other e-commerce and internal operations content.

- Expanded integration with SAP - The Broadvision integration with SAP mentioned earlier with regard to the infrastructure will allow sales partners to place orders through the partner portal and have those orders cross-checked against inventory levels before the order is finalized. Once an order is placed, then the inventory can automatically account for the new order. This feature should help drive down partial order shipments and backorders (and maintain some degree of harmony with sales partners by preventing the perception that a given partner's channel is a distant second in importance to Acme as compared with the new direct sales model). Also, by monitoring inventory levels, Acme can promote products that are on the verge of becoming obsolete via targeted campaigns (e.g., reduced pricing, increased partner rebates, etc.) to partners.

- Electronically bonding with sales partners - Acme's new B2B environment will enable partners to "electronically bond" with them for ordering products, paying, and so on. This will be done via an XML interface (see Chapter 7).

- Extending the knowledge management system to partners - The knowledge management system, though initially intended for internal and external users in the B2C realm, can be extended to B2B partners.

- Electronically bonding with shipping carriers - On the B2C side of Acme's e-commerce initiative, customers will be able to track a shipment online. The closely related B2B capability automatically schedules product shipments—customer-direct or to channel partners—as well as product returns coming back to Acme. Ideally, this capability will eliminate the paperwork and phone calls that are required today. It is anticipated that the interface to the shipping companies will also be implemented via XML.

- Utilizing online auction exchanges to obtain best prices on supplies - Acme has made a decision to utilize freemarkets.com (*www.freemarkets.com*) and possibly other online auction sites in an effort to obtain the best pricing for parts and supplies. At a minimum, they will gather strong insight into pricing when negotiating offline purchases. Data applicable to their marketplace will be loaded into the data warehouse along with related data (pricing, shipping statistics, quality metrics, etc.) from nonexchange B2B supply channels as well as data from before the online B2B initiatives commenced, the purpose being ongoing analysis and guiding future procurement decisions.

Human Resources Initiatives

Though not directly applicable to either the B2B or B2C sides of Acme's e-commerce initiatives, Acme does decide to proceed with the set of B2E (business-to-employee—see Chapter 6) initiatives that had been proposed to upgrade their HR processes. A separate data warehousing environment will be constructed in concert with—and be closely integrated with—the B2E transactional capabilities.

Summary

This chapter brings together many of the topics we've discussed on a one-by-one basis throughout this book and presents a consolidated, integrated picture in the form of a case study as might be found in a real-world company.

The most critical points to note with regard to this chapter include the following:

- The overall e-commerce strategy drives the e-commerce data warehousing strategy.

- The e-commerce data warehousing strategy drives the architecture and design choices that are subsequently made.

- Data warehousing in an e-commerce environment should not be done in the classical manner, that is, disjointed from and after the transactional environments with which it is linked. Rather, every aspect—from strategy to architecture to closely integrated development projects—needs to be done in concert with one another to ensure that the desired integration of transactional and business intelligence functionality occurs.

- For many data warehousing practitioners, e-commerce opens up an entirely new and often confusing world of Web servers, ASPs, networking infrastructure, and other technologies that previously had been part of the behind-the-scenes, "unimportant" systems infrastructure. e-Commerce data warehousing practitioners should not expect to become experts in all facets of e-commerce and related technology, but rather should at least possess a working familiarity with the complexity to ensure that systems they build are adequately suited to "new economy" business operations rather than those of the early 1990s.

Endnotes

1. No reference is intended to any real company, anywhere in the United States or worldwide, that is or has ever been known as Acme Computer—our case study is purely fictitious.

Index